Gravel Pit Restoration for Wildlife

A Practical Manual

John Andrews and David Kinsman

Tarmac
Quarry Products

RSPB

Gravel Pit Restoration for Wildlife

A Practical Manual

John Andrews and David Kinsman

Gravel Pit Restoration for Wildlife is produced by the RSPB. The Society gratefully acknowledges the generous sponsorship of Tarmac Quarry Products Limited.

Published by The Royal Society for the Protection of Birds, The Lodge, Sandy, Bedfordshire SG19 2DL.

Great care has been taken throughout this Manual to ensure accuracy, but the Society cannot accept responsibility for any error that may occur. Any comments or corrections should be addressed to the authors at the RSPB address above.

Typesetting by Bedford Typesetters Ltd, Bedford
Cover illustration and artwork: Dan Powell
Design by: Patsy Hinchliffe
Printed by: KPC Group, Ashford, Kent.

RSPB Ref: 24/562/90

ACKNOWLEDGMENTS

The authors wish to express their thanks to the following, whose support, advice or assistance was invaluable:

Tarmac Quarry Products Chairman and Chief Executive J Mawdsley, and its staff, especially Ron Parry, Val Shields and John Bowman (now of Bowman Planton Associates).

and in addition:
British Geological Survey.
Butterley Aggregates, A D Lamond and Mike Jones.
Tom Cook, Sennowe Hall, Guist, Fakenham, Norfolk.
The Cumbria College of Agriculture and Forestry, Penrith.
Game Conservancy ARC Wildfowl Centre, Dr Nick Giles, Mike Street.
The Institute of Freshwater Ecology, Windermere.
The Institute of Terrestrial Ecology, Grange-over-Sands, Dr R Bunce.
Robert Mandale, Old Wolverton, Milton Keynes.
Minerals Planning Division, DoE, London.
Minerals Planning Unit, Scottish Development Dept.
Minerals Unit, Planning Service, Northern Ireland.
RMC, Bryan Frost.
RSPB staff, especially Kevin Bayes, Peter Makepeace, Steve Rook and Diana Ward.
The Ryton Sand & Gravel Co, Newcastle on Tyne, Ian Hornsby.
St Albans Sand and Gravel Co Ltd, John Spreull and Jim Gooch.
The Sand & Gravel Association, Mr G Thirlwall, CB, Director.

CONTENTS

AUTHORS:
John Andrews, MIBiol, Chief Advisory Officer, The Royal Society for the Protection of Birds, The Lodge, Sandy, Bedfordshire, SG19 2DL.
David Kinsman, PhD, ARCS, Environmental Consultant, Windy Hall, Crook Road, Windermere, Cumbria, LA23 3JA.

LIST OF CONTRIBUTORS:
Amphibians, snakes and lizards: Tom Langton, Director, Herpetofauna Consultants International, PO Box 1, Halesworth, Suffolk, IP19 8AW.

Barn owl: Colin R Shawyer, Director, The Hawk Trust, c/o Zoological Society of London, Regent's Park, London, NW1 4RY.

Butterflies: Dr Marnie Hall, Cambridgeshire Countryside Centre, Newland, Chatteris Road, Somersham, Cambs, PE17 3DN.

Chironomids: Dr Clive Pinder, Institute of Freshwater Ecology, Eastern Rivers Laboratory, Monks Wood Experimental Station, Abbots Ripton, Huntingdon, Cambs, PE17 2LS.

Dragonflies and damselflies: Dr Norman W Moore, The Farm House, Swavesey, Cambridge, CB4 5RA.

Fish, tufted duck and pochard: Dr Nick Giles, The ARC Wildfowl Centre, Great Linford, Milton Keynes, MK14 5AH.

Mallard and other dabbling ducks: Mike Street, The ARC Wildfowl Centre, Great Linford, Milton Keynes, MK14 5AH.

Mammals: bats, water vole, harvest mouse, otter: R E Stebbings, The Robert Stebbings Consultancy, 74 Alexandra Road, Peterborough, Cambs, PE17 2LS.

Wildflower grasslands: Dr T C E Wells, Ecologist/Botanist, Institute of Terrestrial Ecology, Monks Wood Experimental Station, Abbots Ripton, Huntingdon, Cambs, PE17 2LS.

Birds: staff of The Royal Society for the Protection of Birds, as follows:

Canada goose: Dr James Cadbury, Dr Ceri Evans, Dr Graham Hirons.

Grey heron, migrant and wintering birds: Mike Everett.

Kingfisher, sand martin, sedge and reed warbler: Dr Lennox Campbell.

Little grebe, great crested grebe, mute swan: John Andrews.

Redshank, lapwing: Dr James Cadbury.

Ringed and little ringed plovers, common tern: Tony Prater.

FOREWORD

by The Rt Hon Michael Heseltine, MP
Secretary of State for the Environment

I am very pleased to be able to welcome the publication of this practical manual *Gravel Pit Restoration for Wildlife*. I hope it will be read, and used by a wide range of people who are involved in creating new natural habitats out of former mineral workings.

My Department attaches considerable importance to the proper restoration and recycling of land following mineral extraction. This avoids future dereliction and helps to make acceptable the inevitable disturbance which mineral activities involve. The practical achievement of this approach depends on the parts played 'on the ground' by the minerals industry, local authorities, landowners and farmers, nature conservation, sporting and leisure interests and also local people interested in their surrounding environment.

For many years much of this restoration has been carried out to enable productive agriculture to take place again after workings have ceased. However, there is increasing interest in conserving and protecting the diversity of Britain's wildlife and related habitats. This new Manual is a timely and valuable addition to the guidance available on creation and management of such habitats and shows how former gravel sites can provide opportunities for making new sites for wildlife. I commend it to all concerned.

LIST OF FIGURES

INTRODUCTION

The minerals industry is a significant land user. Current operational land and land for which planning permission has been obtained but not yet taken up totals roughly 114,000 ha in England, plus an unknown area in the rest of the UK. The industry takes in about 5,000 ha per year for new workings of which 30% is for sand and gravel extraction. Most mineral workings disrupt the land surface to such an extent that active restoration is required and the subsequent end-use is thus a subject for intelligent selection amongst alternatives.

The industry is by no means unique in having an impact on the countryside. For several thousand years, man has cleared forests and drained wetlands in order to increase the area of agricultural land and has managed all kinds of habitats, both natural and man-made, to produce utilisable crops of one sort or another. In recent times, urban development has been a significant demand on land. However, unlike most other activities, the sand and gravel industry is unusual in creating a range of potential options for after-use with a spectrum of associated social benefits.

Sand and gravel deposits often underlie good quality farmland and in the past it was frequently a condition of planning permission that pits were restored for agriculture. For some mineral workings, the subsequent productivity of the restoration has hardly justified the cost, although for others, the restoration has successfully returned the land to the original levels of productivity. The land area available for restoration each year (about 1,500 ha) comprises less than 0·01% of the utilisable agricultural area of the UK. This compares with current farming surpluses of 10% or so in certain products and with an EC 'set aside' policy for the removal of 3% of arable land from production by 1992. Thus, guidance from government departments indicates that in future agriculture may receive lower priority and other after-uses, including wildlife conservation, may become more important.

Operational aspects of the sand and gravel industry, particularly cost of transport, mean that whenever possible sites are close to urban areas as these are where the bulk of the production is used. This proximity has suggested a spectrum of alternative end-uses for mineral workings, ranging from short-term waste disposal to long-term uses such as industrial and urban construction sites, recreation

1

and amenity, or wilderness areas with managed public access. The social benefits derived from most of these include local employment, usually at a higher level than agricultural after-use. This range of options needs careful consideration in new planning proposals, in the restoration of derelict land left over from past mineral workings and in the re-evaluation of end-uses for active workings in the light of changed social and economic priorities. When structure and other relevant plans are under review, these changing priorities for restored land should receive serious consideration.

Despite the past emphasis on agricultural restoration, there are many permanent lakes to be found in old workings and as part of the designed restoration schemes of more recent years. These lakes could total 15,000 ha, equivalent to half the area of the UK's reservoirs. In addition, with around 1,500 ha of worked-out pits being produced annually, 400–500 ha of which are likely to be flooded, we have the potential to add a relatively large increment to our total of man-made wetlands each year and thus partly to redress the losses of wildlife habitat which have occurred particularly in the highly populated lowlands, as well as catering for other needs.

This Manual deals with the creation and management of habitats for wildlife, and their use for public enjoyment. Its purpose is to show the great potential which exists and how this can be achieved at acceptable cost.

Managers' Summary

The precise landform created during extraction and restoration is of vital importance. Decisions affecting water depth and ground levels, drainage and the treatment of soils will control the subsequent development of all plant growth and colonisation by wildlife. Wrong decisions may be prohibitively costly to correct. Planning for conservation should therefore take place from the outset wherever possible.

Different kinds of wildlife have different requirements, which may vary with the seasons. For best results, a restoration scheme will concentrate on selected kinds of wildlife and tailor landform, planting schemes and visitor access to their precise needs. This maximises the chances of success and value for money.

This section of the Manual summarises the main factors to be considered and makes general recommendations. Obviously, operational circumstances will vary from place to place and initial plans may have to be amended if circumstances change during the extraction phase. Restoration is therefore a dynamic process and one in which the informed judgment of the site manager is of great importance.

More detailed background information is provided in the main text.

Managers' Summary

Table 1

							Sub-merged	Emergent	Rough	Trees &	Islands	Lack of disturb-	
Species	Wind shelter	Sun	Shallow water	Shore-lines	Marsh	Ponds	plants	plants	herbage	shrubs	or rafts	ance	Other
Summary table of major requirements for some wildlife (NB In all cases, refer also to information on Soil, Plants and Productivity (page 111))													
Dragonflies	★	★	★			★	★	★	★	★			
Butterflies	★	★							★	★			Nectar plants
Fish			★				★						Deep water
Amphibians		★	★	★	★	★	★	★	★				
Grebes			★				★	★				★	Fish
Grey heron			★		★							★	Fish and amphibians
Mute swan			★				★				★	★	Short grassland
Ducks	★		★	★	★		★	★	★		★	★	
Waders			★	★	★						★	★	Nesting habitat
Barn owl	★								★			★	Hollow trees or boxes
Kingfisher	★		★									★	Nest banks
Otters			★	★	★		★	★	★			★	Fish and amphibians

4

RESTORATION PLANNING

The Needs of Wildlife

Table 1 indicates the main requirements of some of the wildlife which may be attracted to restored gravel workings. Full descriptions of the needs of these and other species are given in Part II of the Manual.

Prescriptions for the creation and management of the required habitats are summarised in the following pages and presented in full at Part III of the Manual.

For all types of restoration, in addition to considering the specific habitat needs, refer to the section on Soil, Plants and Productivity (page 111) as this affects the development of all aquatic and terrestrial habitats.

The Aims of Restoration

In deciding the aims of restoration, it will be essential to relate the needs of species or groups to constraints imposed by planning conditions, operational factors and the long-term ownership/management of the site.

Other things being equal, restore for wildlife which is uncommon in the locality as this makes a greater contribution to conservation. Guidance on choices for restoration at a given site may be obtained from County Wildlife Trusts or the RSPB.

Preparation of a Conservation Plan

When the objectives of restoration have been decided, it is wise to produce a written plan, supported by drawings. This will confirm that the preliminary ideas are practicable and ensure that the greatest wildlife return is achieved for a given level of restoration expenditure. It will also mean that changes in personnel or operational circumstances do not lead to important aspects of the restoration being overlooked. The plan should include:

(a) a list of species which are the main objective of restoration and the provision to be made for them (eg winter feeding habitat for teal, nectar sources for butterflies, boxes for bats);

(b) brief statements of the status of these species in the UK and the relevant county and the contribution to their conservation which is hoped to result from the planned restoration: this is the justification for what you propose to do (eg up to 200,000 teal winter in Britain but less than 500 in this county and the planned habitat could cater for 50 or more so increasing the county wintering population by 10%);

(c) brief quantified descriptions and plans of the habitats required, including (for example): the extent of all essential habitats/features, local weather conditions especially aspect and exposure, provision of shelterbelts, physical land (or water) form, water depths (including seasonal fluctuation), water quality and nutrient status, water control structures, soil watertable and drainage, subsoil or topsoiling requirements, planting composition, vegetation structure, use of rafts or other artificial habitat enhancement measures, human access arrangements and viewing facilities, and any other relevant factors;

(d) aftercare and long-term management requirements and how they will be met, including any statutory conditions or voluntary agreements;

(e) provision for specialist restoration advice and its timing, if required;

(f) the timescale for restoration related to extraction;

(g) a list of non-priority species (eg wintering mallard) or groups (eg gulls) which are predicted also to benefit from the restoration.

(See photographs 1, 3 & 4)

WIND, SHELTER AND SUNLIGHT

1. Most plants, insects, mammals and birds benefit from wind shelter which results in increased warmth and decreases their energy needs. Winds generate waves, causing erosion and reducing water clarity: important habitat may be destroyed. Wind effects on wildlife and habitats can be reduced by planting tree shelterbelts, reducing water depths and reducing lake length (fetch).

2. The physical effect of wind is related to its force, which is approximately proportional to the cube of its velocity so that reducing the wind speed by 20% almost halves its energy. A reduction of this order is worthwhile.

Table 2

Wind Speed/Energy Relationships	
Wind Speed Reduction	*Wind Energy Reduction*
%	%
10	27
20	49
30	65
40	78
50	87
60	94

3. Good shelterbelts are permeable, absorbing wind energy as it passes through them. Dense, impenetrable barriers direct almost the entire force of the wind over their tops, giving little downwind shelter. Woodland is almost impermeable and should not be planted where downwind shelter is required.

4. Shelterbelts should be planted at right angles to the prevailing wind direction(s) and installed as early as possible in the development of a site. A structure with medium permeability and a height of 10 m will give useful shelter for up to 300 m downwind. (Windspeed is progressively regained downwind of the shelterbelt, the effect of which reaches no farther than 30 × its height.)
5. It may take 20 years or more to reach 10 m height so early planting is desirable. Ideally, anticipate overall site restoration design or at least create shelterbelts sequentially, working downwind. Details of shelterbelt planting are at page 141.

Table 3

Wind Reduction to Leeward of 10 m High Shelterbelt with Medium Permeability			
Averaged over 50 m	*Averaged over 100 m*	*Averaged over 150 m*	*Averaged over 300 m*
Reduction in:			
(a) wind speed 60%	56%	48%	28%
(b) wind energy 94%	91%	86%	63%

6. The proportion of a lake receiving wind shelter becomes greater as the length of the lake along the shelterbelt shore is increased relative to its downwind dimension. Design values should be greater than 2:1 and preferably 3 or 4:1.
7. Variations in wind direction will expose areas of the lake. This may be countered by extending the shelterbelt laterally, wrapping it around the lake shores or creating lakes which are roughly triangular.
8. Wave size is modified by the waterbody fetch and, to a lesser extent, by its depth.

Table 4

Effect of Lake Fetch and Depth on Wave Size			
(Wind speed approx. 60 kph)			
	A	B	C	D
Lake Depth (m)	1·5	1·5	7·5	7·5
Lake Fetch (m)	150	600	150	600
Wave Height (m)	0·20	0·33	0·20	0·39
Wave Length (m)	2·8	4·7	2·8	5·5

9. Installation of barriers between phases of excavation or peninsulas, islands or submerged shallow banks all oriented at right angles to the prevailing wind direction will reduce potential fetch and hence erosion. Ideally these should be at not more than 200 m spacings.

10. Sheltered, sunlit areas are excellent for plant growth, butterflies and dragonflies. They are also much appreciated by mammals and birds. Shelterbelts create shade close to them, so areas of land which gain shelter but are beyond the extent of shade should also be created. Set shelterbelts back from the shore or create sunlit spits or islands in a sheltered lake. Glades and rides in woodland or scrub also provide shelter for butterflies.

(See photographs 5, 6 & 8)

Table 5

Shadow Extent at Different Seasons			
Season	*Sun Elevation Above Horizon*	*Shadow (m) Cast by E–W Shelterbelt*	
		10 m High	*20 m High*
Midsummer (midday)	62°	6	11
Equinox (midday)	26°	21	42
Midwinter (midday)	18°	31	62
Especially in winter, even a 10 m high shelterbelt aligned E–W will shade a substantial area.			

LANDFORM FOR WETLAND HABITATS

1. The relationship of water level to ground surface is the main factor controlling numbers and variety of plants and animals in wetland habitats.
2. Shallow-water areas less than 1·5 m deep are very productive and are colonised by a wide variety of plants, support many breeding invertebrates and fish and are the favourite or essential feeding areas for many waterfowl and their young. Marshland, seasonally-flooded wet grassland and small ponds also have considerable value for specialised plants and animals.
3. Water over 1·5 m deep is the least valuable habitat for most wetland wildlife. Most modern workings go below this depth and the aim in conservation restorations should be to maximise the extent of water areas less than 1·5 m deep.
4. Surface and ground-water levels vary seasonally, being high in winter and early spring, and low in summer and early autumn. It is important to take account of final water levels and their fluctuations before planning the location, extent and exact form of physical features such as shallows, ponds and marshes. Thus, an area of shallows with a 1:15 slope to a depth of 1 m will be 15 m wide: to provide the same extent of feeding habitat after summer draw-down by 0·3 m, the area of shallows would need to extend to 20 m and a maximum depth of 1·3 m. Allowance must be made for the addition of 30 cm topsoil where available.

5. Extensive shallows should be designed into the restoration. Where overburden is insufficient, inert fill should be considered. Ideally, shallows will be created on shores in the lee of the prevailing wind and/or protected by shelterbelts. Where this is not possible, marginal habitats will either require physical protection by islands, booms or bunding or to be so extensive that the outer part will absorb wave energy (page 95).

6. It is better to create one broad area on a sheltered and disturbance-free shore than to produce a narrow 'bench' of shallows around the whole perimeter of the pit, as the broad sheltered area will be more productive of plant and animal life.

7. Many emergent plants, such as reeds, can grow in water depths down to 1 m or somewhat more. Separate areas of shallows by leads of water 5 m wide and more than 1·5 m deep as a means of inhibiting the spread of beds of emergent plants onto the areas of shallow open water required for submerged plants, waterfowl feeding, etc.

8. The shoreline is a favoured feeding area for waterfowl. Shores not adjoining shallows and not exposed to erosion should be lengthened by creating the most sinuous edge possible (page 105). This is doubly important in sites where it is impracticable to create extensive shallows.

9. Marshland may be created by profiling the ground surface within the zone of watertable variation so that it is shallowly flooded in winter and less than 15 cm above the summer water level. Extensive areas may also be developed on silt lagoons, or where soil compaction impedes surface drainage. However, marsh is a difficult habitat to retain because of the rapid rate of willow invasion so it is probably best omitted from a restoration plan except where long-term management will be possible.

10. Wet grassland can be created for shallow flooding (up to 15 cm) in the winter months and grazing or mowing in summer to prevent development of scrub or woodland. Flooding is particularly valuable if it can be timed for mid to late winter when wildfowl and wader food resources in the shallows will be much reduced. If the flooding regime cannot be controlled it is important to level the soil surface so that it will be free of standing water by the end of March. Otherwise the grass sward will be killed.

11. Ponds provide conditions which are particularly favourable to invertebrates and amphibians. Siting will depend on the management aim. Dependent on fluctuations in the watertable, summer draw-down may be used to expose margins for feeding by waders or wildfowl. The ideal site for amphibians is one which dries out completely about one year in five, so destroying any competing fish populations which may have colonised.

12. Ponds should be less than 1 m deep and be excavated with variable though generally shallow-gradient margins. The length of the margin should be maximised by making the pond of irregular shape. Leave excavated surfaces uneven rather than smoothly graded.

13. Shallow water, marginal habitats, marsh or wet grassland, pond sides, islands and shoals will need precise grading after excavation and de-watering have ceased and the watertable has stabilised. Access for requisite machinery must be maintained.

14. Slopes of designed shallow areas around lakes, islands or peninsulas should be no steeper than 1:15. For marsh and flooded grassland habitats slopes of 1:50 to 1:100 are required. Aim to develop a very gently undulating surface with pockets which flood slightly more deeply and elevations which remain less deeply flooded or unflooded. This variety of micro-topography (5–10 cm in tens of metres) will add considerable diversity to habitat development.

(See photographs 3, 4, 7, 8, 9, 13, 14, 15 & 16)

SOIL, PLANTS AND PRODUCTIVITY

1. Soil management is of vital importance because it controls the development of plants. Plants form the basic food resource for all wildlife, directly or indirectly, as well as providing physical shelter and concealment. Soil's value for plant growth will be damaged or destroyed by incorrect handling

2. Soil structure is particularly prone to damage during stripping or reinstatement operations. The two principal causes of damage are compaction and smearing, both of which are related to moisture content. Damage can be caused readily when soils are wet and so handling should be restricted to the drier periods of the year (predominantly May to September) and operations should be halted during rain and for up to 48 hours afterwards. As a rough guide, do not move soils or permit vehicle traffic over them unless the soil is sufficiently dry to crumble when rolled between the fingers. Guidance based on rainfall criteria is given at page 114.

3. Before stripping soils, bulky surface vegetation should be removed. Topsoil, subsoil and overburden should each be stripped and stored separately. Topsoil should be stripped from areas to be used for storage of subsoil or overburden. If soils or overburden vary significantly across the site, material of differing characteristics should be stripped and stored separately. Loam is particularly valuable for plant growth.

4. Earthworms are of great importance in maintaining good topsoil conditions for plant growth. When soil is stored, few worms survive below a depth of 50 cm. Cultivation of restored soils also kills many worms. Ideally, topsoil should be moved directly from the area being stripped to the area being restored, as this saves double handling and also minimises loss of the earthworm fauna. Some topsoil should be stored in small piles around the

10

site for final spreading after the detailed grading of the marsh and other shallow water and shoreline areas is carried out.

5. Any topsoil stored for appreciable periods should be seeded with a low maintenance grass seed mixture or clover to stabilise the surface and protect against erosion and loss.

6. Poor soil drainage and check in tree growth are often caused by soil compaction. Some degree of compaction during soil handling is almost inevitable but it can be minimised by use of a back-acter to spread subsoil and topsoil in successive 'panels' which can be worked without tracking over them at any stage (see page 115). If compaction occurs, it may be relieved by subsoiling but this is not always wholly successful. Normal agricultural cultivation is likely to be inadequate except on original surfaces which have been compacted by light vehicle traffic only. Once spread and treated, the surface should not be driven over when wet, even after vegetation cover has developed.

7. During restoration, use soils as follows:
    (a) for margins, shallows and marshland areas provide 30 cm of topsoil to create the initial high nutrient conditions required.
    (b) for deeper water areas a 15 cm topsoil layer spread over the bottom will slowly release nutrient elements and help support a high level of aquatic productivity. This is desirable but not essential in most lowland areas of Britain.
    (c) for shelterbelt areas, 20–30 cm uncompacted topsoil may be used, but will lead to strong growth of weeds competing with newly-planted trees and shrubs. This will require control (see page 141).
    (d) for most other terrestrial areas supply little topsoil or perhaps mix some topsoil with subsoil.
    (e) for non-shelterbelt tree and shrub planting, subsoil is preferred as this will not generate competitive weed growth.
    (f) for wildflower grasslands (see page 130), no topsoil should be provided.

8. Should additional nutrients and other soil conditioners be required, they may be added in various ways:
    (a) by artificial fertilizers.
    (b) by farmyard or other manures, mushroom compost, etc. Although the nutrient content of most such materials is generally rather low, the addition of the organic matter may significantly improve the productivity of the soil.
    (c) by sewage sludge, to land or water, preferably as de-watered sewage sludge cake.
    Seek specialist advice on appropriate levels of application.

9. Silt deposits may be used in development of restored landform contours. Alternatively, if the silt pond infilling can be developed close to the final restored water level, the low-angled surface can be used for a shallow water and marsh sequence of habitats. It may require wind shelter to prevent wave action causing severe erosion and water turbidity.

(See photograph 2)

11

AQUATIC AND WATERSIDE PLANTS

1. Abundant and diverse wetland plant growth is essential to fuel the food-chains on which all aquatic wildlife depends. As well as providing a direct food resource for many species, it creates the necessary physical structure in which innumerable micro-organisms, invertebrates and fish-fry find shelter.

2. Water depth is a critical factor controlling wetland plant establishment and growth. Marginal plants will grow in soils up to about 15 cm above the watertable with emergents extending into water depths down to about 1 m. Submerged plants usually grow best in depths of less than 2 m. Contouring of the restoration should therefore provide broad, gently sloping (less than 1:15) marginal shelves wherever possible, and peninsulas, islands and shoal banks out in the lake should also be formed with similarly shelving margins.

3. Fifteen centimetres of topsoil at depths of over 1·5 m and 30 cm in shallows will provide a valuable, nutrient-rich substrate increasing the rate of growth and spread by both submerged and marginal plants, particularly where the new, shallow lake floor or margins are of coarse gravel or rather compacted.

4. The commoner submerged, floating and marginal plants are listed on page 122 with some comments on their value for other wildlife. Always use native plant materials, preferably those available close to the site. Do not introduce exotics. If there are wetland areas within the site before excavation starts then these plant materials should be carefully protected and moved into the early phases of the restoration. If such plant sources are not available, possible alternatives include other wetland restorations, farmers clearing out ditches and ponds, County Wildlife Trusts and Internal Drainage Boards or the National Rivers Authority. As many aquatic plants grow and propagate themselves vigorously, the initial introduction need not be vast and early planted material may be thinned for planting later restoration stages.

5. Aquatic plants must not dry out. Plants should be covered with polythene sheeting or bagged up during transit. Tuberous or rooted submerged plants should be inserted into the bottom sediment at water depths of 0·3–1 m, and allowed to extend into deeper water as they become established. For planting in deeper water, plant material should be weighted, eg with roots or stem bases in clay balls or firmly tied in clumps to stones, and dropped into the water.

6. Marginals may be planted individually or as clumps of material either by spade or by back-acter. Cohesive clumps are less likely to be washed out before the root system gains anchorage. In most instances, it is easiest to put marginal plant material into soft soil just on the waterline, when it can spread into the shallows. Where possible, it should be firmed into the ground to prevent it washing out before it has gained a hold. Reeds

must be planted above the waterline and, as their new shoots
are particularly sensitive to pressure, they should be firmed in
with care.

7. Planting should take place in late spring when the plants have
    started into active growth, and light levels and water
    temperatures are high; the new plants then have the remainder
    of the growing season in which to establish themselves.

8. Avoid mixing the more vigorous species with those which are
    slower to become established. By having separate blocks of
    different species, plants in each can become established before
    there is competition from adjacent stands. If some plants are not
    available in enough quantity to create large stands, try to group
    them near species of similar size and rate of spread.

9. Where a shoreline is subject to wave erosion, planting may
    have to be protected, either by a boom moored off shore or by
    use of artificial fabrics such as Enkamat. Once established,
    emergent vegetation may absorb moderate wave energy and
    prevent further erosion.

10. Marginals, including reeds and great reedmace, spread rapidly
    in sheltered waters less than 1 m deep, or form floating mats
    extending over deeper water. There are few circumstances in
    which complete cover by these plants would be desirable,
    owing to the loss of habitat diversity.

11. Herbicides can offer precise and cost-effective methods of
    control of marginal plants, though physical control is also
    practicable. Grazing and trampling by cattle will break up
    stands. Cutting is rarely effective unless repeated or followed
    by flooding to 'drown' the plants. Dredging or scraping the
    vegetation away is preferable in older sites where many years of
    plant litter have accumulated, raising the bed level and
    reducing the extent of shallows. In any event, the need for
    control should be anticipated, so that it can be carried out in
    limited areas of a site on rotation, rather than all at once.

12. Herbicide formulations currently available and their spectrum
    of weed control are listed on page 128. It will be seen that
    herbicides may be target-specific or broad spectrum. The latter
    have more potential for inadvertent damage. Intending users
    should read *Guidelines for the use of herbicides on weeds in or near
    watercourses and lakes* (MAFF, 1985), which gives
    comprehensive information on consultation, choice of
    formulations, the range of plants which may be controlled,
    appropriate timing for applications, toxicological data and
    instructions to operators. Current lists of brand names are best
    obtained from *Pesticides*, published annually by HMSO.

(See photographs 10, 11 & 12)

ROUGH GRASS AND TALL HERBAGE

1. Rank vegetation 0·3–1 m tall is used by butterflies, reptiles and amphibians, small mammals, birds of prey and nesting wildfowl.
2. Such cover often develops naturally on uncompacted subsoil or topsoil and can be planned into a restoration, ideally to occupy a warm, south-facing slope extending down to the water's edge.
3. Linear strips of cover are less valuable as they are more easily searched for nests by ground predators such as foxes.
4. If natural cover does not develop quickly, sparsely sow a mix of native grasses in late summer. Aim for an open sward which wild plants can invade later. Do not use perennial rye-grass.
5. Management should be restricted to preventing succession to scrub by periodic clearance or by rotational management, with one-third or less of the site cut or grazed each year.

(See photographs 8 & 9)

WILDFLOWER GRASSLANDS

1. Relocation of existing grasslands rich in wildflowers prior to overburden stripping is practicable and very desirable on conservation grounds. Creation of new wildflower grassland has less conservation value but is much more beneficial for wildlife than the conventional rye-grass sward.
2. Existing grasslands can be relocated by transferring turves together with topsoil in an excavator bucket or on pallets. The receptor site must provide conditions favourable for turf growth; in particular, the watertable must be at the correct level. Measurements must be made at the donor site, at least to establish typical levels in the summer months, and the receptor site profiled to match, with allowance for the thickness of the turves themselves (30–50 cm). Typically, the restored summer watertable should be within 70 cm of the final soil surface.
3. The receptor site should be of subsoil, free of compaction and without weeds. Freshly-exposed subsoil is likely to be weed free but if weeds have colonised, herbicides should be used prior to the transfer operation.
4. For best results, the soil profile should be maintained throughout pickup and set-down operation. Turves 30–50 cm thick should be cut using a bucket with half-arrow cutting edge and side plates. The thickness of the turves is necessary to maintain the existing root system as intact as possible and to retain the associated soil fauna. For these reasons, care must be taken not to break up turves in handling.

5. To prevent unwanted weeds becoming established, subsoil from the donor site should be used for filling interstices between the laid turves. These gaps will rapidly be colonised by the plants in the turves.

6. Creation of new wildflower grasslands from seed requires selection of species which are suitable to site conditions. A list of species for clay, alluvial or sandy soils is given on page 131.

7. Ideally, obtain seeds from local sources such as surviving hay meadows. A mix of 85% wild grasses and 15% wildflowers is sown at about 2·5 g/m^2 together with about 3 g/m^2 Westerwolds rye-grass as a nurse crop.

8. A firm seedbed with a good tilth and good drainage is essential. Repeated harrowing and rolling will be required. The bed must be weed-free and of low fertility so freshly-exposed subsoil is ideal. The best sowing time is late August to mid-September.

9. In the following year, cut at least three times and remove cut material. Subsequently, cut once or twice annually depending on the conservation aim.

10. On free-draining gravel-pit soils expect an open sward: this is beneficial, permitting other native plants to colonise.

11. Existing swards can be improved for wildlife and amenity by inserting pot-grown specimens or by slot-seeding in herbicided strips. The latter technique is still experimental so seek specialist advice first.

WOODLAND, TREES AND SHRUBS, SHELTERBELTS AND HEDGES

1. Retain existing woodland or hedgerows if possible. Unlike much wetland wildlife, many forms of woodland wildlife are not good at colonising new sites. Woods and hedges may be many decades or centuries old and their wildlife value may be impossible to restore if they are destroyed. Old timber is especially valuable. Do not remove standing dead timber unless there is a safety problem. Leave fallen timber to rot in place.

2. Take advantage of natural regeneration. Willows and alders will readily colonise damp areas, and birch and Scots pine will appear on well-drained ground. Natural regeneration often outperforms planted trees.

3. If planting is necessary, favour a diversity of locally native trees and shrubs. For the most part, native species support a much wider variety of wildlife than do non-natives: willows, oak and birch are invaluable. By creating diversity, the planting will benefit a wider range of creatures. Incorporate at least four tree and five shrub species, with at least 10% of the area occupied by shrubs and plant in single-species groups, each the same extent as the anticipated canopy width of one or two mature

specimens. Otherwise faster-growing trees will suppress slower species. To achieve woodland conditions rapidly, space trees at 1·5–2 m intervals and shrubs at 1m .

4. The three-dimensional structure of woodlands is extremely important to wildlife. Depending on the specific aim, it may be necessary to produce a ground layer (low-growing plants), a field layer (tall flowers and grasses, young shrubs and tree saplings), or a shrub layer (mature shrubs and young trees) and the canopy (older trees). In planted, even-aged woods, thinning will be needed so that ample light can reach the lower layers, otherwise they will be shaded out and lost.

5. Tree-plantings can fail, wasting time and money. Reasons for this include:
   (a) bad soil conditions, especially compaction below cultivation depth (see page 139);
   (b) allowing roots to dry out during planting;
   (c) use of trees which are too large, given the low levels of aftercare which they usually receive;
   (d) selection of inappropriate species for local site conditions;
   (e) inadequate staking;
   (f) lack of protection from rabbits and other herbivores;
   (g) competition by weeds;
   (h) planting at the wrong level relative to final watertables.

6. The choice of tree and shrub species to be planted must be appropriate to their required function, eg for a hedge, a shelterbelt or for specific wildlife conservation values. The species selected must also be appropriate for the site in question. The values, tolerances or requirements of most species likely to be planted are listed on page 145.

7. Younger plants, such as two-year forest transplants, are considerably cheaper than older plants and tend to develop a good root system well before the crown of the tree becomes large and affected by wind. Thus, they tend to be much more stable, to require little staking and to establish themselves well. In fact, a two-year old tree often quickly overtakes a tree which was several years older when initially planted. Where an initial visual impact is required, larger standard trees may be planted but they will be much more expensive to buy, plant and maintain, difficult to stake securely and vulnerable to drought in their initial year.

8. Broadleaved trees and shrubs are best planted when dormant, in November–March. Evergreens should be planted in October whilst the soil is still warm, or in April when it is warming up. Any planting in March or April may, however, be at risk from drought. Containerised stock may be planted in late spring or summer but will need repeat watering. Planting should not take place when ground is frozen, water-logged or very dry.

9. Grass and herbs within 50 cm of any tree compete with it for moisture and nutrients, reducing the growth rate. If allowed to grow unchecked, taller weeds will also compete for light. Healthy, well-planted trees and shrubs will get away in time – it is a state of affairs with which trees cope in nature. However, to

maximise growth in the year or two after planting, weeds should be controlled by cutting, weeding, mulching or use of an appropriate herbicide.

10. If livestock are present, erect a stock-proof fence 2 m away from the outer rows of planting. Tall (1·8 m) plastic grow-tubes offer protection for hardwood transplants from browsing animals up to roe deer size. Protection from rabbits and hares can be achieved by using individual tree guards, grow-tubes or surrounding the planting with a 25 mm mesh wire fence, 60 cm high, the base being turned outwards so that grass and weeds grow through it and make a reasonably rabbit-proof join.

11. Watering of trees and shrubs should not normally be necessary after their first growing season, but if exceptionally dry weather occurs in their second season then watering may save trees, particularly those planted in free-draining soils. With small numbers of standards, it is more economical to water than to replant. Trees and shrubs should be kept mulched and weed free for 2–3 years. Rabbit guards, fences and tree stakes should be regularly checked. Trees which rock in their planting holes often die: loose stakes should be firmed well in and tree-ties adjusted.

12. The composition of a shelterbelt should reflect its physical state when shelter is most required. For optimum performance against winter winds, an evergreen species is desirable. For summer shelter a screen of deciduous trees or mixed deciduous/evergreen planting is best. Mixed plantings are usually very effective and are visually pleasing, but do not work well as single row screens.

13. As a general rule, a hedge has greater value for wildlife if it:
    (a) contains a wide variety of native shrubs rather than just one or two species.
    (b) has a dense bushy structure with foliage virtually down to ground level: this can be created by management.
    (c) contains standard trees, the older the better.
    (d) has a ditch at its foot. Whether wet or dry, this will extend the area of cover and foraging habitat for wildlife.
    (e) has wide margins with a varied community of herbs.

14. In sites where shading of agricultural crops is not a problem, hedges can be encouraged to grow tall and bushy. Avoid trimming hedges during the nesting season (March – July inclusive), or before berries have been eaten by birds. Wherever possible, undertake cutting or trimming in January or February. Do not cut all hedges during a single season. Where possible, manage on a two or three-year rotation to ensure that flowers and fruit are carried on a proportion of the length each year.

(See photographs 16, 17 & 18)

ISLANDS AND OTHER BIRD NESTING SITES

1. Predators take a toll of nesting birds, their eggs and young. Birds thus seek concealment in cover or holes and, in the case of ground-nesting species, the relative safety of islands. Provision of good nesting sites greatly increases breeding success.

2. Duck nests in vegetation less than 0·5 m tall are much more likely to be found by predators than nests in deeper cover which is most simply created by allowing patches of ground to be colonised by tussocky grass, scrub, bramble, dog rose or tall herbs and managing these on a rotation to maintain their density of growth at ground level. In particular, areas of tall growth should not be cut down for tidiness in the autumn or winter as the dead, standing stems provide the necessary early spring concealment.

3. Islands are favoured for nesting by waterfowl because they are less affected by human disturbance and less accessible to predators such as foxes. They are also attractive to birds which are resting, particularly during the moulting season when wildfowl are flightless and a sense of security is essential.

4. Islands should be as far offshore and as widely spaced as possible, bearing in mind that those in exposed locations will require protection against erosion. Several small islands will hold more nesting birds than a single island of the same total area. A minimum practicable size is probably 100 m² but larger islands, up to 0·1 ha, may be easier to manage. Where visitor viewing is a priority, island location and form must not obstruct sight lines: alternatively, they may be deliberately used in order to screen feeding or resting areas from any form of visual disturbance.

5. In general, the shoreline length of islands should be maximised as the land/water interface is a favoured feeding area for waders and dabbling ducks. Fine-scale modelling will erode but atoll, horseshoe and cruciform island shapes are all excellent in this respect. The landing beach should be as flat as possible, particularly to allow easy access by ducklings. Overall, slopes should be no greater than 1:4 for use by wildfowl.

6. In exposed situations, islands should have bank protection or be profiled to absorb wave effects on the windward side and to provide shelter for wildfowl in the lee. Typically, the exposed shore should have a slope of 1:10, to a depth of 1 m. The lee shore may be shallow for dabbling ducks or shelve steeply to prevent the establishment of emergent vegetation and enable diving ducks to find the sheltered open water they favour for safe roosting. The island profile should rise towards the downwind end to a height of up to 2 m above water level and might ideally be capped by scrub to give the best shelter effect.

7. Methods of erosion prevention include booms such as telegraph poles chained to spaced piles, use of rip-rap, willow staking, treated timber or sweet chestnut palings used as piles and backed by brushwood.

8. For nesting wildfowl, a dense vegetation cover is required. The selected islands should therefore be topsoiled and seeded or, better, allowed to vegetate naturally. For nesting by black-headed gulls, lapwing and redshank, a tussocky sward may be achieved by cutting once or twice in autumn and clearing the litter.

9. Terns, ringed plover and little ringed plover require islands surfaced by shingle and ideally only a few centimetres above the water. After initial profiling to a low and gently sloping or level form rising not more than 50 cm above summer water level, the surface should be covered by heavy duty plastic sheeting or old farm fertiliser sacks, ideally to three thicknesses, to prevent deep-rooting plants becoming established. This is then covered with a depth of at least 10 cm of unwashed aggregate – the natural mix of gravels and sand is usually ideal. The outer edge of the plastic must either end above high water level or be weighted and protected with larger stones. Periodic autumn weeding or herbicide treatment may be necessary.

10. Trees should not be planted or permitted to grow on islands. They will be used as lookout places by predatory birds and shade out nesting cover.

11. On sites which have been worked wet or where it is desired to create islands in workings now flooded, a spit may be constructed by tipping progressively into the lake: this can then be cut into islands by working backwards towards the shore and using the excavated material to increase the area of marginal shallows. Where old workings contain peninsulas, they may be treated similarly.

12. Trees felled into the water, for instance when clearing over-shaded banks, or rough faggots of branches wired together and staked into position, may be used as nest anchorages by grebes and coot, and as roost sites by wildfowl.

13. Where islands cannot be created to the extent desired, for instance due to extreme water depth, cost or lack of overburden, rafts provide an acceptable alternative for breeding and roosting, though they lack the adjoining feeding areas for wildfowl and waders. A compensatory advantage on waters where levels fluctuate widely is that nests on rafts are protected from inundation. Designs are given on pages 154–6. They may be surfaced with vegetation (for use by wildfowl), or with shingle (for terns).

14. Artificial sites for sand martins can be created by bedding 1 m lengths of 10 cm polythene pipe at 0·2 m spacings and with 0·3 m between rows into a bank constructed from sand and gravel. A sheer front face can be created with a weak or dry mix of concrete built up against shuttering, which should then be removed. The face should drop into fairly deep water both to prevent colonisation by tall emergent vegetation which would obstruct the birds' flight paths and also to restrict access by predators and humans. Each pipe should be filled with sand and the entrance half blocked with a cement filler. The birds will then excavate their typical oval tunnel along the top half of each

pipe. Ideally, pipes should be scraped out and recharged each winter.

15. Nestboxes may be erected for a range of woodland birds and birds of prey (see pages 158–63).

(See photographs 19, 20, 21, 22 & 24)

IMPROVEMENT OF OLD GRAVEL PIT LAKES

Problem	Solution
1. Steep margins; abrupt land-water interface.	Import clean fill to create shallows. Regrade margins by cutting back where land area permits, dumping spoil into lake.
2. Linear margins; minimum shoreline length.	Make indentations especially along sheltered shorelines, using spoil to make promontories or shallows.
3. Lack of shallow water areas.	Regrade margins. Where spits exist, regrade most to slope from 30 cm below average water level all round, to a top height of 20 cm above it; cut landward trench so that shoal is protected from access.
4. No islands.	Where spits exist, cut off at landward end (trench >5 m wide and 1 m deep). Install nesting rafts.
5. Lack of aquatic plants due to shading by trees.	Selectively fell especially on south side but maintain those providing shelter from prevailing winds.
6. Minimal waterfowl nesting habitat; lack of breeding success.	Create islands or rafts. Coppice trees and shrubs: stack cut material in rows to provide cover. Fell trees into water and leave. Clear shading trees to aid marginal plant growth: introduce marginal vegetation. Do not cut tall herbage, brambles, etc.

7. Poor duckling survival.

Create sunlit shallows and shoals to aid plant growth and boost chironomid numbers. Reduce competition from fish by netting-out.

8. Lack of marsh, pond or terrestrial habitats.

Clear and reprofile silt lagoon or other areas within site.

(See photograph 23)

ACCESS AND VISITOR MANAGEMENT

1. Visitor use will need to be constrained where nature conservation is the main goal of restoration, but with good planning a substantial level of access and enjoyment of the wildlife will be possible. Where public use is the main objective, it will limit the range of species which will co-exist with it but there is always some conservation potential. For instance, grassland can contain wildflowers and tree or shrub planting can be of native species.

2. Most woodland birds are little affected by human activity. Open-ground birds such as partridge and lapwing and other waders are very vulnerable to disturbance. A few species of waterfowl will habituate to humans and become quite tame, but many waterfowl tolerate little disturbance, being most at ease where they can neither see nor hear human activity. Disturbance is at its most severe on a small site with little or no cover, all-round access and no alternative safe areas close by. It has least effect on larger sites, those with substantial cover, and those where birds can withdraw to other nearby waterbodies, returning when conditions are suitable.

3. Sites in which conservation management will be the priority aim should be:
   (a) remote from obvious significant causes of disturbance, notably nearby visible pedestrian movement especially on skylines and intermittent high levels of noise such as clay pigeon ranges;
   (b) capable of isolation from most uncontrolled access, although the ideal is unattainable;
   (c) capable of providing controlled and adequate access for birdwatchers and others without causing disturbance.

4. Boundaries of sites restored for wildlife conservation should be made secure against uncontrolled access. A well-managed hedge of hawthorn or blackthorn is much more resistant to human access than any fence. It will also visually screen the site, offer some degree of wind protection and be of positive wildlife value. Where uncontrolled access is anticipated, a water-filled

21

ditch at least 3 m wide may be constructed and the spoil used to create a screening bank on the inner side. Suitably planted, both ditch and bank will have wildlife value and be visually attractive.

5. The management of visitors within the site is accomplished by the routing of paths, by screening and by the provision of viewing and other facilities. Site facilities – car parking, toilets, picnic areas and interpretative material – should ideally be located together and screened for noise and visual disturbance. At the facility point provide a map showing clearly the location of hides, and the distances involved and indicate the conditions of use.

6. A good path network will provide access to points from which the major concentrations of birds can be seen, enable visitors to sample all the wildlife habitats, cause minimal disturbance to shy species and be intrinsically pleasing to walk. Paths should be reasonably level, wide and well-drained. Even in late summer, when herbage is at its most luxuriant, one should still have easy access. Bear in mind the need for access also by management machinery.

7. Where necessary, water-filled ditches or strips of marsh no more than 1 m wide will keep most people on a path without them realising they are being deliberately constrained. Thickets or hedges of hawthorn, blackthorn, bramble, dog rose or gorse are excellent wildlife habitat, delightful when in flower and virtually impenetrable. The aim is to avoid people realising that they are being excluded from places, as they may then deliberately trespass or at least feel shut in and lose the pleasurable illusion of being in wild and natural places.

8. As an invariable rule, the very shallow-water areas used intensively by ducklings, waders and other waterbirds should be effectively inaccessible to the general public, though always capable of being viewed from hides.

9. For visual screening, broad bands of shrubs or trees will be effective, bearing in mind that an evergreen component or fringe may be necessary to give adequate winter cover. Earth embankments are excellent both for noise and visual screening provided that people cannot obtain access to them. They are tempting viewing points which maximise disturbance by putting the viewer on the skyline. They should therefore be sited behind broad ditches or covered by thorn scrub.

10. Hides should be sited to provide good viewing conditions of all the main areas likely to be used by waterfowl. As looking into the sun across water is particularly difficult, especially when the sun is low in the morning, evening or during winter, ideally there should be several hides with different orientations. However, hides should not be sited where visitor access would cause unacceptable levels of disturbance, nor where inadequate views encourage trespass. Approaches must be screened by 2 m high earth banks, formal solid fencing or evergreen planting reinforced by a wire fence. Hides can be set well back from the water's edge and raised on stilts if necessary.

Photographic Summary

1. *The de-watered void of active workings often contains areas of shallow water and sparsely vegetated ground attractive to nesting and migrant waders, some scarce dragonflies and other wildlife. These conditions may be deliberately created on a limited scale as part of the restoration, in order to retain their dependent wildlife.*

2. *Correct soil stripping and reinstatement are vital to create the essential conditions for good plant establishment and rapid growth. However, for most terrestrial wildlife habitats, topsoil is undesirable because of its high fertility and weed seedbank. It should be restricted to particular uses, such as shelterbelt establishment.*

Photographic Summary

3. *Though not unattractive, this restoration has limited wildlife value. The land/ water interface is sharp with steep banks and no shallows. There are no islands and few areas sheltered from wave action. Though it attracts a limited range of diving waterfowl, few birds breed successfully because of poor nesting and feeding conditions.*

4. *This pit has high wildlife value with diverse margins – some muddy, some reed- fringed with willow carr behind. A vegetated island offers good nesting habitat. A wide variety of waterbirds used the site for feeding and many species breed successfully.*

24

5. *On large pits without shelter, wave action erodes shallows and banks, preventing the establishment of plants and reducing the area of productive habitat.*

6. *Ultimately, wave action cuts back the shore and creates a shallow shelf which will absorb wave effects and may become vegetated. Where space permits, the erosion process should be permitted but it is best to avoid the problem by the provision of shelter.*

Photographic Summary

7. *An unsatisfactory bank profile which is too steep and too straight to have value for marginal plants, feeding waders or dabbling ducks. On an exposed shore, it is likely to erode rapidly and result in the loss of the track. Full marks, however, for retention of the trees and old hedge.*

8. *A reasonable shoreline profile, fairly low-angled, not too straight and with a natural herb cover developing. Scrub and trees provide wind shelter but are set back from the shore so that shading will not inhibit the development of the aquatic plant community.*

9. *This shoreline is better still. Note the sinuous form, increasing the overall length of the land/water interface. The vegetation is at an early successional stage, good for some invertebrates but likely to be replaced by scrub unless managed.*

10. *Typical succession on a low-angled shoreline. The marginal plant community is diverse and the present level of willow cover is excellent but will ultimately shade out other vegetation unless managed.*

Photographic Summary

11. *The consequence of neglect is a willow-fringed shoreline with little vegetation diversity, shaded and unproductive shallows, and no nesting cover at ground level.*

12. *Good vegetational diversity with tall herbage in the foreground, dense scrub and tree cover set well back from the water's edge and substantial patches of bare ground or low vegetation leading into sheltered shallow water. The birdwatcher is a source of disturbance, however.*

13. *Winter flooding was a natural characteristic of river valleys and is important for waterfowl and waders. Here, restoration of grassland close to the watertable creates conditions suitable for light summer grazing and partly inundated in winter. The lake shoreline lies immediately to the right of the central belt of rushes, which marks permanently wet ground.*

14. *Patches of standing water make grassland particularly attractive to feeding wigeon and geese or, as spring advances, to breeding waders, notably redshank. A late-summer grazing regime is essential to maintain a suitable sward structure and colonisation by rushes will need to be controlled. However, such conditions should be the result of deliberate design, not poor landfill or restoration practice.*

Photographic Summary

15. *An extensive system of shallow water, low marshy islands and long shorelines which is ideal for waders and dabbling ducks. It will require regular management if the open conditions are to be maintained. If water levels can be varied with a sluice, in winter the area could be shallowly covered, drowning vegetation and providing good feeding habitat. Spring drawdown would then produce extensive areas of wet ground containing shallow pools for waders and ducklings, plus islands with shingle surfaces suitable for terns.*

16. *Accurate prediction of final water levels is essential, not just for tree planting but for all shallow water or floodland habitats. This planting is likely to fail anyway due to competition from grass amongst other problems.*

17. *Most tree-planting schemes fail to produce a natural woodland structure. Ideally, a mixture of native trees and shrubs should be planted at close density on bare ground to create rapidly a thicket in which micro-climate, leaf litter and dappled shade generate conditions suitable for some woodland flora and fauna.*

18. *Self-sown tree cover may develop rapidly in suitable conditions. It can be left to thin itself through competition. Unregenerating areas may be planted with shrubs or developed as sheltered glades for butterflies.*

Photographic Summary

19. *Bad island form, with sides too steep for wildfowl to get ashore easily and no marginal plant growth. The tree cover may hold some woodland songbirds but there is little understorey.*

20. *A good island form with gently sloping sides, which will provide easy access for resting wildfowl and enable marginal vegetation to establish. A dense cover of tall herbage is developing, suitable for nesting wildfowl.*

21. *For nesting by terns, bare shingle is required, though scattered herbage provides useful shelter for the chicks.*

22. *Gulls will nest in short vegetation. Note that willows have been cut back on the near island and there are relatively few birds on the island behind with its dense willow cover.*

33

Photographic Summary

23. *On old workings, peninsulas can be cut off to create islands so reducing human disturbance and predator access.*

24. *A fallen willow provides a resting site for waterfowl and potential nestsites for grebes, coot and moorhen which will build where branches are at the waterline.*

Part I

The operational background

SUMMARY

1. Government policy is that the construction industry should continue to receive an adequate and steady supply of minerals at the best balance of social, environmental and economic costs. Regional Aggregates Working Parties have been set up to advise and to ensure these aims are met in respect of aggregate mineral supply.

2. Sand and gravel deposits are widespread and the material is used in the construction industries roughly in relation to population distribution. Current annual production is 90–100 million tonnes. It is estimated that about 1,500 ha of worked out excavations are produced each year of which 400–500 ha may be flooded. These are concentrated in the south-east of England, East Anglia and the east Midlands.

3. It is estimated that historic production has generated nearly 60,000 ha of exhausted workings in the UK as a whole of which 15,000 ha are flooded (equivalent to about half the area of reservoirs).

4. The general basis for control of mineral workings is the Town and Country Planning Act of 1971, as amended by later legislation (now embodied in the Town and Country Planning Act 1990), an important recent aspect of which has been to empower planning authorities to impose a five-year aftercare period for restoration to agriculture, forestry and amenity, which is defined as including wildlife conservation.

5. The latest government guidance on the restoration of mineral workings recognises that in future there is likely to be a shift away from restoration for agriculture towards other uses which may include wildlife conservation and amenity.

6. Current costs of restoration range from 1–7% of the value of the sand and gravel extracted; good wildlife restorations are likely to lie in the middle of this range.

7. The wildlife value of flooded sand and gravel excavations is considerable. Over 30% of the

Operational Background

UK breeding populations and over 25% of the wintering population of several waterfowl species occur on gravel pits. Some older sites have become, generally by chance, outstanding for wildlife and some are now designated as SSSIs.

8. Active, well-planned restoration for wildlife, as described in this Manual, should speed the colonisation processes immeasurably and will lead to enhanced wildlife habitat, much of which can be available for low-intensity public use and enjoyment.

SAND AND GRAVEL PRODUCTION IN THE UK

Sand and gravel are one class of construction aggregates, ranging from low-grade materials for embankments and foundation-fill to high quality materials for making concrete or for coating with bitumen for road surfacing.

Sand and gravel occur mostly as superficial deposits laid down by ancient rivers or as glacial or fluvioglacial spreads of debris following the retreat of the Pleistocene ice sheets. Gravel is the coarser component of the material, encompassing pebbles ranging in size from 4–64 mm. The term sand is used to describe intermediate sized rock and mineral grains ranging in size from 0·1–4 mm. Mineral grains of even smaller dimensions comprise the silt and clay components, and normally account for 5–20% of the total volume. The natural mixture may be satisfactory for certain purposes but very often needs screening and washing to produce a usable end product. The river deposits, because of their more consistent grading and smaller proportion of silt and clay particles, tend to be the most important, especially in the south and east of England. The river gravel deposits are often of fairly uniform thickness and those ranging from 2–6 m may be readily worked. High quality river gravels are major aggregate sources in the Thames, Trent and Ouse river valleys. The distribution of river-valley sand and gravel deposits in England and Wales is shown in Figure 1.1. Most excavations in river-valley deposits extend below the watertable and are thus of particular interest for their wildlife conservation potential.

Glacial and fluvioglacial sands and gravels are widespread but not all are economically workable, often being poorly sorted. The proportion extending below the watertable is small.

Other sources of aggregate include the Bunter Pebble Beds in the Midlands, offshore sand and gravel, crushed rock and manufactured materials. This Manual is not directly relevant to dry workings. However, the prescriptions for the creation of terrestrial habitats such as wildflower grasslands, or woodland may be applied depending on site conditions.

Prior to about 1970, the aggregates industry comprised mainly a large number of small, often family-owned companies, which met local requirements. Since then, demand has grown and much of the production has been by fewer, rather larger firms, although a large number of small companies still operate. The industry has two trade Associations, the British Aggregate Construction Materials Industries (BACMI) and the Sand and Gravel Association (SAGA). Many tens of thousands of people are employed directly or indirectly by the aggregates industry.

The production of sand and gravel in the UK has grown enormously through this century from probably less than two million tonnes per year in 1900 to 118 million tonnes in 1987, when total aggregates production was valued at close to £1,000 million, with sand and gravel valued at £466 million being produced from just over 900 pits. The most recent compilation for the UK for the period 1900–87 is reproduced in Figure 1.2. For the past 25 years or so, sand and gravel production in the United Kingdom has averaged around 110 million tonnes per year, about 90–95 million tonnes from land-based deposits and 15–20 million tonnes from marine sources. The aggregates industry takes in about 1,500 ha of new land each year for extraction, which is about 30% of the total land intake by the entire minerals industry; the greater part of this land intake by the aggregates industry is for sand and gravel, which currently comprise somewhat under half the total aggregate consumption in the UK.

Future demand for aggregates has been considered by the Department of the Environment (DoE) and the forecast demand for England and Wales to the year 2005, as published in Mineral Planning Guidance Note (MPG) 6, is indicated in Figure 1.3. For the UK one would need to add roughly 11% to include the forecast for Scotland and 5% for Northern Ireland. However, the DoE demand forecast figures are now the subject of review. The expansion in the UK economy in 1987–88 led to a building boom which required a large increase in aggregate supply. Total aggre-

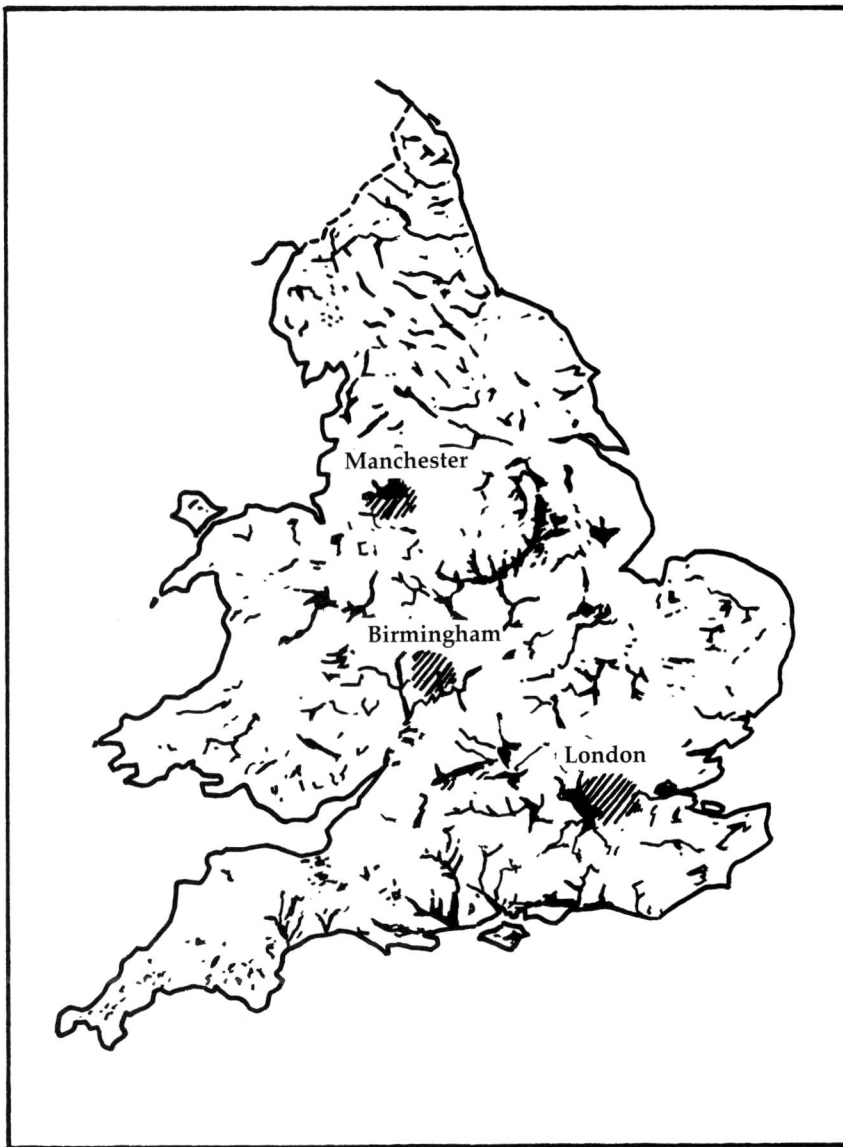

Fig 1.1 Distribution of river
valley sand and gravel
deposits in England and
Wales (from Verney
Committee Report, 1976).

Operational Background

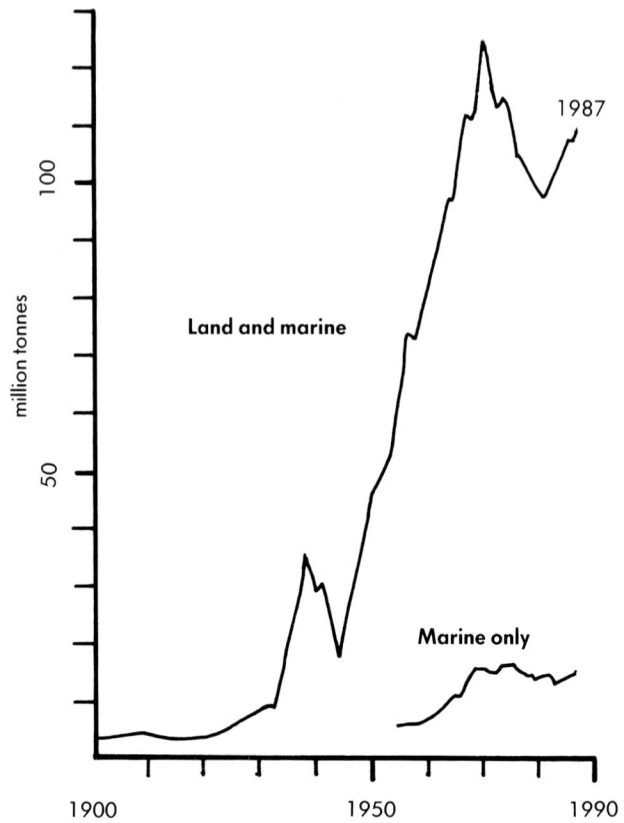

million tonnes

Land and marine

1987

Marine only

100

50

1900   1950   1990

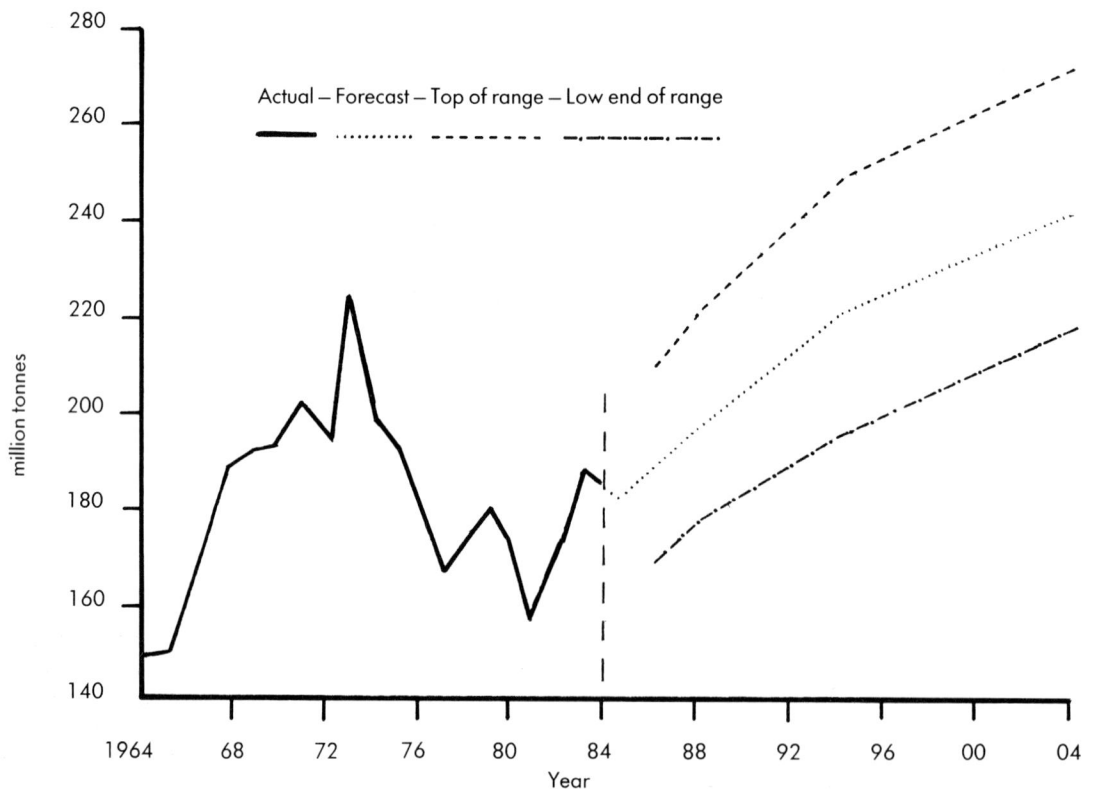

Actual — Forecast — Top of range — Low end of range

million tonnes

280

260

240

220

200

180

160

140

1964   68   72   76   80   84   88   92   96   00   04

Year

gate production in 1988 was 291 million tonnes and in 1989 was approximately 300 million tonnes. It is thought that land-based sand and gravel has maintained its 40% proportion of total aggregate production, ie 1988 – 116 million tonnes; 1989 – about 120 million tonnes. These production figures are already in excess of the 2005 demand forecast. The latest (1989) regular survey on production, consumption and transport of aggregates will be published in early 1991. At the same time a new forecast of national demand for aggregates will be issued.

As stated, nearly all onshore aggregates are relatively thin superficial deposits and, especially in the southern half of England, the deposits lie in river valleys. Working depths are variable. A typical deposit would be 3–6 m thick with a yield of between 40,000 and 80,000 tonnes/ha of workings, ie one million tonnes of sand and gravel derived from between 12·5 and 25 ha. This means that the 1987 production of 99 million tonnes was won from between 1,200 and 2,500 ha of workings.

This total fits reasonably well with the estimated intake of new land for the aggregates industry of about 1,500 ha per year, the major part of which is for sand and gravel extraction.

The regional distribution of current permissions for sand and gravel extraction in England in

Fig 1.4 Areas (ha) of land in England with permission for sand and gravel working in 1988 and, in brackets, areas (ha) reclaimed to amenity afteruses 1982–88 (DoE, in prep).

Operational Background

1988, and the areas in each region reclaimed to amenity after-uses in the period 1982–88, are shown in Figure 1.4. This indicates the dominance of southern England and the Midlands both as sources of the mineral and as potential for development of future wildlife habitats from current (and likely future) workings.

In England during the last forty years or so, about 37,000 ha of sand and gravel have been worked out and reclaimed. Much of this has been restored for agricultural use, but probably about 10,000 ha has been flooded pits. Current workings occupy almost a further 30,000 ha.

The total area of exhausted working from 1900–87 in the UK as a whole is estimated at about 56,000 ha much of which has been restored. To place this seemingly vast area in a wider context, the utilisable agricultural area of the UK is 18·6 million ha which is close to 80% of the total land area of 23 million ha. The likely area of exhausted sand and gravel workings produced during the 20th century represents about 0·4% of the utilisable agricultural area of our country.

Land-won sand and gravel production is likely to continue to provide an important part of the demand for aggregates for the construction industry for the foreseeable future. Such supply will continue to create exhausted pits which will need to be put to a beneficial new use. This suggests that as well as meeting other after-use needs the potential exists to create new wildlife habitats during restoration not on an ad hoc basis but as a planned part of conservation restoration strategies developed on a county basis.

References

Department of Environment, 1986, *Transforming our Wasteland; The Way Forward.* HMSO.
Fellow, ME and Highley, DE 1989, *United Kingdom Mineral Yearbook 1988.* British Geological Survey. Keyworth.
Guidelines for Aggregates Provision in England and Wales (DoE and Welsh Office MPG6, 1989).
Scottish Development Dept, 1987, *Survey of Aggregates Working in Scotland, 1985.*
Verney Committee Report, 1976, *Aggregates: the Way Ahead.* HMSO.
Department of Environment, in preparation, *Survey of Land for Mineral Working in England,* 1988.

THE PLANNING CONTEXT

The general basis for the control of mineral workings in England and Wales is the Town & Country Planning Act 1990 and the associated General Development Order. In 1971, the government set up the Committee on Minerals Planning Control (the Stevens Committee); and the report of the Committee was published in 1976, reviewing the operation of the planning system as it related to mineral working. The Town & Country Planning (Minerals) Act 1981 embodied some of the recommendations of the Stevens Committee report and gave the 'mineral planning authorities' important new powers to control the environmental effects of minerals working. The mineral planning authorities responsible for planning control over mineral working were defined as the County Councils and the National Park Joint Planning Boards or Committees; in Greater London and the areas formerly covered by the Metropolitan County Councils, the mineral planning authorities are now the Borough and District Councils.

An important provision brought in during 1982 (Section 5 of the 1981 Act) empowers mineral planning authorities to impose aftercare conditions on planning permissions for mineral working, where the land is to be restored to agriculture, forestry or amenity use. (*The Reclamation of Mineral Workings* (MPG7) defines 'amenity' as including the conservation or promotion of landscape and wildlife). The aftercare conditions can require specific treatment of the land relating to planting, cultivation, fertilising, watering and draining, for a period of up to five years after the land has been restored.

Central government places high priority on ensuring that the construction industry continues to receive an adequate and steady supply of aggregate minerals at the best balance of social, environmental and economic cost. An important element of aggregate mineral planning since the early 1970s has been the work of the Regional Aggregate Working Parties – eight in England, two in Wales and one for Scotland. These have a membership drawn from local government, the minerals industry and central government and are guided in their work by a National Coordinating Group, chaired by the Department of the

Environment (DoE). The Group includes senior representatives of the industry and the chairmen of the Regional Aggregates Working Parties. The Welsh and Scottish Working Parties are respectively overseen by the Welsh and Scottish Offices. In Northern Ireland the aggregates industry is overseen by the Department of Environment for Northern Ireland.

In the light of a 1985 survey and forecasts of demand, the Regional Aggregate Working Parties prepared commentaries on how the demand might be met during the period 1985–2005 inclusive. National guidelines prepared from these commentaries by DoE and the Welsh Office were published in 1989 as Minerals Planning Guidance Note (MPG) 6. These aim to:

(a) provide a clear framework within which minerals planning authorities can develop aggregate policies in development plans and carry out development control;

(b) serve as a national framework for the Secretaries of State, when considering the aggregates elements of development plans and within which the merits of individual planning applications on appeal and any applications called in for determination can be considered;

(c) help reduce the number of cases going to appeal;

(d) provide guidance as to how a steady and adequate supply of material to the construction industry, at a local and regional level, may be maintained at the best balance of social, economic and environmental cost, through full consideration of all resources;

(e) provide the basis for informed consideration at national, regional and local level of the implications for aggregates working of other policies.

A further guideline document was published in 1989 – *The Reclamation of Mineral Workings* (MPG 7). This sets out advice on how the question of restoration of mineral sites should be handled through planning conditions. Taken together, MPG 6 and MPG 7 give guidance on sand and gravel supply and demand issues and on planning policies and controls over extraction of the mineral. Particularly relevant paragraphs are quoted in full in Appendix I. In summary, they indicate that:

(a) good restoration standards should be ensured (MPG 7, paragraphs 1, 2);

(b) environmental assessment may be warranted where the effect on the environment will be significant (MPG 6, paragraph 26);

(c) improvement of restoration standards will

lead to the release of land not so far available for mineral working (MPG 6, paragraph 32);

(d) for sites which will be restored to water space, detailed landscape schemes agreed between the planning authority and the operator should be drawn up including water depths, bank profiles, island creation, planting schemes and subsequent management (MPG 7, paragraph 87);

(e) it is not satisfactory to propose a scheme anticipating in general the creation of a lake without planning specifically for the after-use: mixing of nature conservation and recreational uses is rarely practicable (MPG 7, paragraph 88);

(f) advice on aspects of nature conservation restoration can be obtained from several organisations including the British Association for Shooting and Conservation, the Game Conservancy, Nature Conservancy Council, Royal Society for Nature Conservation (County Wildlife Trusts) and RSPB (MPG 7, paragraph 89);

(g) mineral planning authorities have powers to require aftercare of mineral sites following restoration but voluntary agreements may be more appropriate for ensuring reclamation and initial management of water space, particularly for nature conservation (MPG 7, paragraph 90);

(h) local authorities should have regard to nature conservation in drawing up planning policies and determining applications. Opportunities for creative conservation exist in restoration of mineral workings and new ecological techniques might be included in the preparation of schemes for working and reclamation (MPG 7, paragraph 91).

References

Development Involving Agricultural Land (DoE Circular 16/87: WO Circular 25/87).

Environment Assessment (DoE Circular 15/88: WO Circular 23/88).

Guidelines for Aggregates Provision in England and Wales (DoE & Welsh Office MPG6, 1989).

Nature Conservation (DoE Circular 27/87: WO Circular 52/87).

Stevens Committee Report, 1976; *Planning Control over Mineral Workings. HMSO.*

The Reclamation of Mineral Workings (DoE and Welsh Office MPG7, 1989).

Town & Country Planning Acts, 1971, 1990.

Town & Country Planning (Minerals) Act, 1981.

RESTORATION OF SAND AND GRAVEL WORKINGS

In the first half of this century, many exhausted sand and gravel workings were left derelict, but in more recent years nearly all worked-out sites have been restored to some agreed end-use. This has occurred for three main reasons: (a) an agreed restoration plan has become an essential part of any planning application to extract sand and gravel; (b) as a response to the present-day pressure of a more environmentally-aware public; and (c) the residual value of the restored land is an important consideration.

Modern production methods are designed to limit the period of activity at any single site, to minimise disturbance by the screening of machinery and workings, and to carry out progressive restoration during active extraction or even commence landscaping before extraction has begun.

During European Conservation Year 1970, the Sand and Gravel Association set up a Restoration Awards Scheme whereby restored sites were to be assessed for merit by a panel of independent judges comprising ex-county planning officers, landscape architects, officers of national conservation organisations and others. The sites have to (a) satisfy all aspects of the planning conditions imposed, (b) demonstrate excellence in design, planning and execution of the restoration, and (c) in the case of agricultural restorations to have been restored for the full five years' aftercare period before consideration.

Between 1970 and 1988 a total of 284 awards was made, covering restoration of about 6,000 ha of workings, sites ranging in size from 1 ha to nearly 200 ha. Restoration categories are recognised for agriculture, forestry, leisure, urban development and, more recently, nature conservation; a few restorations have been made for joint use, such as agriculture plus leisure.

The conservation category brought in during 1986 represents an interesting development. Amwell Quarry in Hertfordshire, a 43-ha wildlife refuge created by the St Albans Sand and Gravel Company, was judged the outstanding restoration in that year.

In the past, most dry sites were ultimately restored to agriculture, sometimes being used for landfill before final restoration. However, the limited availability of inert fill, such as building rubble, has led to most wet sites being restored to some agreed water-based leisure or nature conservation end-use. In some areas, where there is already a concentration of flooded workings, local planning authorities are now, however, objecting to additional water areas as acceptable restoration propositions.

The current costs of restoration average £10,000–12,000/ha and range from a minimum of £2,000–3,000/ha to around £20,000/ha for the highest practicable standards of agricultural reinstatement. If one takes the approximate value of sand and gravel produced in the UK in 1987 as £466 million, then restoration costs range from 1–7% of this value. In general, restoration to agriculture lies toward the higher end of the cost spectrum whereas restoration for low intensity leisure use or for nature conservation lies toward the lower end. However, with some creditable exceptions, much wildlife conservation restoration has been to a low standard and the deliberate creation of good wildlife sites is likely to involve costs in the middle range.

The best currently available information suggests that half or perhaps two-thirds of the worked out sand and gravel area has been restored to agriculture (30,000–45,000 ha this century). The wet excavations which comprise perhaps a quarter of the total have generally not been used for landfill and have been either restored to a water-based end-use or, in the case of some older sites, abandoned. If this is correct, then there could be as much as 15,000 ha of old wet mineral workings in the UK, resulting from sand and gravel extraction. Their cumulative contribution to wildlife conservation is considerable, and their potential is very great.

WILDLIFE VALUE OF GRAVEL PITS

The fertile, natural wetlands which once existed in the lowlands of the UK have largely been drained or their wildlife value has been reduced by pollution, changes in water regime or disturbance. Flooded gravel pits have provided compensation for some of this loss. Indeed they probably provide conditions similar to those in our river valleys in the post-glacial period when gravels were being successively deposited, vegetated and then eroded or shifted wholesale by spates. This dynamic system will have provided habitat for most of the same wildlife species which live in today's gravel workings. Best known for their birds, particularly waterfowl, these man-made waterbodies also support important populations of plant, insect and other animal species.

In general, it is the older pits which are more interesting. The sites were usually operated with an excavator, normally a dragline, extracting the overburden and depositing it in the adjacent worked-out area. The water area is broken up by spits or islands, thus providing shelter and a long shoreline which tends to compensate for rather steep shoreline profiles – shallow water being important for much wetland wildlife. In the 20 years or more since they were dug, these pits will have been colonised naturally by a range of wild plants, while scrub and young woodland may have developed on adjoining ground. A few such sites have become notably important for scarce plants, insects or birds. By contrast, modern workings are often deeper and larger and have straighter shorelines; these characteristics result in minimal development of productive shallows and a high degree of exposure and general lack of shelter. The general range of wildlife is small, though some sites with suitable water quality have developed interesting aquatic plant communities, or support large numbers of diving duck in winter.

There are several gravel pit sites which have developed sufficient wildlife interest to have been notified as Sites of Special Scientific Interest by the Nature Conservancy Council. In many localities, wet pits and other surroundings are the best areas of wildlife habitat in an otherwise intensively managed agricultural or semi-urban landscape.

The wildlife interest of gravel pits in the UK was first highlighted by a 1931 survey of the great crested grebe, which found that many of these spectacular birds were nesting on flooded workings. At that time the great crested grebe was relatively scarce, still slowly recovering from the destruction of Victorian times when its plumes were used in the millinery trade. Later surveys showed that 26% (1965) and 34% (1975) of these birds were to be found nesting on gravel pits.

A survey of 448 inland waters carried out in 1980 (Owen *et al*, 1986) shows clearly the importance of gravel pits (Table 1.1). Close to a third of the British breeding populations of Canada goose and tufted duck as well as great crested grebe are

Table 1.1

The percentages of British inland populations of breeding waterbirds[1]
found on gravel pits during the 1980 survey of enclosed inland waters.
(Adult numbers are based on pre-breeding populations.)

Species	Total adults inland	% on Gravel pits
Mallard	6,568	18·7
Teal	188	2·1
Pochard	538	10·0
Tufted duck	4,793	29·7
Mute swan	700	16·1
Canada goose	2,772	34·2
Moorhen	1,360	18·0
Coot	6,240	20·8
Great crested grebe	1,429	33·7
Little grebe	287	21·2
All waterbirds	33,289	20·8

1. *Waterbirds are wildfowl, grebes and rails. (Modified from Owen et al, 1986)*

Operational Background

Table 1.2

**The percentages of British inland populations of wintering wildfowl[1]
found on gravel pits. Percentages are mean maxima for the three years
1979–80, 1980–81 and 1981–82.**

Species	Estimated total population inland	% On gravel pits
Mallard	500,000	12·1
Teal	100,000	5·8
Wigeon	200,000	1.7
Gadwall	4,000	26·9
Shoveler	9,000	11·8
Pochard	50,000	29·2
Tufted duck	60,000	25·2
Goldeneye	15,000	4·2
Goosander	5,500	10·7
Mute swan	18,000	16·1
Canada goose	33,000	27·5
All wildfowl	2,000,000	7·0

1. *Wildfowl are ducks, geese and swans. (Modified from Owen et al, 1986)*

to be found on gravel pits, and the disproportionate value of this environment is obvious from
the fact that although gravel pits comprised only
11–12% of the number of sites and of the area of
water surveyed, they supported over 20% of the
breeding waterbirds. The tufted duck is now a
widespread breeding species in Great Britain,
largely owing to its colonisation of gravel pits; in
the late 1960s the total breeding population was
around 1,500–2,000 birds, increasing to 4,000–
5,000 pairs in the early 1970s and in the 1980s to
around 7,000–8,000 pairs.

Wintering populations of waterfowl also make
extensive use of gravel pits (see Table 1.2) which
are especially important for Canada goose, gadwall, pochard and tufted duck, over a quarter of
the wintering populations of these four species

being found on them. Wildfowl wintering populations have been generally increasing in Great
Britain over the past 20 years or so, with the
proportion to be found on gravel pits also progressively rising (Figure 1.5).

The value of gravel pits is not confined to
flooded sites. Almost as soon as extraction commences, colonisation by plants, insects and birds
begins to take place. Sand martins are often quick
to exploit exposed sand faces. The scarce blue-
tailed damselfly *Ischnura pumilio* and an uncommon dragonfly, the keeled skimmer *Orthetrum
coerulescens*, occasionally breed in seepages in the
floors of pits being worked dry. Wading birds also
find the intricate mix of shallow pools, wet
ground and sparse vegetation which develops in
active workings very much to their liking, and

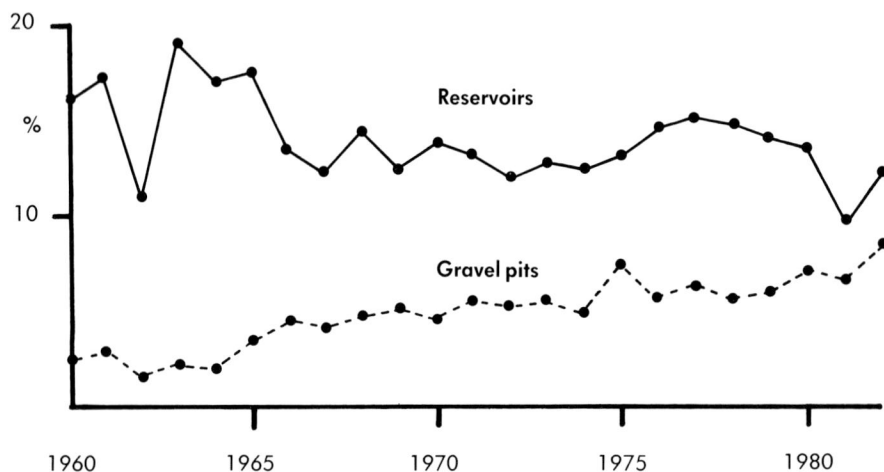

*Fig 1.5 Proportion of counted
wildfowl in Britain on gravel
pits and reservoirs (from
Owen et al, 1986).*

many species may be seen on spring and autumn migration. Redshank, lapwing, ringed plover and little ringed plover may all breed. Indeed, the little ringed plover, which first colonised England about 50 years ago, nests mainly on shingle in gravel workings, and has steadily increased in numbers, to about 400 breeding pairs in 1984, of which 58% were using gravel and sand pits.

As a gravel working develops, the earliest colonists move from the first dug areas and progressively occupy the youngest areas of the workings. These colonising species are normally lost when extraction is completed and the site is flooded and restored. The colonists then usually move on to any new areas where extraction is starting up. However, the loss of colonising species capable of occupying the often raw and unstable early habitats need not necessarily occur. Careful planning and design can accommodate them as well as creating suitable condi-tions for much other wildlife of both aquatic and terrestrial habitats.

References

Hughes, S, Bacon, P, and Flegg, J, 1979, The 1975 census of the Great Crested Grebe in Britain. *Bird Study* 26, 213–26.

Owen, M, Atkinson-Willes, GL, and Salmon DG, 1986, *Wildfowl in Great Britain*. Cambridge University Press.

Parrinder, E, 1989, Little Ringed Plovers *Charadrius dubius* in Britain in 1984. *Bird Study* 36, 147–53.

Tydeman, C, 1982, Gravel pits as wildlife habitat in Great Britain pp 6–12. In Svedarsky, WD, Crawford, RD (eds) *Wildlife Values of Gravel Pits*. Misc Pub 17 Univ Minnesota, Agric Exp Station.

Part II

The needs of wildlife

DETERMINING CONSERVATION PRIORITIES

Different kinds of plants and animals have different habitat requirements. For plants, soil type and fertility, drainage and grazing pressure are amongst the most important considerations. For animals, the structure and composition of the plant community is very influential and so are matters such as shelter and disturbance. A gravel pit restored with no particular wildlife conservation aim in mind will be colonised by plants and animals which it chances to suit. Not surprisingly, they are usually common species with needs which are easily met by the typical conditions of most flooded workings. Adding to the stock of common wildlife is of limited value. Instead, restoration for wildlife should focus on species which it would be beneficial to encourage. However, the creation of habitats can be costly in terms of direct expenditure or income foregone, plus any long-term management commitment, so it may be necessary to limit the extent of such work, concentrating resources on the requirements of one species or on an assemblage of plants and creatures which, in their different ways, can all exploit one habitat type.

Two factors are most important in determining the conservation status of an individual species which might be the focus of restoration. One is the actual population size. The other is any trend in numbers or range. Thus a widespread, abundant species with a stable or increasing population would be a low priority, whereas a species with a small population or suffering a significant decline might rank amongst the highest priorities for action.

We are fortunate in the British Isles in having good information on the relative abundance and distributions of most plants, butterflies, dragonflies, fish, reptiles and amphibians, mammals and birds. There are also generally accepted criteria by which species can be ranked as internationally, nationally, regionally or locally important. These criteria value not only scarcity but also large concentrations of commoner species and, in the case of migrant birds, take separate account of population sizes in summer, winter and during migration itself. Guidance on priority species which it would be desirable and practicable to foster in any given gravel pit restoration can be obtained from the regional offices of The Royal Society for the Protection of Birds and the Nature Conservancy Council, or from the County Wildlife Trusts.

Where it is impracticable to restore for any priority species, consideration should still be given to designing for the needs of selected commoner species or groups of species rather than merely producing so-called 'habitat' with no clear idea of its purpose. Thus the emphasis might be placed, for instance, on providing ideal conditions for dragonflies, for breeding mallard or for migrating waders. Management for diversity has become a catch phrase. It is not recommended as an end in itself. Creating a mishmash of habitat types and hoping that it will chance to fit the requirements of a variety of unspecified wildlife all too often means expenditure for no good result, the habitats created being in the wrong place, having the wrong structure, plant composition or extent to meet the needs of all but the commonest and least demanding wildlife.

A master plan for a wildlife conservation restoration scheme should be produced and include:

(a) a list of species or groups of species which are the main objective of restoration, and the provision to be made for them (eg winter feeding habitat for teal, nectar sources for butterflies, boxes for bats);

(b) brief statements of the status of these species or groups in the UK, and the relevant county contexts, and the contribution to their conservation which is hoped to result from the planned restoration;

(c) brief quantified descriptions and plans of the habitats required, including (for example): the extent of all essential habitat features, local weather conditions (especially aspect and exposure), provision of shelterbelts, physical land (or water) form, water depths (including seasonal fluctuation), water quality and nutrient status, water control structures, soil water table and drainage, subsoil or topsoiling requirements, planting composition, vegetation structure, use of rafts or other artificial habitat enhancement measures, human access arrangements and viewing facilities, and any other relevant factors;

(d) aftercare and long-term management requirements and how they will be met, including any statutory conditions or voluntary agreements;

(e) provision for specialist restoration advice and its timing, if required;

The Needs of Wildlife

(f) the timescale for restoration related to extraction;

(g) a list of non-priority species (eg wintering mallard) or groups (eg gulls) which are predicted also to benefit from the restoration.

Such a plan has four benefits: (a) the greatest wildlife return is achieved for a given level of restoration expenditure; (b) the cost and management implications of the aims are fully understood at the outset; (c) the end product can be objectively measured against the original plan; and (d) management continuity is assured even if personnel or circumstances change.

To aid the process of planning, in this part of the Manual information is provided on the status and habitat requirements of a range of wildlife. The species and groups included:

(a) are nationally uncommon and have needs which may be met within gravel workings, eg little ringed plover, barn owl, otter;

(b) have needs which are often overlooked in restoration design, eg feeding areas for ducklings, dragonfly habitat, breeding sites for butterflies;

(c) are important in the food-chains on which desired species depend, eg chironomids, fish.

In each case, clear prescription for habitat creation and/or management are provided. These are summarised at Table 2.1.

Examination of Table 2.1 reveals that certain features recur as of major importance for many species or groups of wildlife. Shelter from wind is valued not only by waterbirds but also by insects, including dragonflies and butterflies, and by bats. Tall herbage and rough grass are required for breeding-cover or hunting by a wide range of creatures. Shallow water is also essential: it is the zone most productive of food resources and most accessible to waterbirds. Finally, freedom from human disturbance is vital for successful feeding and breeding by many birds and mammals. These four conditions are notably absent from the majority of modern gravel pit restorations and, as Part III of the Manual shows, can all be provided if planned from the outset.

The following sections are recommended as essential reading because they give a good insight into the range of needs of aquatic wildlife, and the interactions between different species or groups: chironomids; dragonflies; fish; great crested grebe; mallard; ringed and little ringed plovers and common tern; mammals.

Plants are, of course, crucially important both directly in food-chains and indirectly because they provide the physical structure on or in which many creatures live. In addition, many aquatic plants are rare and opportunities for their conservation may exist in gravel workings. However, as they are one of the main elements capable of direct management – their needs and management are considered in Part III which deals with restoration techniques.

Table 2.1 Summary table of major requirements for wildlife

Species	Wind shelter	Sun	Shallow water	Shore-lines	Marsh	Ponds	Submerged plants	Emergent plants	Rough herbage	Trees & shrubs	Islands or rafts	Lack of distur-bance	Other
Chironomids	★	★	★				★	★		★			Organic detritus
Dragonflies	★	★	★			★	★	★	★	★			
Butterflies	★	★							★	★			Nectar plants
Fish			★				★						Deep water
Amphibians		★	★	★	★	★	★	★	★				
Snakes and lizards	★	★							★				Compost heaps, rocks and log piles
Little grebe			★				★	★				★	Fish
Great crested grebe			★				★	★				★	Fish
Grey heron			★		★							★	Fish and amphi-bians
Mute swan			★				★				★	★	Grazed grassland
Canada goose											★		Grazed grassland
Mallard	★		★	★	★		★		★		★	★	
Other dabbling ducks	★		★	★	★		★		★		★	★	
Tufted duck and pochard	★		★				★	★	★		★	★	
Redshank			★	★	★	★			★			★	
Lapwing				★								★	Short grass or bare ground
Ringed and little ringed plover and common tern			★	★							★	★	Bare shingle
Migrant and wintering waders			★	★	★	★						★	
Barn owl	★								★			★	Hollow trees or boxes
Kingfisher	★		★									★	Nest banks
Sand martin												★	Nest banks
Sedge and reed warblers								★	★	★		★	
Bats	★									★			Hollow trees or boxes
Harvest mouse									★				
Water vole			★	★			★	★	★				
Otter			★	★	★		★	★	★			★	Fish and amphi-bians

CHIRONOMIDS (Non-biting midges)

This is the most widely distributed and frequently the most abundant group of insects in freshwaters although species diversity is generally lower in waters with a pH outside the range 6–9. Probably in excess of 600 species occur in the British Isles. Many are very adaptable, while others are much more specific in their ecological requirements. They are important components of the food-chain of most aquatic ecosystems. Larvae of some species are predatory on small invertebrates, such as worms, mites and small crustaceans, but the majority feed on detritus or diatoms. Larvae, pupae and adults are all eaten by fish and birds, as well as by other predatory invertebrates. The survival of some species of ducklings during the first few days after hatching is closely related to the numbers of midges that are emerging at this critical time. The preference of migrating swifts, swallows and martins for particular ponds has also been related to the abundance of larger species of adult midges, which are apparently preferred to smaller insects.

As might be expected from their great diversity, chironomids exhibit a range of life-cycle characteristics. In temperate regions many species have only one or two generations a year, but the occurrence of three or four is not uncommon and a number of species are capable of completing a larger number of generations, often with more or less continuous emergence for much of the year. In many species, rate of development is closely related to temperature but quality of available food may also be of importance in this respect. For example, certain species grow and develop more rapidly on a diet that is rich in diatoms than on one that is predominantly organic detritus, and in certain situations population densities are closely correlated to abundance of diatoms. However, there are many species that thrive on organic detritus alone, including those with the large, red larvae familiarly known as bloodworms. In soft sediments, most larvae are to be found in the surface layers, thus sediments thicker than about 10 cm do not necessarily support more larvae than thinner deposits.

When fully developed, pupae swim to the water surface and the adult emerges through a split in the pupal thorax, the whole process being completed in a matter of seconds. It is at this stage that they are a vital source of food for young ducklings.

Immediately following emergence, wings and body surface are soft and the newly-emerged insect is then very susceptible to desiccation. The adults therefore select initial resting sites that are humid and sheltered from wind.

Males of most species form aerial mating swarms to attract females, and locate a female that enters the swarm by virtue of the different tone produced by the vibration of her wings. Pairing occurs almost immediately, the mated pair dropping out of the swarm. Hence swarms are almost exclusively of males. Whereas some species swarm low over the water surface, often very close to the bank, the majority do so over land, using features such as bushes, posts or trees, often some distance from water, as markers. Swarming behaviour is strongly inhibited by even a slight breeze. Dawn and dusk swarming is very common and is triggered by changing light intensity. This behaviour may be related to the fact that wind speed is often reduced at these times of day.

There are species of chironomid that colonise virtually every type of substratum that is to be found in freshwater. However, population densities in sand are generally very low, and gravel and rock usually only support high densities when densely covered with algae. By contrast, organic sediments and plant surfaces can support high population densities. Plants are important in that their surface area may be many times greater than that of the underlying pond or lake bed and hence they may increase, considerably, the extent of colonizable substratum. Aquatic plants are also used for egg-laying by many species and are a food resource when they die and decay.

Egg-laying behaviour varies between species; many simply deposit masses of eggs on the water surface, whereas others attach eggs to trailing vegetation or floating plants.

Habitat creation and management

1. Since the timing of the emergence of any particular species is likely to vary from year to year, as is the date of duckling hatching, a high level of chironomid species diversity is desirable in order to maximise the likelihood of a plentiful supply of emergent midges as food for ducklings during the first few critical days after hatching.
2. Adjustment of pH may be necessary to bring it within the favourable range of 6–9, for example by addition of calcium carbonate. Outside this range, chironomid diversity is much reduced.
3. During the early years of establishment, gravel pits are likely to be relatively poor in organic detritus and aquatic plants. While the spreading of topsoil in shallows will be beneficial, two additional strategies for increasing chironomid production during the early years may also be helpful. The first involves the addition of relatively intractable organic material such as straw. Probably, the most important effect of this is that it increases the surface area for colonisation on the bottom of the pit while natural organic detritus is accumulating. Secondly, the addition of phosphate and nitrate to lakes that are nutrient-poor will serve to stimulate the development of phytoplankton and attached algae, which will in turn increase the amount of food available for chironomid larvae.
4. Low, dense vegetation close to the water's edge provides protection for adults from desiccation. Shrubs and trees are useful as swarm markers and in providing shelter from wind that readily inhibits swarming behaviour. Some species selectively swarm in woodland glades and, where pits are surrounded by woodland, clearings could usefully be provided for this purpose.
5. Deciduous trees and shrubs, especially willows and alder, are a valuable source of food as their submerged, fallen leaves rapidly degrade and develop a microfauna of bacteria, fungi and protozoa.
6. Presence of submerged plants has, in general, been shown to be correlated with higher population densities and diversity of chironomids. Aquatic plants are therefore to be encouraged.

Clive Pinder

DRAGONFLIES AND DAMSELFLIES

Adult dragonflies catch their prey in meadows, marshes, moorland, scrub and in woodland rides and edges, but all British species require fresh water in which to breed and pass a larval existence which may well be up to several years long. Before man changed the landscape, dragonflies were dependent upon slow-flowing rivers, oxbow lakes, meres, bogs, and pools created by beavers. Many of the original habitats have been lost through drainage or pollution, but the losses have been partly offset by water-filled ditches, farm ponds and clay and gravel pits. Of these, gravel pits are particularly important as they cover a wide area and provide a great range of habitats. Therefore, it is not surprising that about half of the British species of dragonflies have been recorded from gravel pits and about 14 species are commonly found in them. There are more species in the south of Britain than in the north. Those marked * in the next paragraph are restricted wholly or mainly to areas south of the Humber.

When a gravel pit is dug it is usually colonised quickly by the black-tailed skimmer *Orthetrum cancellatum** and the common blue damselfly *Enallagma cyathigerum*. Then, as the aquatic vegetation develops other species occur, notably the emperor dragonfly *Anax imperator**, the southern hawker *Aeshna cyanea**, the migrant hawker *Aeshna mixta**, the common darter *Sympetrum striolatum* and the azure damselfly *Coenagrion puella*. The red-eyed damselfly *Erythromma najas* often colonises pits where floating-leaved plants such as broadleaved pondweed or waterlilies are abundant. The common blue damselfly and the emperor dragonfly are found at large waterfilled pits, but most prefer small channels and pools or narrow backwaters. The four-spotted chaser *Libellula quadrimaculata*, the variable damselfly *Coenagrion pulchellum** and the emerald damselfly *Lestes sponsa* are much more abundant in such places.

53

The Needs of Wildlife

Habitat creation and management

Much can be done to make gravel pits better for dragonflies, both when restoration work is done after extraction and in the years that follow:

1. Dragonfly larvae require warm, shallow water. Therefore the edges of the pit should not be left steep-sided but gently sloping. A sinuous shoreline will lengthen the total extent of shallows. Shallow water in embayments will gain added shelter from wave action and thus from mixing with the main body of the lake so that warming will proceed more rapidly and warm conditions will be better maintained.

2. For most species, abundant submerged vegetation is important, to provide the larvae or nymphs with both cover and hunting habitat: the abundance of prey – other insects, fish-fry and tadpoles are all taken – is influenced by the amount of plant cover to provide habitat. Again, extensive areas of shallow water are ideal.

3. When emerging to become adults, most dragonflies use the stems of emergent plants on which to climb above the water. Stands of emergents are therefore required but should not be allowed to spread and dominate the whole area of shallows. Reedbeds are not suitable habitats for British dragonflies and so should not be allowed to develop in pits where

the conservation of dragonflies is the main objective.

4. Trees and bushes should not be planted by the water's edge as they shade the water, inhibiting plant growth and lowering temperatures. An excess of dead leaves can prevent the growth of waterweed. Trees and bushes which have seeded themselves should be controlled in subsequent years.

5. The edges of waterbodies are used by dragonflies, therefore a series of small, sheltered pools is better for them than a large sheet of open water of equivalent area. These may be created by cutting back bays or infilling on a lee shore, or as separate pools.

6. Dragonflies tend not to be active in cold, windy or wet weather. Though many of the larger species stray far from water and will readily find shelter in which to settle at such times and at night, the smaller damselflies mostly remain close to their emergence site so that suitable shelter should be provided: tall herbage and shrubs provide this and also offer a good foraging habitat with much of the hunting being done by flying between the tall plant stems rather than in the open.

7. Dragonflies are susceptible to pollution and so gravel pits should be protected from contamination by nutrients and pesticides from farmland and from dumping rubbish.

Norman Moore

BUTTERFLIES

Butterflies need two basic commodities if they are to complete their life cycles successfully. First, adults need a source of nectar on which to feed. (Some species exhibit distinct preferences for particular nectar plants, for example in late summer peacocks will often be seen feeding on teasels.) Second, butterflies need foodplants on which the female butterfly will lay her eggs each year and on which the larvae will feed.

The quality of foodplants, their structure and location are all crucial points which are assessed in some way when female butterflies are searching for plants on which to lay their eggs. The female may alight on many plants but not select them because they are growing in unsuitable conditions. Sometimes the reason for a plant's rejection may be obvious: for instance, if it is in too shady a place and therefore too cool. More often, it is difficult for us to discern why a plant is unsuitable. Certainly an abundance of foodplants is necessary in order to support a colony of butterflies over many years. The greater the number of foodplants, the better chance a female has of finding one which is suitable to receive her eggs.

Detailed studies of some species of butterflies have revealed their exact requirements, many of which are compatible with the type of vegetation one might expect to develop after mineral extraction. Banks of gravel and spoil create a variety of aspects on which food and nectar plants can grow. In addition, the soils around mineral workings are sometimes thin and well-drained. These skeletal soils, and the sparse vegetation which often develops on them, usually have a warm micro-climate, conditions much favoured by many species of British butterfly. In southern Britain one might reasonably expect about 24 species to be found in disused mineral workings. These may be divided into three groups: those whose larval foodplants are:

(a) herbaceous: 11 species, green-veined white, orange-tip, small copper, common blue, peacock, red admiral, painted lady, small tortoiseshell, comma, grizzled skipper, dingy skipper;

(b) grasses: 11 species, marbled white, meadow brown, ringlet, small heath, speckled wood, wall, hedge brown, Essex, large and small skippers, grayling;

(c) shrubs: two species, brimstone and holly blue.

In the process of mineral extraction, most populations of butterflies which originally occurred on the site will be severely depleted or destroyed. Some, such as the very mobile whites, the peacock, small tortoiseshell and brimstone may quickly recolonise suitable areas. Others will be much slower to reappear. Unlike birds, many species of butterfly are incapable of travelling even short distances in search of new breeding areas, so that reintroductions may be required.

If foodplants are scarce or absent on the restored site, they may be increased by spreading seed from existing plants into bare areas or by collecting seed to spread from a nearby site. Pot-grown plants can also be planted into suitable areas. This method has some advantages over seeding. First, new plants are immediately available to female butterflies and second they can be selectively planted into areas which are known to be suitable such as south-facing banks or sheltered places. Lastly, survival of mature plants is often better than that of seedlings. However, seeding is cheaper and less time-consuming than planting-up new areas.

If recolonisation by the desired butterfly species does not occur naturally within, say, two years, specimens of the common butterflies may be collected from nearby areas where they are known to be abundant. These can be released into the suitably restored areas, provided adequate foodplants are present. However, in the case of more local species, it may be necessary to collect a few females and rear one generation on foodplants in captivity in order to boost numbers prior to release. Where reintroductions are being considered, expert help should always be sought. The British Butterfly Conservation Society, Tudor House, Quorn, Loughborough, Leicestershire, LE12 8AD, has a national network of members able to help with such projects.

It is also advisable to inform the Biological Records Centre and the Regional Office of the Nature Conservancy Council of any reintroduction.

Habitat creation and management

1. Shelter is essential, both for nectar-producing plants as food for the adults and for food plants on which females will lay their eggs and on which the larvae will feed. Most species prefer both food and nectar plants in full sunny conditions.

The Needs of Wildlife

2. A wide variety of flowering plants is used as nectar sources with thistles, teasels, dandelions, clover, knapweed and brambles being particularly important. These should be retained where they naturally colonise suitable sites, or introduced.

3. For caterpillar foodplants, native grasses such as the fine-leaved bents, fescues and bromes, Yorkshire fog and cocksfoot, together with plants such as lady's smock, field garlic, bird's-foot-trefoil and sorrels should be introduced if not present, either by seeding, by turf transplants or by insertion of pot-grown plants. Buckthorns may also be planted for the brimstones, and holly and ivy for the holly blue.

4. Introduction of selected, less mobile butterfly species may be considered, if they have not appeared naturally within two years of restoration. The marbled white, small copper, common blue, grizzled, dingy and large skippers, and grayling would be suitable for this type of project.

M Hall

FISH

Depending on whether they are dry-dug or suction-dredged, the resultant flooded sites will have different characters. Dry-dug pits are normally clear-watered, with hard bottoms and luxuriant aquatic weed growth. Wet-dug pits have a deep, soft bottom layer of clay silt which is continually disturbed by feeding fish (carp and bream) and wind action, making the water turbid, often with dense algal blooms, poor light penetration and little submerged aquatic vegetation.

As most gravel workings which are restored to lakes lie along lowland river valleys, it is not surprising that they are often subject to winter flooding. With the floods come the fish. River-dwelling fish of most species adapt well to life in still waters though they often fail to breed successfully. Carp, crucian carp, tench, bream, silver bream, roach, rudd, perch, ruffe, eels, pike, chub, bleak, dace, minnows, sticklebacks and bullheads all occur in gravel pits. In addition to these species, gravel pits are often stocked with rainbow trout, brown trout and even salmon as 'put-and-take' game fisheries. Whilst most coarse fish thrive in warm conditions (>20°C) and shallow (1–2 m) water, salmonid fish are adapted to cold waters (<15°C) and need depths of at least 5 m somewhere in the lake to avoid the warm surface layer of summer. In older lakes, where decaying organic detritus leads to summer deoxygenation in deeper water, there may be large-scale deaths of salmonid fish.

Dry-dug lakes are most suitable for tench, rudd, roach, perch and crucian carp, all of which thrive in weedy conditions. Wet-dug lakes, with their silty beds, are perfect for bream and carp which dig in the sediments to winnow midge larvae, worms and mussels for food. Pike, which grow to large sizes (more than 10 kg) in those lakes with large (>0·5 ha) areas of open water, prey actively on all of the other fish species and are often cannibalistic.

Flooded gravel workings start out with a limited supply of the decaying organic matter which many invertebrates need as a food source. As the lakes age they change, within a few years, into more productive waters which support both invertebrates and the fish which eat them, but only at low population densities (ie a total of perhaps 50 kg of fish per hectare). These populations gradually build up as more food becomes available, so that 20-year-old gravel pit lakes can support total fish standing crops of 300–500 kg per hectare. The latter density equates with a 50-g fish living over every square metre of lake bed. Fisheries management to improve the quality of angling usually involves stocking a few large specimens and netting out large numbers of small fish to reduce food competition which would otherwise cause 'stunting' of growth potential. Lakes appear typically to have a peak of fish growth rates a few years after their initial flooding, and this then subsides to a lower, stable level thereafter.

Fish – bird interactions
These take three principal forms:

1. Predation by fish on birds.
 This is probably a common and widespread phenomenon, with ducklings, young grebes, coots and moorhens all being vulnerable. Medium-sized (2–3 kg) pike are the usual culprits but large eels (>2 kg) also take ducklings. The European catfish (wels) introduced into gravel-pit fisheries by specialist anglers can grow to more than 20 kg and is another likely bird predator.
2. Predation by birds on fish.
 The large shoals of young roach and bream which live in the shallows and weedy areas of gravel pits provide an abundant food supply for a wide range of piscivorous birds. Great crested grebe, little grebe, heron, kingfisher, common tern, common gull, black-headed gull, cormorant,

goosander, smew, goldeneye, greenshank, spotted redshank and other species all eat fish from gravel-pit habitats at various times of year.
3. Food competition between fish and waterfowl.
 Where the primary management aim is waterfowl conservation, research by Game Conservancy scientists at Great Linford has shown that the invertebrate food supply for waders and wildfowl can be increased substantially by netting as many adult fish as possible from gravel pit lakes. It is most efficient to draw down the lakes and concentrate fish in any remaining deeper pools before attempting to net. Small fry go through the seine net (mesh 2 cm) and therefore remain as food for fish-eating birds. A two-to-threefold increase in midge larvae was achieved at Great Linford in this way: before they were netted out, bream, tench and perch had been eating the chironomids. A very wide range of birds may potentially benefit from this simple management technique, namely dabbling and diving ducklings, adult ducks, wading birds (both breeding and on passage), swifts, swallows, martins and reedbed nesting passerines which feed on midges and other aquatic insects. The fish removed from the lake can be sold for stocking into waters used for coarse angling.

The ARC Wildfowl reserve (17 ha) lake at Great Linford which was de-fished in 1987 (producing six tonnes of fish) subsequently grew abundant beds of submerged plants for the first time in its 25-year history, producing a food source which attracted many more gadwall, pochard, coot and mute swans than ever before seen at the site. The small cyprinid fish would need to be netted out on a cycle of around three years to ensure that the lake bed was not dug up continuously by large adult fish recruiting to the population.

Habitat creation and management

1. If fish are not naturally washed in during river flooding, selected coarse fish species may need to be introduced to those waters where fish-eating birds are to be attracted. Aquatic weeds, chironomid and other aquatic invertebrate populations need to be developed, by active management if required, to provide food resources for the fish.
2. Aquatic weed beds in shallow water will provide shelter and feeding for fish-fry.
3. When fish populations reach high levels, the fish will destroy aquatic plant beds and compete with ducklings and other birds for invertebrate food resources; in addition, the larger fish (pike and eels) will eat ducklings and small grebes. Where breeding waterfowl

production is the primary aim, every three or four years water levels should be drawn down and all large fish netted and removed. Periodic drawing down of a lake increases aquatic productivity after re-flooding through the release of oxidised inorganic chemical plant nutrients from the sediments of the lake bed. Water level regulation is, therefore, a potent habitat management technique.

N Giles

AMPHIBIANS

Six native amphibians occur in Britain, though there are a few colonies of other amphibian species introduced from mainland Europe. The six native species are: the common frog, common toad, natterjack toad, and smooth, palmate and great crested newts. All are widely distributed throughout Europe, though the great crested newt and natterjack toad are localised and declining and have been classified as endangered species. In Britain, both are protected under Schedule 5 of the Wildlife and Countryside Act 1981 which makes it an offence to damage or disturb their breeding or resting sites.

Each spring amphibians require still or slow-flowing water in which to lay their eggs or spawn. Natural spawning sites such as those created by springs or flooding are now quite rare and it is estimated that at least 60% of artificial ponds existing one hundred years ago have been lost as a result of infilling or drainage; others have been polluted by industry and agriculture.

Having rested in a torpid state for several months since the onset of the previous winter, frogs and toads usually become active in February or March when they emerge from hibernation and return to their breeding pond. There males and females will pair and spawn, frogs a few weeks earlier than toads. The warm, shallow edges of ponds are preferred for spawning, as eggs develop faster in such places. Toads wind their strings of eggs around submerged plants or the bases of emergents, and frogs and toads will often spawn together in one particular place in a pond, usually the warmest spot.

The tadpoles feed on dead animal and plant remains and micro-organisms at the edges and bottom of ponds. As they develop, the tadpoles grow legs, absorb their tails and leave the water in summer, seeking habitats such as marshes, bogs and meadows where the ground is slightly damp. These places will provide cover, and the large numbers of tiny invertebrates on which they feed. Tadpoles, young and adult amphibians are preyed on by many other animals.

Many of the requirements of newts are similar to those of frogs and toads, though newts tend to spend longer periods of time in the water. Peak breeding is usually in April and early May, eggs being laid individually or in small clusters, on the leaves and stems of aquatic plants, the roots and branches of submerged trees and even on algae and mud. Newt tadpoles look and behave like small fish. Great crested newt tadpoles spend more time in open water than the two smaller species which tend to hide in dense vegetation. The tadpoles develop legs, absorb the gills which have enabled them to breathe under water and then leave for dry land in late summer.

Frogs and toads spend only a few weeks or months in the water and live on land for most of the year. Places covered with dense vegetation in which they can find food and shelter are ideal. Woodlands and rough grassland with brambles are often found around amphibian ponds. Natural rock piles, hedgerows and fallen trees will also provide good shelter for them.

Adult newts feed both on land and in the water, depending on availability of food. Newts may move out of ponds at night to hunt on land, returning to the water before light. In the water, where newts are most agile, they will feed on small animals like Daphnia (zooplankton) and other small invertebrates on plants or in the surface layer of pond sediment. On land, they will catch and eat invertebrates such as slugs and earthworms. The adult great crested newt will prey upon frog tadpoles and the tadpoles, young and even adult smooth and palmate newts.

Habitat creation and management

1. Ponds of any size up to 0·1 ha may be created with a maximum depth of 1–2 m. Ponds should have shallow margins and, where the size of the pond permits, these should gently slope to a depth of about 2 m at a distance of 5 m from the edge. Alternatively, this depth can be reached by a series of steps. Larger ponds are also used by amphibians.

2. A series of three or four small ponds is often most successful, as it gives opportunity for a greater variety of bank profiles, which will provide more types of microhabitats and a greater variety of amphibian species.

3. In gravel pits, marginal lagoon pools can be created either by excavating outside the final worked face or by infilling with overburden. Such sites need protection from waves.

4. Ponds which dry out from time to time are often very good for amphibians because this reduces the numbers of aquatic predators, especially fish. Autumn and early winter drying is most common and is ideal. Having the capacity to be long-lived, amphibians can miss an occasional breeding season without jeopardising the population. If site water levels fluctuate sufficiently, locate and design ponds accordingly.

5. If ponds do not dry out, avoid stocking them with fish, particularly sticklebacks, perch and pike which are voracious predators of amphibians.

6. A diverse range of emergent vegetation should be established around no more than half of the edges of a pond or lagoon. Avoid reedmace, which is invasive and difficult to manage. Emergent vegetation provides habitats for insects which in turn provide food for frogs, toads and other aquatic life.

7. Submerged plants should be introduced to provide cover from predators, spawn deposi-tion sites and support the food chain on which amphibians depend.

8. Avoid planting trees near the water's edge as they will cause shading, affecting water temperature and plant growth. To benefit amphibians, the sunniest aspect to the south and east should be left exposed, so that the temperature of the water can increase as much as possible.

9. Once the pond or lake has been created or restored, any further heavily disruptive management should only be carried out during winter months and kept to as small an area as possible. Disturbance should be kept to a minimum from the start of February until the end of September.

10. Ditches are often good places for amphibians. They should be as deep as they are wide, with the above-water edges cut back at a shallow angle. They can be dammed to create pockets of deeper standing water.

11. Rock and log piles will benefit amphibians, as will compost heaps and piles of leaves. These provide food and shelter, and should be positioned within 200 m of the edge of a pond.

12. Sites can be stocked with amphibians by introducing spawn or tadpoles from thriving colonies elsewhere. As amphibians may take three years or more to mature, a new colony may take up to 10 years or more to attain maximum numbers.

Thomas Langton

SNAKES AND LIZARDS

There are six species of reptile in Britain; the grass snake, northern viper or adder, smooth snake, viviparous or common lizard, sand lizard and slow-worm. The smooth snake and sand lizard are endangered species, confined to a few sandy heathland locations in southern England. The other four species are widespread but declining on mainland Britain, while the common lizard is the only reptile to occur in Ireland. Like amphibians, reptiles can be very abundant when their habitats are properly managed. They provide an important food supply for many mammals and birds of prey.

Being cold-blooded, reptiles need sunny places in which to bask and raise their body temperature so as to be able to move, hunt and breed. Snakes and lizards do particularly well on south-facing banks and slopes, especially those which are sheltered from strong breezes. They are found on less fertile soils where grasses and heathers flourish. Plants such as gorse, broom, bracken, birch, hawthorn and blackthorn are species which often make up low, open vegetation which holds sheltered but open areas that act as warm suntraps.

Adders, common lizards and slow-worms are live-bearing. Grass snakes lay small bundles of up to several dozen white, leathery eggs in late summer. These are hidden under rotting logs, in stacks of grass cuttings, manure heaps and other warm, humid places. Usually laid in July, they may take ten weeks or more to develop before hatching.

Grass snakes feed mainly on amphibians and fish, while adders prey on small rodents and other small animals such as lizards. Legged lizards feed almost exclusively on invertebrates such as flies and spiders, while the slow-worm, a legless lizard often mistaken for a snake, eats slower-moving prey such as slugs.

Reptiles require dry places underground to overwinter, usually between October and March.

Habitat creation and management

1. In general, the bigger the area available, the more scope there will be to establish and maintain reptiles. Sites of over 2 ha offer greatest potential.
2. Create variation in the detailed topography of an area, so that a mosaic of surface environments is formed, some moist, others well drained and dry; some in full sun to provide basking areas, others more shaded and sheltered from sun and wind.
3. Reptile colonies can be most easily established away from disturbance by humans or domestic animals, especially from cats which may systematically destroy reptile populations. To control human disturbance during the reptiles' active season may require careful screening with dense plantations of prickly growth such as gorse, blackthorn and hawthorn. Within such screening, the open area should be at least 0·25 ha in extent, to avoid too much shade. Banks and ditches can also be used to control access to areas. Raised hedge banks can be made from piles of rocks filled with topsoil, which will also create refuges for reptiles.
4. Low-nutrient soils are ideal as the basis to create fairly open habitats of dwarf vegetation. Often sites can be left to vegetate naturally but low-growing grasses and herbs can be sown, and on sandy, low-pH sites, heather may be established to provide plenty of cover and basking spots. Grasslands may need to be mown or grazed from time to time and a management plan is advisable. Avoid summer mowing and disturbance in the smaller patches where reptiles are becoming established, around hibernation sites and favourite basking places. Manage these places during winter or during other cool spells when reptiles are not likely to be active. Small areas of bare ground, stone piles or rocks may be created to provide basking sites.
5. Piles of brick rubble, broken paving slab, crushed concrete, old pallets and railway sleepers can be buried to create overwintering sites. These should be packed sparingly with loose soil to create a warren of small gaps of 2–3 cm diameter. They must be above the normal high watertable and flood level.
6. For grass snakes, basking areas should border marshy wetland areas and lakes. Public access in such areas should be carefully controlled. Raised board-walks can allow access across marshy ground and help to leave the edges of wetlands undisturbed.
7. For grass snake breeding, 'compost heaps' can be constructed in sheltered spots from materials such as grass, reed and rush cuttings, vegetation from ditch and pond dredgings, sawdust and farmyard manure. Avoid large amounts of tree trimmings or other fibrous material which will not break down easily. The

optimum size of these heaps of vegetation is a cube of about 1 m; this size heats up well as the plant materials decompose and will normally stay reasonably aerobic throughout. The heaps

should be topped up each year with new materials in spring.

Thomas Langton

BIRDS

Their power of flight means that birds are usually quick to find new areas of suitable habitat and because many waterbirds tend to travel along river valleys, whether on daily feeding forays or seasonal long-distance migration, gravel pits are usually ideally placed to be discovered. In the course of a year thousands of birds of many species can be expected to pass through or over a site but whether they choose to stay depends on whether they find food and security.

In designing restoration for birds it is important to bear in mind the full range of their requirements.

Feeding

(a) Summer: Resident bird populations are augmented by large numbers of summer migrants exploiting the seasonal flush of invertebrate food. Despite its apparent abundance, there is considerable competition between birds especially when rearing broods and this can be particularly acute during spells of poor weather such as continuous rain, leading to the death of many chicks and fledglings. Good quality feeding habitat is the key and this means creating the right physical conditions, such as shallow water, or vegetation cover such as trees and shrubs to support abundant suitable invertebrates. Making the right decision is critically important – for instance, most native trees and shrubs support much greater numbers of invertebrates than non-native species.

(b) Passage: Most migrants need to stop periodically in order to feed and restore energy for the next stage of the journey. Some of these birds are travelling short distances, for instance from the UK coast to the uplands, but others may be en route between west Africa and the Arctic: for them to complete the demanding journey and arrive in fit condition to breed, they must be able to find sites where abundant food is easily available.

(c) Winter: Songbird numbers are much reduced

by migration. For wintering species food supplies are progressively depleted and may become very difficult to obtain in conditions of hard frost, snow cover or ice. There is often high mortality of birds. Large numbers of waterfowl from northern Europe winter here and disturbance may dangerously reduce their feeding opportunities and deplete their energy reserves. Habitat design, planting and management are very important. In particular, estate management work which must take place in winter should avoid inadvertent destruction of vegetation or non-essential tidying-up as this often substantially reduces the amount and quality of feeding habitat.

Nest sites

All birds require nest sites which provide safety from predators or accidental destruction and many species also select sites which provide protection from the weather. Most birds find safety and shelter by nesting in holes or cavities, on islands or in a dense vegetation cover. A few species such as lapwing and little ringed plover nest in the open, and rely on camouflage. Their eggs and chicks are particularly liable to physical destruction due to trampling by humans or domestic livestock.

Human disturbance of nesting birds greatly increases the likelihood of desertion or of the nest being drawn to the attention of predators.

Good nesting habitat can be created by the establishment and correct management of vegetation, plus the provision of islands, rafts, nestboxes and other artificial sites.

Moult sites

All wildfowl become flightless in late summer and congregate at sites where there is abundant food and a high level of security from human disturbance. Such sites are scarce and of great importance. To develop and maintain suitable conditions requires careful control over visitor access at this season.

Roosting

When not feeding or engaged in courtship, birds seek undisturbed and sheltered conditions, with safety from predators, where they can rest, preen and sleep. In winter, when temperatures are low, shelter from wind is particularly important. Waterfowl congregate under lee shores. Most small birds seek dense cover and often favour evergreens. Large flocks can build up in favoured locations which have a very important survival value and can be created by the provision of shelterbelts, land forming and appropriate planting schemes.

The following sections summarise the distribution, habitats and requirements of a selection of those birds which it should be possible to support in a gravel pit restoration. The selection was made to illustrate the range of requirements of wetland birds and is far from exhaustive, but detailed information on species not discussed is available in ornithological literature or from conservation organisations.

A restoration plan will achieve more for conservation if it seeks to benefit good numbers of a few of the less common birds rather than attracting small numbers of everything. However, if the main aim is to provide birdwatching entertainment, then it is often practicable to achieve both benefits for scarce birds and year-round variety and interest.

LITTLE GREBE

A very widely distributed bird, the little grebe's range extends from the British Isles through much of Europe, Africa and Asia. Despite the extent of its total range, it is not very numerous because it is restricted to shallow, productive waters with ample marginal cover. Thus, though it occurs throughout Britain and Ireland, our total breeding population is probably less than 14,000 pairs.

In the breeding season, little grebes feed mainly on aquatic insects such as water beetles and the larvae of dragonflies, midges and caddisflies. In winter, when insects are less abundant, about half the diet consists of all kinds of fish up to 7 cm long.

Little grebes nest on both still and running water and will occupy sites of well under 1 ha in extent. Average territory size is 0·1 – 0·2 ha but, perhaps because of interaction between adjacent pairs, the maximum recorded density is five pairs per hectare.

Three factors are critical for successful breeding. The first is water depth – the birds feed by diving and the deeper the water the more energy they must use, so depths of about 1 m are probably ideal. The second is abundant submerged vegetation to provide habitat for the insects and small fish which form the little grebes' prey. The third is stands of emergent vegetation in which the birds can make their nest and themselves take cover, as they are shy of humans.

Breeding can start in late February but there are rarely eggs before early April. The nest is built of water plants, often the dead remains of last year's growth, gathered to create a floating platform anchored amongst emergent vegetation, on mats of waterweed or on branches which dip below the water's surface. Usually several platforms will be made before one is selected to hold the nest, a cup only about 5 cm above the water's surface and therefore vulnerable to inundation.

Four to six eggs are laid and both sexes share incubation. Normally, if one bird leaves the nest without being relieved, it will cover the eggs with plant material but if sudden disturbance causes a sitting bird to flee, the eggs will be left uncovered and may be taken by crows or magpies. Young birds are also taken by predatory birds and pike. There are usually two broods produced each year from which, on average, each pair raises 1·7 young.

Many little grebes desert their breeding waters in winter, perhaps because of food shortage or, more obviously, because of freezing. Small groups may be found on larger waters which remain open all year.

Habitat creation and management

1. A continuous area of at least 0·2 ha should have a water depth 0·75–1·25 m overall. At this depth, there will be good light penetration aiding submerged plant growth and high productivity of insects and small fish.
2. Each such area should contain, at the shore or surrounding islands, shallow shelving margins to provide for the establishment of beds of emergent vegetation. The precise total area

necessary to provide adequate choice of nest sites is not known but it is suggested that shoreline shallows of at least 40 m length and 1–2 m width should be treated in this way and surfaced with topsoil to aid rapid growth and spread of the emergent vegetation. The site should be distant from sources of disturbance by people.

3. Though dense stands of emergents interfere with the birds' foraging, quantities of floating plants such as lilies do not appear to present a problem. Trees at the margins are also tolerated and indeed trees growing, standing dead or fallen in the water may help to provide the

cover which these birds like as well as increasing the choice of nest sites.

4. In natural sites, little grebes seem to favour those with muddy bottoms but use of topsoil for this purpose is probably unnecessary as stands of submerged plants will develop readily on normal worked substrates.

5. Though the nest can rise or fall with limited water level changes, large fluctuations are likely to cause breeding failure and should be avoided if possible. Nests may also be swamped by powered craft.

John Andrews

GREAT CRESTED GREBE

The world distribution of this bird is less extensive than that of the little grebe. Thus though it reaches to south-west Australia, it is found in few areas of Africa, is absent from most of south and south-east Asia and has a very patchy presence in western Europe. In the British Isles it is a bird of the larger waterbodies in the lowlands.

Brought almost to extinction here in the last century, when it was killed in the breeding season so that its handsome feather tippets might adorn millinery, the population fell to 42 pairs by 1860 but there has been a steady recovery in this century, aided greatly by the creation of flooded

gravel workings which can provide ideal conditions, and the present resident population in the British Isles is probably over 10,000 birds.

Great crested grebes feed mainly on fish which they pursue by swimming under water, usually in depths down to 4 m. All fish species seem to be taken; presumably the main prey species are those which are most abundant and visible. Size ranges from 3–21 cm, and the birds probably need about 150–250 g per day.

For breeding, a pair of birds requires a site of about 1 ha or more, with beds of emergent vegetation. On larger waterbodies they will distribute themselves in bays or inlets, particularly those screened by islands or stands of reeds. Marginal tree cover is accepted but so are open banks. However the former, by screening them from human activity on the shore, may help to reduce disturbance of incubating birds.

The nest is a substantial pile of aquatic vegetation, built up from the bottom in shallow water or floating and tethered to growing vegetation. It is usually well concealed in emergent plants, most often *Phragmites*, or amongst the trailing branches of willows overhanging the water. The nest cup is 4–7 cm above the water surface and is susceptible to swamping by sudden increases in water level, waves or boat wash.

There are usually three or four eggs, laid from early April onwards and incubated by both adults. As with little grebe, the eggs are covered with weed to protect them from predatory birds if both adults have to leave the nest. Two broods are normal, but there are substantial losses to pike and other large fish, starvation due to inadequate supplies of small fish and insects, and bad weather conditions.

Habitat creation and management

1. Most gravel workings offer adequate feeding habitat for the adult grebes but may lack the abundance of small fish and insects required by the young. Good conditions for the production of such food will be provided by areas less than 2 m deep, where submerged vegetation can flourish.
2. Stands of emergent vegetation are required for nesting. These can be created in water to a depth of about 1 m and should be as broad as practicable to distance the birds from human disturbance on banks and from mammalian predators. The total extent for nesting habitat is not known: birds will use small patches in undisturbed sites but larger areas may increase the chances of breeding.
3. Fluctuations in water level should be minimised and wash from power boats prevented over the nesting period (normally between early April and mid July).

John Andrews

GREY HERON

The grey heron breeds in most of Europe, in parts of Africa and right across Asia to the Far East. Essentially a lowland bird, it is largely confined to regions free of intensive frost and snow cover. It is widespread in Britain and Ireland, but has a breeding population of only some 10,000 pairs. Numbers have increased recently, but are depleted during long, hard winters with prolonged freezing; short periods of freezing weather may cause heavy mortality among first-winter birds, but the more experienced adults normally survive.

Coastal habitats may be frequented outside the breeding season, or in some areas throughout the year, but in most of Britain herons occur on inland freshwaters. They have a broad tolerance of habitat types: easily accessible shallow water with a good food supply is the basic requirement. This can be standing or slow-flowing and includes rivers, marshes and lakes, as well as a wide range of artificial habitats such as canals, reservoirs, gravel pits, ditches and even garden ponds.

Throughout the year, the main food is fish: the species taken will reflect what is available at a given site, but fish of roughly 10–16 cm in length represent a normal catch. Damage to fish stocks is often alleged, so it is important to realise that an adult heron requires 330–500 g of fish per day, or up to about 25% of its own body weight. Herons regularly take other prey (including on dry land), such as insects, amphibians, reptiles and small mammals and, less often, crustaceans, molluscs, worms and small birds including ducklings.

The usual fishing tactics are to stand motionless at one point, or to stalk slowly and patiently through the shallows. Herons feed largely by day, especially in the mornings and evenings, but also around dusk and sometimes later. Flights to and from preferred feeding places are normal – herons are accomplished and powerful fliers and if necessary may travel 30 km to feed.

Herons are colonial breeders and many heronries have a long history of use. The largest British heronry regularly holds over 200 nests, but most are far smaller and the national average is about 20. Most heronries (probably all in likely gravel pit country) are in trees. Dense woodland is avoided, but more open woods may be used, as well as groups of trees of varying size. Freedom from disturbance is important, but the proximity of water is not; nevertheless, some heronries are beside water or on islands in lakes, reservoirs and old gravel pits.

Eggs are laid very early, in February or March in normal years, but even in late January in very mild weather. By around mid to late June, the breeding cycle has normally finished for the year.

Habitat creation and management

1. Invertebrates and fish soon appear in most flooded sites and, later, fish stocking may occur. In any event, herons quickly find and explore new sites. Any form of stocking specifically for herons is probably unnecessary.
2. Because herons have such a broad tolerance of habitat conditions, sites managed for other wetland birds and aquatic wildlife are likely to suit them if,
   (a) there are reasonable lengths of open, gently shelving shore (herons tend to avoid dense cover and steep banks) and adjoining shallow water up to 30 cm in depth. About 20–25 m of open shore is a probable minimum to aim for.
   (b) there is freedom from disturbance. Herons tend to be wary and will make most use of areas well away from regularly used paths and active excavation.
3. Herons will not normally use steep banks with a drop of 60 cm or more to the water surface.
4. An existing heronry on a proposed excavation site will almost certainly be deserted at an early stage, unless it is possible to give it a wide berth or to avoid disturbance altogether. If short-term work is feasible, however, it could be confined to the non-breeding period – roughly July to December inclusive: the re-occupation of heronries will begin in January in most years.
5. New heronries cannot be easily 'planned' – it is unlikely, for instance, that sufficient mature trees (eg willows) will exist in suitably undisturbed places until about 25 years after excavations finish. Much depends on existing heronries and heron populations locally – and other factors beyond a site manager's control.

M J Everett

MUTE SWAN

Their conspicuous, white colour and large size – they are the biggest wild birds in the UK – make mute swans so noticeable that it is easy to form a false impression of their abundance. The British Isles population totals about 20,000 birds in winter of which only about half are of breeding age. Numbers in other European countries are much smaller, though there is a substantial population in central Russia. In the British Isles, in the recent past some 3,000–4,000 birds died each year through ingesting lead fishing weights. Mortality from this cause has greatly declined since the bans on import, sale and (in England and Wales) the use of all but the smallest shot sizes (below 0·06 g).

Mute swans feed mostly in water, taking submerged vegetation: small numbers of invertebrates must be consumed incidentally. In water up to 45 cm deep the birds can feed by dipping the head and neck but they can also reach down to 1 m by up-ending. Where undisturbed, they come ashore to graze natural grasslands, farm pastures or young cereals. The range of plant material taken is wide, including leaves and stems, roots and stolons. Common food plants include *Myriophyllum, Potamogeton, Chara, Callitriche, Rorippa palustre, Agrostis stolonifera* and *Glyceria fluitans*. The amount of food required by so large a bird is considerable, and may reach 4 kg of wet plant material a day.

Most individuals do not breed until they are three or four years old, then normally mating for life. Pairs are territorial from about February until November, defending an area the size of which depends on the richness of food resources and availability of suitable nesting habitat but may average around 4·5 ha. Water depths must be sufficiently shallow to support extensive, accessible beds of plant material. Mute swans rarely occur on steepsided areas of deep water.

The nest is usually built at the water's edge, an obvious structure which the adults can defend effectively against natural predators. However, up to 40% of eggs laid fail to hatch and in the first two weeks of life about 30% of chicks die, mainly due to starvation. The food requirements of the young have not been fully studied. They are fed by the adults on fragments of plant material but may also require supplies of invertebrates.

Adults which have failed to breed successfully, and birds too young to mate, may congregate in large numbers from mid-summer for the annual moult, when they become flightless. The sites chosen are usually traditional, offering both security and reliable food supplies.

Habitat creation and management

1. For successful breeding, sites should offer extensive beds of submerged waterplants, either growing in depths of less than 1 m or readily accessible at that level by birds up-ending. Expanses of water less than 4 ha in extent are unlikely to support breeding pairs.

2. As the birds negotiate steep slopes with difficulty, banks should be cut back at a shallow angle (<40°) to give access to suitable marginal nest sites and to grazing habitat.

3. Nesting places should be protected from human disturbance and vandalism. Islands are ideal. Alternatively, open areas of shore may be screened by scrub or tree cover on the landward side.

4. Areas of short grassland (mown or grazed by livestock) may be provided adjoining the water to give additional feeding habitat.

John Andrews

CANADA GOOSE

A native of North America which was first introduced into large estates in Britain in the second half of the 17th century, the Canada goose has become thoroughly naturalised. Since the 1950s the feral population has greatly increased at an average rate of 8% per year and the rapid upward trend continues. The total population in Britain is probably about 50,000 birds with large concentrations in East Anglia, the Thames Valley, Midlands and Yorkshire.

The main habitat is open standing water in the lowlands, lakes in parkland and flooded gravel pits with islands. For most of the year they feed mainly on grass near water, often in areas used by the public for recreation. In some areas, geese feed in cereal crops and often frequent stubble fields in the autumn. In summer they will also feed on aquatic plants.

Pairs arrive on their breeding territories during March and frequently breed in loose colonies. Nests are built on the ground, often in the shelter of a bush or at the base of a tree, close to water. Islands are much favoured, such nests suffering markedly less predation than those on the mainland. The normal clutch of 5–7 eggs is laid in April and early May. Replacement clutches are laid after early egg loss, but only one brood is reared. The goslings fend for themselves, but are cared for by both parents which defend them against predators and sometimes human intruders. The males can be very aggressive.

The young are about 10 weeks old before they can fly. They graze the spring growth of grass in May and June. The adults undergo a complete postbreeding moult, becoming flightless in June when the goslings are about a month old. Canada geese are rather sedentary during the late spring and summer; their flights to feeding areas rarely exceed 5 km. However, about 1,000 immature and older non-breeding birds from Yorkshire and the Midlands perform a northward migration of c500 km in order to moult on the Beauly Firth on the east coast of Scotland. Flocks of moulting Canada geese occur near breeding sites in several areas. During the winter, the birds form flocks and become more mobile, often flighting from lakes and flooded gravel pits where they roost to feed on farmland (pasture, crop waste, and young winter wheat).

Habitat creation and management

Canada geese are the subject of some controversy. They have been rapidly increasing in some areas. It is claimed that they may cause damage to crops and pasture and disrupt the nesting of other birds on islands.

If Canada geese are to be encouraged:
1. For nesting, well-vegetated islands, surrounded by enough water to deter foxes, should be constructed.
2. Geese thrive on good quality grassy swards with a low fibre content and nutritious species. They can be encouraged to gravel pits by creating goose lawns using agricultural seed mixes of species such as perennial rye-grass, meadow fescue, Timothy grass and white clover, the stolons of which form an important part of their diet. Indigenous species such as common and creeping bent, and rough

meadow-grass will also tend to invade the sward in time, and these are valuable food plants too.

The goose lawn should be kept short, ideally about 5 cm high. This is best achieved by grazing tightly in the autumn with sheep or cattle at a stocking density of 5–10 sheep or 1·5–2 cows per ha. Management by introducing grazing stock may be unnecessary if sufficient numbers of geese are present to graze all year round, although in the summer they will also feed on aquatic plants and emergent vegetation in and around the gravel pit. Mowing the sward in the late summer is also beneficial as this removes any remaining dead flowering stems.
3. The edges of the gravel pit should be sculptured to have gently shelving banks in close proximity to the grazing areas, so that birds have easy access to the goose lawns. This is especially important during the moulting period when the birds are flightless. These banks will also provide good loafing areas.
4. The ideal feeding area should contain large fields with relatively few hedges, ditches, trees and buildings, since wildfowl require good visibility. Visitor paths should be at least 200 m away from the main feeding area.
5. Avoid disturbance in the form of people landing on islands in the goose breeding season (mid March–June) and shooting at dusk during the inland wildfowling season (1 September–31 January) when the geese may be coming in to roost.

If Canada geese are to be discouraged:
1. Islands capped with bare shingle (favoured by nesting common terns) or with tall vegetation cover (attractive to nesting ducks) are less attractive to geese than those with a lawn-like grass sward. Two strands (wire or binder twine) set at a height of 20 and 40 cm around the periphery of islands discourages geese from landing from the water and should be erected where the aim is to enable other species to nest.
2. Where conditions are attractive to the birds, there are no easy ways of reducing their numbers. The Canada goose is a quarry species which may be shot within the wildfowling season (see above). The Wildfowl and Countryside Act 1981 also allows it to be shot under licence in the close season if it can be shown that the birds are responsible for serious damage to crops. However, shooting is often not a practicable option where there is public access or interest.

3. Unwanted Canada geese may be rounded up (at the time of the moult) and moved to other sites provided that a licence is obtained. In practice a licence is unlikely to be granted as translocation merely establishes a problem elsewhere. Attempts to control a local flock by reducing its breeding success (eg by egg removal) may be carried out under licence and, if contemplated, advice should be taken from the Nature Conservancy Council. However, the effects of such control will only be seen in the long-term as the adults are long-lived. Even then, the population may be replenished by immigration.

C J Cadbury, C Evans and G Hirons

MALLARD

A very widespread and abundant duck, the mallard is found right across the northern hemisphere, from the arctic tundra to sub-tropical zones. The large British breeding population is swollen over winter by immigrants from farther north.

The mallard is an opportunist omnivore, with very catholic tastes. It feeds mostly in water, preferring areas less than 1 m deep, by pecking and dabbling (sieving food from the water) sometimes with the head or head and neck immersed, or by up-ending. Occasionally it will perform shallow dives down to 2 m. It also feeds on land, the main foods in autumn and winter being crop residues, arable weed seeds, acorns etc. In the spring and summer, mallard need high quality proteins and switch to a diet composed principally of freshwater invertebrates – insects, molluscs, crustaceans and worms. Later in the year, they take more vegetable material, such as shoots, seeds, leaves and tubers of aquatic plants. The ducklings, from hatching to three weeks of age, feed almost entirely on aquatic midges (chironomids) and other invertebrates taken from the water surface and from vegetation.

The winter flocks on larger, more open sites disperse widely by March to smaller, more vegetated and sheltered waters. The breeding pairs occupy a home range which includes an invertebrate-rich feeding area and the nest site. The nesting pairs are usually well dispersed, though in some cases they tolerate another nest as close as 2 m, and the nest may be a considerable distance (2 km or more) from water.

Like most ground-nesting birds, mallard are very vulnerable to predation, losing eggs and sitting females, so dense ground cover is important. Nests are usually made in tall herbaceous plant cover such as nettles, thistles, docks and willowherb, in tall grasses, sedges and rushes, under bramble, dogwood, willow coppice or thorn scrub, and sometimes in woodland edges and the crowns of pollarded trees, but in general they prefer to nest away from dense tree cover. They are very often early nesters, so dead plant stems standing from the previous year are important as cover for first nests before the new spring growth appears. Nest losses to predators are also reduced by nesting on islands for which they show some preference.

For preening, resting and sleeping they prefer areas of sheltered, bare ground or short grass very close to open water to which they can easily move if in danger.

From late summer, mallard congregate on the larger, more open waters of gravel pits, reservoirs and estuaries which provide a safe daytime roost. They will also move into areas with abundant cover such as tree-fringed islands and shores.

Habitat creation and management

1. Mallard are tolerant of considerable disturbance and rapidly exploit any suitable habitat. Parts of most wet gravel pits can easily be modified to meet at least some of their needs. For feeding, the principal requirement is to make extensive areas of water less than 40 cm deep; water deeper than 1 m is used almost solely for roosting, so the maximum area possible should be restored as shallows. The deeper roosting waters should include parts which are sheltered from wind, either in the lee of islands or by a shelter belt; they should also be kept undisturbed.

2. The shorelines should be graded to slopes of less than 1:10. A variety of soil types above and below the waterline – topsoil, subsoil, gravel, sand, mud and rocks – will increase habitat diversity and thus the range of food resources.

3. Landward of the shore, blocks of ground should be managed to provide tall herb or low shrubby nest cover as close as possible to the shallow, brood-rearing habitat, so that ducklings do not have to move long distances on their first feeding foray. Linear strips of nesting habitat are not recommended as they are easily searched by foraging foxes.
4. There should also be sheltered short grass areas, gravel beaches or islands to serve as loafing sites.
5. For breeding, islands should be created. To reduce predation by mammals they should be sited as far from shore as possible. Because breeding drakes are territorial, a large number of well-spaced islands (20–30 m apart) is ideal, and an irregular shoreline also helps to separate birds. In some circumstances, floating rafts planted with suitable turf covering may be the only way to provide enough islands.
6. To maximise the range of food resources, the littoral zone should be planted with a variety of marsh plants (purple loosestrife, gipsywort,

kingcup, flowering rush, brooklime, water forget-me-not etc), and with emergent aquatic species (common reed, reedmace, pond sedge, yellow iris, soft rush and bulrush), each in blocks of a single species. If planted as a mixture, one would eventually take over and dominate the entire planted area, reducing the plant diversity. Shallows should be planted with floating-leaved species (yellow and white water lilies, broad-leaved pondweed, amphibious bistort, starwort) and the deeper spots with submerged plants (eg stonewort, hornwort, milfoil, crowfoots, *Potamogeton* pondweeds).
7. In general terms, a gravel pit restored for mallard and other dabbling duck species should have at least 60% of its total area well vegetated, with a mixed pattern of emergent, floating-leaved and submerged plants occupying almost all of the lake bed. Thus the shallower gravel pits are the best ones to restore for this species.

M Street

OTHER DABBLING DUCKS

Apart from the mallard, four other British dabbling ducks – teal, gadwall, shoveler and wigeon – are all likely to exploit gravel pits restored to create habitat for mallard, but they have some additional requirements that need to be met if conditions are to be ideal.

TEAL

Like mallard, teal are widespread and abundant throughout the northern hemisphere, with around 200,000 birds in north-west Europe, almost half of them wintering in Britain. However, we have only 3,000–4,500 breeding pairs.

Their main foods are small seeds of plants like fat hen, goosefoot, bistort and bramble, grasses, rushes and *Potamogeton* pondweeds, alder and birch trees. Teal also take many invertebrates (chiefly insects like chironomids) in the summer.

Food items are picked from the water surface by pecking, or from the shallows by dabbling. They therefore need very shallow (less than 20 cm deep), still or slow-flowing water, ideally with a sprinkling of shorter emergent and marsh plants (spike rush, brooklime, water plantain, bistort etc) growing in fine muds and sands. They often use small pools in marshland but are quite shy and require undisturbed sites.

Teal breed in most parts of Britain, but only in low densities. For nesting, they like very quiet, secluded sites in shallow marshy habitats with tall, dense ground cover, often under trees. The ducklings take invertebrates for the first three weeks of life, generally eating more small molluscs than do mallard ducklings.

For roosting and loafing, teal favour extensive mud flats and sand bars which are covered by only 3–4 cm of water, with dense fringing vegetation into which they can retreat.

The Needs of Wildlife

Habitat creation and management

Gravel pits restored for mallard can be much improved for teal by increasing the proportion of very shallow water and by using the silt settlement lagoons to make shallow mudflats, planted with a variety of low-growing marsh plants. If there is any spare land around the larger lakes, a large number of small (0·2–1 ha), well-sheltered, shallow marshy scrapes should be excavated, with scattered small (eg 30 m×10 m), densely vegetated islands to provide the feeding and nesting areas. Human disturbance should be minimised.

SHOVELER

The shoveler is another widespread species, but with a generally more southerly range than the other dabblers. There are an estimated 100,000+ birds in northern Europe, but only around 1,500 pairs breeding in Britain, chiefly in the south-east and East Anglia. Our breeding population moves south and west in autumn, and is replaced by wintering birds from north-west Europe and the USSR.

The shoveler has a wide-tipped bill with many fine, fringing lamellae adapted to filter out very small food items such as tiny molluscs, insects, crustaceans (especially zooplankton) and smaller seeds. The specialised filter feeding allows it to exploit zooplankton as a resource in the spring, hence its liking for nutrient-rich waters where plankton blooms are common. The ducklings too benefit from this.

Shoveler feed by bill-skimming the surface or with head and neck submerged, sometimes up-ending and readily diving in shallows. Often a small group will stir up food by swimming rapidly in tight circles. Water depth is not critical provided it is nutrient-rich so that they can feed on the plankton in the surface layer. They do need the seeds of water plants in the winter however, so marshy areas with open, shallow pools and scattered vegetation over soft, fine sediments are also necessary. For loafing, like teal and mallard, they use bare, low mudflats and gravel beaches.

Shoveler nest in shorter cover than mallard and teal, often almost in the open, usually close to the waterside.

Habitat creation and management

This species readily uses gravel pits restored for mallard, but can exploit deeper sites especially if measures are taken to raise the nutrient level of the water in spring to promote plankton growth. If the downwind shore (usually the eastern side) of the lake is scalloped to make bays, shoveler will take advantage of the windblown seeds and insects in the flotsam which collects there. Dense tree and shrub cover should not be developed close to the water margins, better nesting habitat being provided by tussocky grass created by allowing cattle to graze the shores in the latter part of each year, but not in April–June, when nests may be destroyed by trampling.

GADWALL

The gadwall has a rather scattered distribution but has been increasing steadily for many years and spreading northwards through Europe, partly as a result of introductions. The north-west European winter population is around 10,000. It has bred in Britain since the middle of the 19th century and we now have some 500 pairs, with an influx in winter from north-west Europe taking numbers up to 4,000–5,000 birds.

Gadwall feed mainly in the water, usually just with the head under and rarely up-ending. They are almost entirely vegetarian, taking leafy growth, buds, roots, tubers, seeds and rhizomes of water plants, especially the softer ones such as Canadian pondweed, milfoil, starwort, water crowfoot, duckweed and fennel-leaved pondweed. Frequently, they feed alongside other waterfowl such as swans and coot, which bring plant materials to the surface while feeding in greater depths than gadwall can reach. The younger ducklings eat invertebrates (mainly flies) from the water surface, until switching to vegetation at around three weeks old.

Gadwall thrive on clear, shallow waters with extensive dense beds of submerged water plants. Research at the ARC Wildfowl Centre has shown that their use of a gravel pit lake increased significantly with the removal of most of the bream, whose foraging activity on the lake bed had inhibited the plant growth. Numbers of other vegetarian species, especially coots and swans, also increased following the fish removal.

Though mainly in the south and east of Britain, gadwall are extending their breeding range and can be expected to use good new habitats. For nesting, they prefer well-concealed sites in the dense cover of grasses and scrub near water. They share wintering habitat with mallard, using the sheltered parts of larger waters and roosting on bare, open shores.

Habitat creation and management

This species can adapt well to most gravel pits restored to meet mallard requirements, provided there is abundant plant food.

WIGEON

This is a very widespread and abundant Eurasian duck, which breeds mainly in the far north and moves south early in the winter, about 1·5 million birds migrating to western Europe. The British breeding population is only around 400 pairs, mainly in the uplands.

Wigeon are almost entirely vegetarian, eating the leaves, stems, bulbs, rhizomes, roots, stolons and some seeds of a wide variety of aquatic and terrestrial plants, especially the finer, softer grasses such as floating sweet grass and marsh foxtail in wet areas; meadow grass and rye-grass in dry areas. In winter they are mainly flock feeders, spending much time grazing on short pasture. They will also feed on cereal stubbles with mallard. The wintering birds rely heavily on estuaries but are making increasing use of the larger open gravel pits and reservoirs.

Habitat creation and management

In winter, wigeon ideally require sites which offer very good all-round views, with roosting, loafing and feeding areas in close proximity. They will use the larger, more bleak gravel pit lakes for roosting, especially if the shores are not heavily wooded. Adjoining such sites, extensive areas of short pasture should be created, combining suitable grasses with white clover, and maintained by mowing or, better still, grazed by sheep. If feasible, as much as possible of the pasture should be flooded to a depth of 10 cm from December to February. The shores between the roost and the pasture should be free from emergent plant growth, as wigeon like unimpeded pedestrian access to their feeding sites. The prescriptions given for Canada geese should provide acceptable conditions for wigeon.

M Street

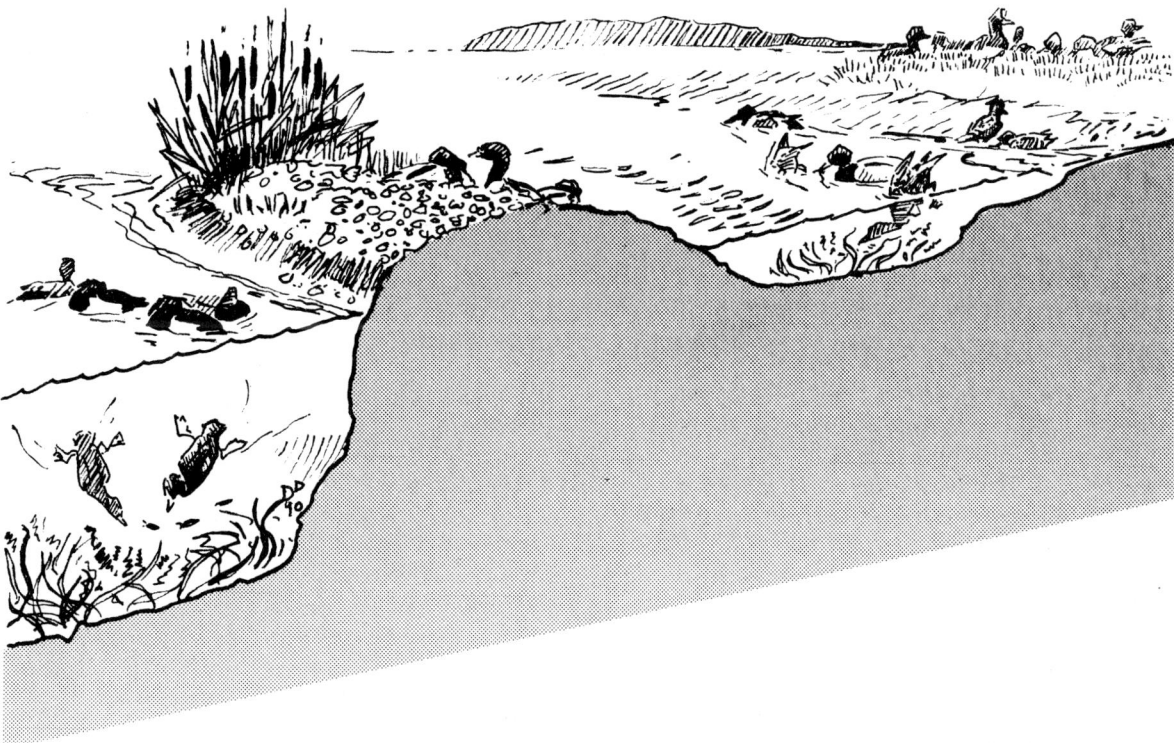

TUFTED DUCK AND POCHARD

Flooded gravel pits now provide an important breeding and wintering habitat for diving ducks in Britain. The principal breeding species to benefit from flooded gravel workings is the tufted duck, with smaller numbers of pochard and feral ruddy duck. These species are joined by goldeneye, smew and goosander in winter.

As breeding birds, both tufted duck and pochard are widely distributed through northern Europe and well across northern Asia. Tufted duck were first recorded breeding in Britain in 1850, and the total had risen to around 7,000 pairs by the mid-1980s. Breeding pochard number about 300 pairs.

More than half a million tufted ducks now winter in north-west Europe with perhaps half as many pochard.

The spread of the tufted duck in Britain has paralleled that of the zebra mussel. First recorded in London docks in 1824, this mollusc now provides a valuable food source for diving ducks on gravel pits throughout lowland Britain.

All birds which dive underwater for their food face the same fundamental problems. The environment is cold, often turbid, and requires the expenditure of much energy in swimming to the bottom and then looking for food in a single breath. Invertebrate-feeders like tufted ducks search for prey which either burrow into the sediments (chironomid larvae, pea mussels), live on weeds (shrimps, water lice), are camouflaged (caddis larvae, mayfly nymphs, snails) or which live in clumps (zebra mussels), making them difficult to find. Carp, bream, roach, perch and tench also eat these animals and deplete their numbers. Pochard wintering at Great Linford have recently been shown to concentrate their feeding activities on areas of shallow water which support higher than average (around 3,000 per square metre) winter numbers of chironomid larvae. The autumn/winter habit of flock-feeding by pochard and tufted duck may help individual birds to find food-rich patches through co-operative searching.

Tufted ducks and pochard delay breeding until late May or June, when the ground cover vegetation (bramble, nettles, sedges, rushes, grass tussocks) has grown to provide adequate nest cover. Both species nest close to the water. Carrion crows take a heavy toll of eggs from all but the most carefully hidden nests.

At the start of feeding, tufted ducklings need about 1,000 large chironomids per day each to meet their dietary requirements. Unhappily, these are not always available as young gravel pits typically have sparse populations of the aquatic invertebrates vital for duckling nutrition. Chironomid larval numbers may peak at only around 2,000 per square metre in mid-summer, whereas mature natural lakes can support 20 times this population density.

On the ARC Great Linford gravel pit site in north Buckinghamshire, tufted duckling broods usually experience an 80% mortality over the first two weeks of life. It seems likely that starvation is the primary cause of death for most of these birds. Food supplies for both dabbling and diving ducks and ducklings have now been increased by removing fish. Bream, carp, tench, perch and roach are competitors for food, and pike are predators on ducklings.

The ideal habitats for pochard and tufted duck also benefit the rarer wintering species. Smew dive in the shallows (<2 m) hunting for small fish or invertebrates; dives usually last for around 20 seconds. Goosander also hunt fish, normally in depths up to 4 m. Goldeneye favour a similar water depth, taking invertebrate prey from the lake-bed and mid-waters.

Habitat creation and management

1. Adult tufted ducks will feed in water 0·5–5 m deep whilst pochard prefer shallower sites up to about 2·5 m deep. Adult tufted duck and pochard usually dive for 10–20 seconds. Tufted duck avoid lakes over 15 m deep, unless there are extensive areas of productive shallows.

2. Large (>2–3 ha) areas of wind-exposed water are avoided by both pochard and tufted duck. Wintering flocks of diving duck need lakes large enough to represent a safe roost (minimum 0·5 ha) but ideally broken up by chains of islands which provide shelter in rough weather.

3. An additional benefit of well-designed islands is provided by the gently shelving shallow water which allows the settlement of fine silt and decaying organic material. Both emergent and submerged aquatic plants thrive along shores sheltered from the prevailing winds. These shallow, relatively productive areas of lake-bed support abundant invertebrate populations.

4. Whilst pochard are known to eat invertebrates (chironomid larvae and other insects) in the

winter and spring, a wide variety of plant material probably forms the bulk of their diet, at least in the summer and autumn. Many plants can be introduced deliberately to young gravel pit lakes to speed up natural processes of colonisation and to break up the natural monocultures of invasive species such as reedmace and reed sweet-grass.

5. Islands are strongly preferred nest sites both for pochard and tufted duck, probably as a defence against fox predation. Pochard show an additional preference for islets with thick, fringing beds of reed where nests are built as floating platforms.

6. Ideal brood-rearing habitat has shallow (<1 m) water, with a diverse mosaic of aquatic vegetation, supporting abundant populations of aquatic invertebrates (chironomid larvae, caddis larvae, mayfly nymphs, shrimps, water lice, mussels, snails). Nutrient-rich waters often provide feeding areas rich enough in chironomids (and other insects) and molluscs to promote high duckling survival. Adult diving ducks thrive in similar conditions but can cope with deeper water (>1 m) than can their ducklings.

N Giles

REDSHANK

The redshank has a widespread but somewhat localised distribution within temperate and sub-arctic regions of Europe and Asia, breeding in wet lowland grassland habitat. About 30,000 pairs breed in Britain and 2–3,000 in Ireland, together totalling about 20% of the European population. Nearly 60% of the total nest in saltmarshes. Inland breeding has declined markedly especially in the lowlands of southern Britain, largely due to land drainage. Most of the breeding population perform short migratory movements to and from coastal wintering sites.

At inland sites, redshank feed in shallow surface water at the edges of pools and ditches (more so than lapwing and snipe which frequent similar wetland habitats inland). Food at inland breeding sites is mostly small insects and aquatic invertebrates, including beetles and fly larvae. These are located visually and picked from the water surface and vegetation. Incubating birds may feed up to 1·5 km from the nest.

Non-territorial and semi-colonial, redshank often nest in loose groups in wet/damp grassland. The nest is usually a deeply cupped depression hidden among grass and sedge tussocks. The vegetation surrounding the nest is generally about 20 cm high, taller than that favoured by lapwings and shorter than that in which snipe nest. Egg-laying peak is in May, but replacement nests are frequent, within a week to 10 days of nest losses due to predation or trampling by livestock. Clutch size is normally four and only a single brood is reared. On hatching, young tend to follow their parents to shallow water where they can feed for themselves. While incubating, adults may sit tightly and even the off-duty bird may be unobtrusive but, once the young hatch, both parents noisily mob intruders and will behave aggressively towards other redshanks with young that are competing for feeding space.

For feeding, redshank require gently graded and, ideally, muddy margins of a flooded pit, providing shallow water (less than 4 cm deep) and allowance for some fluctuation in water levels. The margins should be fairly clear of emergent vegetation. Floating or submerged vegetation, including algal mats, provide habitat for invertebrates on which redshank feed. Shallow water needs to be available from mid March, when redshanks return from wintering areas, until early July, by which time the young are normally flying.

For nesting, redshank require tussocky grassland (but not rank vegetation) within 100 m of the shallow-water feeding areas. The nesting areas should not be subject to flooding or intensive grazing by cattle or sheep between mid April and early June.

Habitat creation and management

Feeding habitat:
1. Shallow grading (<1:20) of gravel pit banks.
2. Control of water levels so that there is a muddy margin and shallow water throughout the breeding season (mid March–early July).
3. If necessary, some control of emergent vegeta-

tion on the pit shore, either by flooding (raising the water level) in winter or occasional treatment with the herbicide glyphosate in late summer to eliminate vigorous perennials.

Nesting habitat:
4. Provision of damp, tussocky grassland, ideally several hectares in extent, adjacent to the gravel pit. If possible, the grassland should be fenced and grazed by cattle (avoid heavy grazing by sheep) to promote a tussocky structure formed by coarser, less palatable grasses (eg tufted hairgrass) and sedges, and to prevent colonisation of willows and other scrub. Cattle should be grazed at a density of about two per

hectare between late June and October, but excluded between mid April and early June when redshank eggs could be crushed. Failing grazing, the grass should be mown at least once a year in the late summer/autumn.
5. The breeding area should be kept free of disturbance by humans, dogs or machinery during the April to July period.
6. The provision of low islands (with some tussocky vegetation to provide cover from crows and magpies) can reduce nest predation by mammalian predators such as foxes. Redshank chicks are capable of swimming to reach feeding areas.

C J Cadbury

LAPWING

Widely distributed through most of Europe and temperate Asia but not in the more mountainous parts, the lapwing is the most widespread and abundant breeding wader in the British Isles. The British population has been estimated to be about 182,500 pairs with another 33,500 in Ireland. Less closely tied to water than the redshank, lapwings frequently nest on arable fields before the crops have grown up, or on intensively grazed pasture. In the more northerly parts of Britain they have been increasing but by contrast, in the eastern and southern parts of the country where autumn sowing of cereals makes farmland unsuitable for them by springtime, lapwing numbers have declined markedly. Lapwings usually feed on open moist ground with sparse or short vegetation where they can find their food visually. Earthworms are the predominant food of adults, but they also feed on surface-living insects, particularly ground beetles. Insects associated with dung are important in drier situations. Since most of the feeding occurs within 200–300 m of the nest, the highest nesting densities tend to occur close to water where food is most abundant.

Birds return to their breeding sites in early spring to establish territories which serve for courtship, nesting and feeding of adults and young. Where the food supply is good, territories may overlap. The nest is a shallow scrape, sometimes with very little lining, but at wet sites the nest may be built up with dead stems and leaves. The normal clutch is four eggs. The main laying period is late March and early April in lowland

southern England, but is later farther north and in the uplands. Lapwings re-lay to replace early clutches lost through predation, trampling by livestock or accidental destruction by machinery on farmland or at gravel pits.

Both parents guard the young, but the female does most of the brooding. The chicks feed themselves on small invertebrates picked from the ground surface or from short vegetation. Chicks hatched in nests on arable fields are frequently led by their parents to damp pastures and gravel pits if they are available nearby.

In lowland Britain, damp permanent pastures now assume increasing importance for breeding lapwings. Not only are their nests on grassland less likely to be destroyed accidentally by farm machinery, but the invertebrates on which lapwings feed tend to be considerably more abundant than on arable land. Small numbers of lapwings may breed at flooded gravel pits, especially those with an apron of short grass.

Lapwings are highly migratory. By the time most breeding birds are leaving the breeding grounds in June, immigrant flocks of birds which have finished breeding or have failed are already arriving from the Continent. Such post-breeding flocks gather at wetlands, including flooded gravel pits.

Habitat creation and management

1. Lapwings may be encouraged to breed at gravel pits by retaining or creating fairly level

and extensive aprons of short grass adjacent to water.

2. Feeding conditions for adults and young may be enhanced by creating low-lying muddy spits and islands along the shores, or by excavating shallow, flooded depressions and lining with topsoil. Such feeding sites should be kept fairly free of vegetation, either by flooding outside the lapwing breeding season (mid March – mid June), or by careful use of a herbicide such as glyphosate.

3. Machinery should be kept off nesting and feeding areas during the breeding season to avoid accidental damage of nests and chicks and disturbance to the breeding birds.

4. Where lapwings are breeding, there should be minimal human disturbance between mid March and mid June (coincident with the close season for coarse fishing).

C J Cadbury

RINGED PLOVER, LITTLE RINGED PLOVER AND COMMON TERN

These three species of birds have several requirements in common. All breed widely across Europe with populations extending well into the USSR and, in the case of the two plovers, to the Far East. Ringed plovers are mainly northern and arctic in their distribution with southernmost breeders in north France, while the closely related little ringed plover has its main populations across southern and central Europe and extending to south-east Asia. British little ringed plovers are believed to winter in central Africa, while British

common terns winter along the coast of west Africa mainly between Mauritania and Ghana. On the other hand, ringed plovers which have bred in the UK spend the winter months on the west coast of Europe, mostly in Britain.

The numbers breeding in the UK are about 8,600 pairs of ringed plovers (1,200 inland, many on gravel pits), up to 650 pairs of little ringed plovers (all inland and most on gravel pits) and abut 16,000 pairs of common terns (perhaps 1,500 inland). The numbers of all three are increasing

The Needs of Wildlife

inland with the increase in the area of suitable habitat available, especially on gravel pits. Because of the similarity between the two plovers, it is not surprising to find that there is aggression between them; the larger ringed plover, which is the more recent colonist of the inland habitat in Britain, seems to be dominant and can push out its relative.

The two plovers feed on small insects on land and mud-dwelling invertebrates at the water's edge. Common terns take small fish up to 10 cm in length by plunging into the water; sometimes they take invertebrates from the water surface while in flight.

All arrive on the breeding areas between March and mid May and generally leave during August or September. They normally choose nest sites which are mostly bare shingle but will use areas of sparse herbage; locations which have a range of stone sizes, including fine pea-gravel or some sand are most likely to attract these birds. Terns will only breed on islands, preferring a flattish surface not more than 0·5 m above the water: they will also use artificial rafts. The plovers will nest on islands and the 'mainland'. Tern islands can vary greatly in their nature from tiny shingle patches just out of the water to quite tall mounds with steep banks. As the breeding season advances, there is likely to be some vegetation growth and if this is over most of the area, the amount of cover will make the site unsuitable for chicks or replacement clutches. The plovers require access to shallow water; for ringed plovers this should be close to the nest site but little ringed plovers appear to be more flexible, even nesting well away from water and leading their chicks for several hundred metres to shoreline feeding grounds.

Territory sizes are variable, depending on the layout of the site. Plovers will nest as close as 10 m to one another but more typically the closest neighbour will be 40–80 m for ringed plovers and 75–150 m for little ringed plovers. Territory sizes are usually about 0·15–0·6 ha and 0·2–2·2 ha respectively. Eggs are laid on bare ground and are very well camouflaged. Though solitary pairs occur, common terns usually nest socially in small colonies inland; most colonies are of 2–15 pairs. They can nest very closely together, only requiring to be out of bill-range and with a small radius in which the chicks can wander. Territories can be as small as 2 m².

For all three species the young leave the nest within a short time. The young plovers move to feeding areas and feed themselves, whereas the terns bring food to their chicks which remain on or near the nest site. The chicks remain motion-less and rely on their camouflage when danger threatens. As the chicks become older, they tend to hide in nearby vegetation if this is available. Tern chicks swim readily and can be dispersed widely if seriously disturbed.

All species, especially the two plovers, suffer high rates of nest failure: this is mostly due to avian and mammalian predation, often exacerbated by disturbance. The plovers may lay up to four clutches before giving up. The total time between laying the first egg and the young flying, assuming breeding is successful, is 8–10 weeks.

Habitat creation and management

1. Both species of plover tend to be early colonists of new workings, nesting on the floor of pumped workings and on other shingle-covered areas, including roadsides and vehicle parks. Where birds are known to be present from March onwards, breeding should be presumed and care taken to avoid disturbance, especially of the little ringed plover. Changes in water levels of working pits should be prevented if possible, to avoid inundation of eggs.

2. To retain or attract birds to restored sites, bare shingle with some fine material is required. For the plovers it should be in patches of at least 0·2 ha. For common terns islands are essential although the provision of rafts can make a suitable substitute. Where wave action could be considerable, islands make better breeding sites but it is probable that some erosion will take place and the islands will require armouring or repairing from time to time. Rafts can be made from a wide variety of material (see pages 152–3) and are best covered in a thin layer of shingle, although there are many instances where terns have nested on bare wood. Square compartments of 50 cm × 50 cm will hold a nest each, particularly if the side of the dividers are at least 15 cm high. It is essential that there is a fence at least 40–50 cm high around the perimeter of the raft to prevent the chicks leaving it; once they are in the water, they will not be able to get back on board unless there are ramps leading up each side from below the waterline.

3. To keep shingle bare will require annual maintenance during September–March: physical pulling of plants, using herbicides or winter flooding with a March drawdown are some well-tried techniques. To minimise plant growth, a plastic layer (overlapping fertiliser bags make a cheap method) a few centimetres below the shingle surface will help; this keeps

the surface layers very dry and prevents deep root growth. Note, however that the techniques can only be used on the flat. Sloping plastic sheds its shingle cover! Scattered, small patches of vegetation can be very helpful, providing hiding places for the chicks when danger threatens.

4. Trees and other woody vegetation need to be kept well away from the breeding areas, preferably at least 100 m. Predators such as crows use such areas as look-out points and mammalian predators can lurk in the undergrowth.

5. Water level control needs to be considered: substantial fluctuations can destroy many nests and cover bare shingle. If tern islands become attached to the mainland, it makes access easy for predators.

6. The feeding areas of the chicks should be kept free from marginal emergent vegetation. This prevents access to the water's edge where much feeding takes place. Ideally shorelines should be scalloped and have a very shallow slope (1:100).

7. Although some disturbance can be tolerated, it must be minimised. Eggs and young are cryptically coloured and are vulnerable to being trampled if access is allowed to the breeding areas. The little ringed plover is a specially protected species on Schedule 1 of the Wildlife and Countryside Act 1981 (see page 177). This means that it is an offence to disturb the birds at or near their nest.

A J Prater

MIGRANT AND WINTERING WADERS

'Waders' is a general term covering a large number of closely-related birds, such as plovers, sandpipers, stints and snipe, but specifically excluding some others which also 'wade', such as herons, moorhens and gulls. Waders vary in size from sparrow-sized stints to quite large birds such as curlews and whimbrels, and in structure from fairly compact, short-billed and short-legged birds to others with very long legs and very long bills. As a group, they are able to exploit a wide range of mainly invertebrate prey in both wet and dry situations. Insects and their larvae, worms, crustaceans and molluscs are the main foods, although some species also take very small fish and small amphibians. Essentially, prey is either picked from the surface of land or water, seized in water or probed for in mud, sand or wet soil.

In theory, about 60 species of wader could occur at gravel pits, but about half are rarities or vagrants. As discussed elsewhere, a few species are present as breeders: some of these will also occur as migrants passing through in spring or autumn, or may overwinter. The number of species likely to overwinter is small (about 5–10), but the best sites used by migrants can record 20 or more species in a year. At most sites, however, the total will be far smaller. In general, the number of individual birds is also likely to be small at most sites; some species may be represented only by singletons. Nevertheless, the cumulative total of migrant waders at all sites can be important for some species and thus gravel pits can make a positive contribution to the provision of a suitable network of habitats for them.

Habitat creation and management

1. New excavations, either kept open by pumping or with their floor at or just above the water table, soon become suitable for use by waders, especially where they contain a mosaic of shallow pools, channels, islets and low mounds all in the process of being colonised by plants and invertebrates. Likely visitors include greenshank, green and common sandpipers and dunlin, ringed and little ringed plovers – the last two may also breed. These are essentially temporary habitats, continually being created and destroyed: where pumping is unnecessary, they could be maintained, but this would involve vegetation control to preserve their open nature.

2. Apart from common sandpipers, few waders use steep pit sides or artificial banks on flooded, superficially restored sites. Such pits, which are often large, will attract migrant or winter waders only if suitably landscaped. This involves creating (preferably along the sheltered side) long shorelines (50 m or more, if possible) complete with small bays and promontories, sloping into several metres width of very shallow water – a range of about 0–10 cm over about 5 m (1:50 slope) would be very suitable. On sites where the watertable fluctuates on a seasonal cycle, these conditions should apply relative to April and to September water levels for passage migrants, or to January levels for wintering birds. Ideally, stretches should be constructed relative to the three seasonal levels, to provide maximum benefit.

3. Pure sand or gravel shores are generally less valuable than those with organic soils because they contain fewer invertebrates. Shores should therefore be over-excavated to allow for surfacing by 20–30 cm of topsoil.

4. Plant growth should be sparse or absent. Higher water levels in winter will check plant colonisation to some extent, but it may be necessary to control vegetation to maintain an open shoreline.

5. Broadly similar principles should be applied, on a smaller scale, to the shores of islands. Islands also provide useful roosting and loafing places for waders.

6. Some working sites include habitat fragments of possible value to waders: small pools and shallow depressions are good examples, especially where they have been left alone and plants have colonised naturally. Such sites can also be created easily and inexpensively. Ideally, they should include areas of open mud or sand, sloping very gently into water only 1–3 cm deep, with indented shorelines and a series of miniature bays and promontories. Such areas should be sheltered from prevailing winds, for better plant growth and to benefit invertebrate populations. The ideal is a network of very shallow pools, at different levels relative to the watertable so as to be subject to seasonal flooding and drying-out, or with water levels controlled by a simple sluice system. In the long term, vegetation control is necessary to maintain open areas.

7. Wintering snipe seek areas of rank vegetation over wet or shallowly flooded ground. This

may be created as a strip at the upper margin of winter wader habitat. Better still are areas of rough grassland with the watertable within 20 cm of the soil surface or even shallowly flooded.

8. Ditches or other watercourses on site should have some open 'edge' in the form of a shelf

approximately level with the spring or autumn water level to benefit green sandpipers and, occasionally, other species.

9. The maintenance of wet carr (eg willow) will benefit woodcock in winter.

M J Everett

BARN OWL

The barn owl is one of the most widely distributed land birds, present in almost all temperate and tropical countries of the world. Although considered relatively common in many of the latter, it has declined throughout most temperate regions of Europe and the northern states of America over the last 50 years. Major population declines are apparent north of latitude 48° where January temperatures average 4°C or below and where winter snow cover is often prolonged.

In Britain and Ireland, it is still widely distributed as a breeding bird except in northern Scotland, the Outer Hebrides, Shetlands and Orkneys. A recent survey by The Hawk Trust indicated a total breeding population of about 5,000 pairs in Britain and Ireland. In England and Wales it currently numbers some 3,800 pairs. This

represents a 70% decline since the first national census in 1932.

Barn owls feed mainly on small field mammals such as voles, shrews and mice, but young rats, small birds and even insects are taken, particularly during winter months. In some areas, frogs can constitute a significant part of the diet in spring.

Since 1940, agricultural intensification, coupled with an increased severity of winter snowfall, has reduced the availability of prey. Modern farming methods (and urbanisation) have led to the disappearance of prey-rich rough grasslands. Not only whole fields, but perhaps more importantly the grassy margins alongside hedges, ditches, rivers and streams have been lost as field sizes have increased to maximise crop yields. In addition, barn owls could once depend on the old

The Needs of Wildlife

farmyard, complete with cornricks, straw-bedded cattleyards and stables, to provide its food needs, especially during winter. Following the introduction of the combine harvester in the early 1940s and more sophisticated methods of grain storage, the modern farmyard no longer provided the dependable source of prey which cushioned this bird during times of shortages.

Although not territorial in the true sense, it will range over an area of 100–300 ha. However, where linear grassland is the only suitable habitat, such as in the fenlands of Lincolnshire, it will travel 4 km from the nest site. Maximum recorded density in the British Isles is 27 pairs per 10,000 ha but, in regions where the barn owl can still be found, 2·5 pairs per 10,000 ha is the average population density.

The main factors which are critical for successful breeding are the availability of 15–25 km of rough grassland edge within its hunting range, and a nesting site close to the most productive feeding grounds. Perennial tussocky grassland in lowland valleys is the prime habitat and some of the most favoured grasslands are those alongside watercourses.

An undisturbed nest site in the form of a dry platform or ledge at least 0·5 m wide, 2·5 m or more above the ground is the second requirement. Barn owls nest in buildings, trees, nestboxes and, in some parts of Britain, rock crevices. There is a significant regional variation in the type of nest sites selected. In western regions, the bird shows a strong preference for buildings whilst in eastern counties, tree cavities are its favoured site. Nestboxes, old chimneys or empty water tanks (the tall sides of which prevent the young from falling out, and also reduce the risk of predation) provide some of the most productive sites.

The barn owl usually pairs for life. It is a sedentary bird normally remaining faithful to its chosen hunting grounds and nest sites throughout its average life of three years. Where habitats have remained largely intact and productive,

many sites have been used by successive generations of owls for decades.

Breeding begins in April although winter and spring weather can influence the laying date and subsequent productivity. On average, three young fledge successfully. Sometimes two broods are reared but this usually occurs only in years of high vole abundance following a very mild winter and a good spring.

About half of all barn owls vacate the breeding site in the winter and roost elsewhere, often in haybarns which presumably provide the necessary shelter and food.

Habitat creation and management

1. An uninterrupted network of grassland corridors at least 5 m wide should be created throughout the site. These should follow natural features of the land in question such as along margins of lakes, rivers, streams, ditches, hedgerows, shelterbelts and woodland. These strips of perennial grasses should be lined every 20 m or so with standard height fence posts to provide vantage points for 'perch hunting'. About one-third of the total length should be grazed or cut on rotation in the autumn. This will create a mosaic of mixed height grassland and reduce the unwanted development of scrub.

2. If nestboxes (see page 163) cannot be provided in nearby buildings or old trees, boxes on stout poles can be used. To increase the chances of occupancy, two should be erected, facing away from the prevailing wind and positioned on islands to discourage unwanted human disturbance.

3. Attempts should be made to site the grassland and nestboxes away from major roads as many barn owls, hunting along the verges, are killed by cars.

Colin R Shawyer

KINGFISHER

Widespread throughout central and southern Europe, the kingfisher is scarce in most of Scandinavia, and the breeding population within the British Isles lies at the northern limit of its range. It breeds beside still or slow-flowing freshwater in England, Wales and Ireland, but is much less common in Scotland.

It is not an abundant species, the total breeding population within the British Isles being 5,000–9,000 pairs. Although basically resident, wintering birds may be forced by freezing weather to find unfrozen water elsewhere and estuaries are especially favoured. This susceptibility to hard weather is reflected in the periodic crashes in the breeding population following cold winters although, because of its high reproductive capacity, it is usually able to recover again quite rapidly.

During the breeding season kingfishers feed mainly on small fish, such as minnow, stickleback and fry, supplemented by a variety of aquatic insects, including caddis flies and the nymphs of dragonflies. Fish are caught by diving, either from a perch over the water, or from hovering flight. Although prey may be taken from a depth of up to 1 m, shallower water is preferred. Clear water is essential, since the kingfisher must be able to see its potential prey.

Although the nest site may occasionally be as far as 250 m from the waters where the birds feed, it is usually found in a vertical or steep earth bank at or very close to the water's edge. Suitable substrate for tunnelling – firm, stable and without large numbers of big stones – may also be found amongst the overhanging roots of some trees. The nest tunnel which is excavated by both parents over a period of 7–12 days, is usually 1–2 m above the normal water level. It is horizontal or upward sloping and as much as 1 m in length. Two and very occasionally three broods may be reared in a single season.

Pairs are solitary and territorial and, although feeding may take place up to 1 km from the breeding territory, each pair usually occupies a length of watercourse or shoreline of 0·8–1·5 km.

Habitat creation and management

1. Shallow peripheral areas of clear water are required for feeding. Basically, kingfishers feed in the sort of habitat favoured by small fish and fry. These areas should be free of emergent vegetation.
2. Suitable perches from which to fish are necessary at the water's edge or in the water, over or very close to areas of shallow water. Overhanging branches or posts driven into the shallows will be used.
3. Vertical or very steep bare earthbanks at least 1·5 m high, preferably at the edge of the water, but otherwise within 250 m, are essential for nesting. The actual extent of the bank may not be critical, although the more that can be provided, the greater the chance that kingfishers will find it attractive. Banks may be created during excavation or result from wave action, but active erosion during the breeding season is undesirable. On the other hand, small-scale winter erosion is beneficial in maintaining steep faces largely free of plant cover.
4. Fluctuating water levels, particularly rapid rises during the breeding season, may cause nests to be lost by flooding.

Lennox Campbell

SAND MARTIN

Sand martins occur widely throughout the British Isles, only being very scarce or absent in the western and northern isles. They are one of the group of migratory species which are known to be severely affected by droughts in the Sahel regions of Africa and population levels may fluctuate considerably from year to year. In good years there may be up to a million breeding pairs, but less than 250,000 in years of high winter mortality.

They are highly opportunistic in their choice of nest sites which are usually found in sandy banks along rivers, in coastal areas and increasingly in man-made habitats such as quarries, sand and gravel pits. Sand martins are by no means exclusively waterside birds and breeding colonies may occur wherever suitable banks occur. Such banks are often highly unstable and colonies may be forced to move from year to year. Where substrates are more stable, they may re-use a site for many breeding seasons.

Colony size ranges widely, from fewer than a dozen pairs to large groups of several hundred. The height of banks used for nesting also ranges widely, from less than 2 m along some rivers to 4–5 m or more in sandpits. The nest hole is usually 35 cm–1 m long and is excavated over a period of two weeks by both parents. In stable substrates, the same hole may be used in several years and it is difficult to estimate how many pairs are present each year simply by counting the total number of new or old holes.

Two broods may be raised each year. Although they will feed on airborne insects over water or reedbeds close to the colony, sand martins tend to roam very widely to exploit abundant insects wherever they may be available. Their presence as breeding birds at a particular site is most likely to be determined by the presence of a suitable nest bank, rather than any particularly rich local feeding conditions.

In late summer, reedbeds may be used at dusk by large flocks of roosting sand martins, and gravel pits or reservoirs may be especially important as feeding areas for early returning migrants in spring.

Habitat creation and management

1. If sand martins are already present at a site, the most effective measure would be to preserve and protect the banks that they are using. The long-term value of this will depend on the stability of the bank and measures may need to be taken to stabilise them and to prevent erosion.
2. Where no sand martins are present it may be possible to retain or create suitable banks, although there is no guarantee that they will ever be used. To maximise success, banks must be vertical, stable and, to minimise the possibility of predation or other interference, should be 3–4 m high (see page 156). The area in front of the banks should be kept clear of tall vegetation such as bushes and trees and, whilst public viewing from a distance can be encouraged, there should be no direct public access to the banks.
3. Where nesting occurs in low waterside banks, it is important to prevent rises in water levels during the breeding season.
4. Development of extensive areas of reeds and marginal emergent vegetation which encourage insect populations may help to attract feeding or roosting sand martins, even if they are not breeding in the immediate vicinity.

Lennox Campbell

SEDGE AND REED WARBLERS

The sedge warbler is one of the characteristic small breeding birds of marsh and wet scrubby wetlands and is particularly common around lakes and lowland rivers. It is migratory and, although numbers may vary considerably from year to year in response to drought-related winter mortality in Africa, is a widespread and relatively common breeding bird throughout the United Kingdom. The breeding population is probably of the order of 300,000 pairs.

Favouring tall vegetation, it is relatively inconspicuous and is more easily heard than seen. Whilst marshy habitat at the margins of rivers or lakes is preferred, sedge warblers may breed at sites some distance from water provided that there is tall herbage and scrub. The nest is usually built low down in clumps of sedges or in scrub, such as bramble or low willow, and two broods may be reared, particularly in the south. Sedge warblers are insectivorous and feed on a wide variety of insects and other invertebrates found in wet and rough waterside vegetation associated with marsh and the edges of lakes and rivers. Reeds seem to be particularly favoured.

The reed warbler is much less widespread and abundant than the sedge warbler, although like the latter it is migratory and subject to similar population fluctuations as a result of drought in the African wintering grounds. It is mainly confined to the south and east of England, being scarce in the South-West and in Wales and absent as a breeder from Scotland. The breeding population probably numbers 40–80,000 pairs.

As befits its name, the reed warbler normally breeds in reeds, where the nest is woven around a group of several reed stems. Two broods may be reared each season. They are most abundant where there are extensive beds of reeds and are usually found close to open rivers or lakes, in wetter habitat than may be used by sedge warblers. Feeding on a range of insects may take place within the reeds but the main feeding habitat is adjoining scrub, particularly willows.

Habitat creation and management

1. For reed warblers, provide stands or marginal strips of reeds, adjoining areas of willows and alders.
2. For sedge warblers, provide patches of low (<3 m) scrub and bramble mixed with tall herbage and, where the watertable is high enough, marshy ground with sedges and other marginal vegetation.
3. Resist cutting or grazing rough vegetation in autumn as it will be required to provide cover in the spring before new growth has developed.
4. Keep such areas free from disturbance by humans.

Lennox Campbell

MAMMALS

Almost all British mammals can occur in or around gravel pits. Many of the small species – shrews, voles, mice and rats – are common and widespread. Their main conservation importance is as a food resource for predators such as adders, weasels, stoats, barn owls and kestrels. Specific management for them should rarely be necessary as they will colonise a wide range of habitats, with rough grassland, tall herbage, scrub and woodland being utilised. Short grassland, however, has little value for any of them though it will be used, or created, by rabbits.

A few mammals are of sufficient local or national rarity to justify the creation and management of gravel pit habitats with their particular needs in mind. They are the bats, water vole, harvest mouse and otter.

Bats

All 15 resident species of bat in Britain are regarded as threatened or endangered. The greater horseshoe bat is known to have declined by over 99% this century and even the most common species, the pipistrelle, declined by 64% in the decade to 1988. Bats feed on insects which they catch in woodland and over pasture and loss of these habitats (including hedgerows) is an important cause of their severe decline. The loss of hollow trees has also been a contributory factor.

All bats can be regarded as forest-dwelling animals living in tree holes and exploiting insect food gathered over, around or within the canopy. A few species such as the widespread Daubenton's bat and the rare barbastelle specialise in feeding over water, picking up emergent insects. All species are known to drink from gravel pits especially in hot weather.

Habitat creation and management

1. Creation and maintenance of glades surrounded by trees provides suitable habitat for most species of bat. Some feed over water and here too tree shelter is important to provide relatively calm, warm air in which their insect prey is most readily active.
2. While trees are needed for shelter and feeding, holes are needed for roosting. Therefore, old and hollow trees are a vital component for bats' requirements. Woodpecker or rot holes are used as well as splits and even spaces behind ivy.
3. Pollarded willows are most valuable and this important resource has been disappearing through decay and removal of riverside trees. Planting of willows and subsequent pollarding should be a long-term management goal for areas around gravel pits to create cavities for bats and other creatures.
4. In the intervening period before hollows develop, bat roostboxes may be placed on trees of about 15 years old or more. Essentially the boxes are about 100 mm^3 internally, and have 25 mm walls of untreated, rough sawn timber, with a slit 15–20 mm wide beneath for access (Fig 2.1). Roosts may contain tens of bats and they will feed over a wide area, at least up to 5 km away.

Water vole

Although widespread throughout England, Wales and much of Scotland, the water vole appears to be in decline due to loss of habitat, pollution and possible predation by feral mink. Voles are absent from many rivers and marshes where once they were common. Nevertheless, disused gravel pits are colonised and may provide valuable refuges, especially if they are near rivers and marshes with ditches.

Water voles are found in a wide range of wetland habitats where the most important prerequisite is dense vegetation spreading into the water, giving cover from the aerial predators, together with banks of soil in which tunnels leading to resting and breeding places can be excavated.

Habitat creation and management

1. In Britain the species is mostly semi-aquatic, usually living within a few metres of water. Management of banks must ensure scrub does not become dominant as water voles feed entirely on vegetation, mostly grass stems and roots. Grassy vegetation should be tall and dense.
2. Banks should be constructed of top soil (not sand or gravel), so that the voles' extensive burrow systems may be excavated and not run the risk of collapse. A low (about 0·5 m) vertical bank is ideal, enabling the animals to pass direct from the water into tunnel entrances.
3. Water voles usually have linear territories along banks, ranging from about 80 m for

84

Plank: 1, 110×15×25 mm (10 mm allowed for marking and cutting)

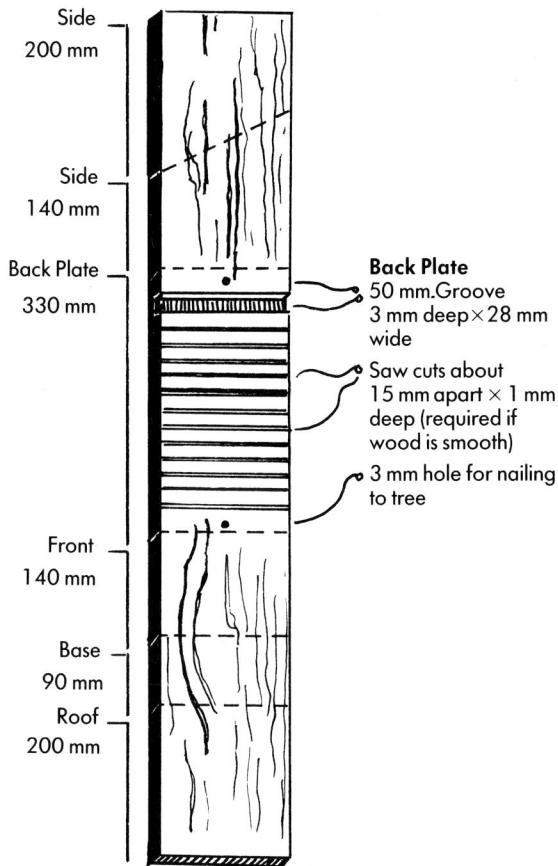

Side
200 mm

Side
140 mm

Back Plate
330 mm

Back Plate
50 mm. Groove
3 mm deep × 28 mm
wide

Saw cuts about
15 mm apart × 1 mm
deep (required if
wood is smooth)

3 mm hole for nailing
to tree

Front
140 mm

Base
90 mm

Roof
200 mm

Section

Front

Slit 15–20 mm wide

additional strength for back plate – two battens:
30×20×150 mm

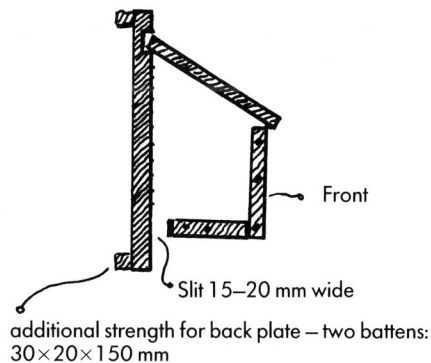

Fig 2.1 Standard bat box construction (from Stebbings, R & Walsh, S, 1988 Bat Boxes, Fauna and Flora Preservation Society).

Softwood should be very rough all over. Saw cuts on the back plate are necessary only if the wood is smooth.

The groove cut in the top of the back plate is to take the lid, which snaps into it firmly. Some people find it easier to make a hinge for the lid. A strip of car tyre inner tube may be tacked to lid and back and a wire hook can be fitted to the front. A hook will help prevent animals or wind removing the lid, especially if it shrinks or warps. Elastic bands made from car tyre inner tubes may also be used to hold on lids. A well-fitting lid greatly improves the chances of the boxes being used by bats. Alternative construction suggestions: (a) Fix top firmly and provide a loose fitting bottom hinged at the front. This is held in place by a length of galvanised wire (about 3 mm diameter) placed in an oversized drill hole at one side. When the wire is withdrawn the bottom drops by gravity. Take care from March to July because birds could be nesting. (b) A vertical partition of 10 mm thick rough timber can be inserted side to side in the box leaving 40 mm space above the base. It is best to provide this only in large boxes.

The Needs of Wildlife

females to 130 m for males. Therefore, if these voles are to be encouraged, long lengths of habitat need to be created or links made with surrounding wetlands.

Harvest mouse

Harvest mice are uncommon or absent in the west and north, but in suitable habitats in south and east England they can become abundant. Gravel pits have the potential to provide important refuges for these diminutive mammals which are believed to have declined due to changes in agricultural practice and more particularly through loss of habitat such as hedgerows, marshlands and old pasture.

They are short-lived creatures, on average living less than one year, but can breed rapidly (litters of five young every 20–21 days) from June–October, and when present in high numbers they can become a useful food resource for predators.

Habitat creation and management

1. An area as small as 0·1 ha could support a population of harvest mice. They are omnivorous, feeding mostly on insects and seeds. Habitats created for other species are likely to present suitable conditions for nests and plentiful food.
2. The species requires areas of marsh or grassland with dense stands of long grass or reed in which it makes spherical, woven nests attached to flowering stems. In tussocky grassland nests may rest on top of tussocks. Nests may be built over water and in reeds and have been recorded over 1·5 m above the surface.
3. All kinds of dense grass, reed and sedge vegetation are suitable for nests, providing stems are robust enough to support this 6–9 g mammal.
4. Control of scrub encroachment in marsh or grasslands is needed. This can be achieved by cutting and removing vegetation every second or third year in a rotation.
5. Harvest mice are often associated with ditches and banks, topped by a hedge and this is especially important if the area is subject to flooding. The banks may provide safe winter sites above water level, whereas low-lying nests may be inundated.

Otter

The otter has disappeared from water courses over much of lowland Britain, due to pollution and lack of suitable habitat. Much of this loss has been since the 1950s but there are encouraging signs that the species is slowly returning in some areas. Positive conservation efforts involving reduction of pollution and sympathetic management of riparian habitat is helping this re-establishment. Also, in a few selected rivers, otters are being reintroduced and the initial trials appear to be successful.

Otters range widely, with territories stretching over 10 km or more of river. In suitable conditions they will forage up side-streams and into nearby waterbodies. They require secluded areas for lying up and for breeding.

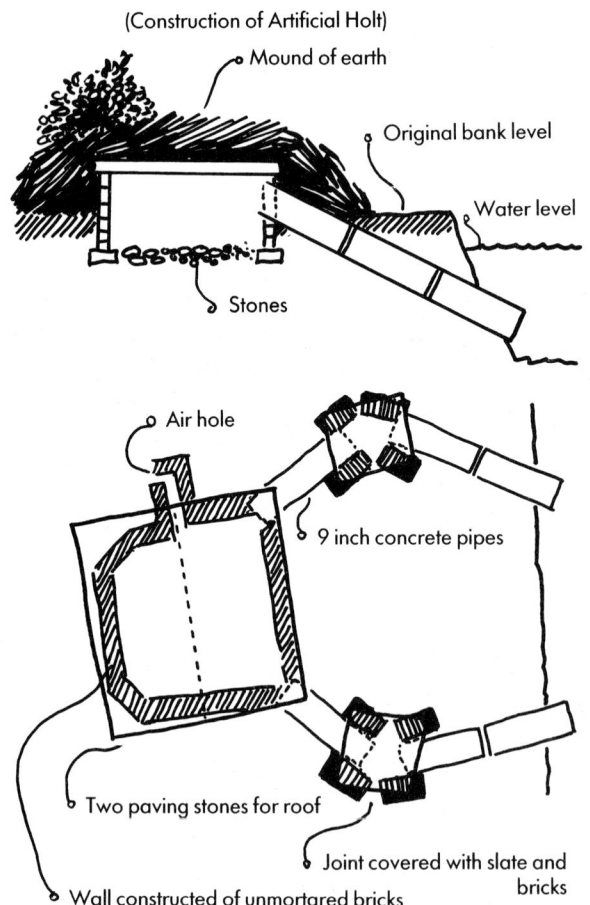

(Construction of Artificial Holt)
Mound of earth
Original bank level
Water level
Stones
Air hole
9 inch concrete pipes
Two paving stones for roof
Joint covered with slate and bricks
Wall constructed of unmortared bricks

Fig 2.2 Construction of an artificial holt (from Wood, M 1978, Artificial Holts).

Habitat creation and management

Most gravel pits lie in river valleys often with short distances between the river and pit. In these cases, otter havens may be created in which otters will be secure from human disturbance.

1. A haven needs at least 0·5 ha of tall marsh plants, eg reed mace, reed, brambles, dense scrub or a mixture of such cover. If not adjoining the pit, then undisturbed linking corridors of dense cover are desirable. Such a haven could be used for lying up or even as a breeding site.

2. Havens must be entirely free from human disturbance. They need to be fenced on the landward side and preferably isolated by ditches.

3. Artificial holts may be built of piles of logs (which will rot) or, preferably, of mortarless bricks with rough concrete pipes radiating from a central raised chamber, all covered with soil and planted with shrubs (see Fig 2.2). If holts are likely to be used for breeding, they need to be adjacent to at least 6 ha of open water, surrounded by cover and ideally containing islands.

4. Otters feed primarily on eels and sticklebacks, but also eat a wide variety of other food, both aquatic and terrestrial. Most large water bodies will have adequate food within easy reach.

5. Specialist advice may be obtained from the Otter Haven Project, RSNC, The Green, Nettleham, Lincoln, on siting and the likelihood of otters being in an area.

6. Otters, their holts and lying up places are specially protected under the Wildlife and Countryside Act 1981 and it is an offence intentionally to disturb otters in their places of shelter.

R E Stebbings

Part III

Habitat creation and management

DESIGN PRINCIPLES

Most conservation management is a matter of growing plants to provide year-round food supplies, cover and breeding places to support wild creatures. Though it derives many of its techniques directly from agriculture and forestry, it tends to be more complex for several reasons.

First, it is normally aimed at sustaining several different species of plants and animals, each with somewhat different requirements. Second, the animal species may themselves depend on other creatures and the food-chain back to the plants which initially sustain it may be several stages long. Third, the plants or animals may be in competition with each other for nutrients or food. Fourth, the aim is to set up systems which require minimal management intervention. This final point is particularly important, and not just for practical or financial reasons. Self-sustaining natural systems have more value than the preservation of species in an artificial, 'farmed' or zoo context. Our aim in restoring gravel workings for wildlife is to mimic the physical structure which would exist in some natural wetlands and then to let plant and animal processes largely have their head. If we understand what plants and animals need, and we design the basic structure to meet these needs, the system should largely run itself.

However, the smaller the site or the larger the number of species it is desired to conserve, the harder it becomes to apply this principle. For example, in the huge extent of a natural wetland system such as the original Fens of East Anglia, it would not matter that one mere became choked by vegetation because there would probably be compensatory changes occurring elsewhere across the system, with, say, another waterbody opened up by flood. In a small site, it is unlikely that events will balance each other out neatly, so sometimes intervention may be necessary.

Finally, most habitat types are successional, that is to say they tend to change their character without management. The rate of succession varies with the habitat. For instance, grassland may quickly become scrub, whereas scrub turns more slowly to forest and forest sustains itself indefinitely wherever rainfall is adequate. This should be borne in mind when deciding on the range of habitats to be created and managed.

In gravel pits, the first objective will be to create good conditions for wetland wildlife. Wetland plants flourish where the watertable remains at or no more than about 10 cm below the soil surface year round, or in water depths to a maximum of

about 2 m. Because of high light penetration and rapid warming by the sun, shallows less than 1 m deep are particularly productive areas. With plants providing the primary food resource and the physical structure in which to live, invertebrates and fish flourish, in turn creating rich feeding conditions for birds. Most waterfowl have evolved physical or behavioural adaptations which mean that they are either confined to feeding in shallows or can only feed in water deeper than about 2 m with disproportionate expenditure of energy. In excavation and/or in restoring ground profiles, watertable and water depth are the key considerations.

Plant growth is most vigorous where nutrient levels are relatively high and where root penetration is unobstructed. In some situations, the rapid development of plant cover or tree growth will be required. However, high nutrient levels tend to favour the strongest-growing species which will suppress less robust ones. For this reason, a greater variety of plants, including many of the scarcer species, will develop in less fertile conditions. The productivity of both aquatic and terrestrial habitats can be modified by the correct handling and restoration of topsoil and, where appropriate, by the application of organic or chemical fertilisers. The degree of soil compaction and the level of the soil surface relative to the watertable are also factors which can be controlled to inhibit or encourage particular terrestrial plant communities.

Shelter is a particularly important consideration in wetlands as wind generates wave action which affects the productivity of aquatic habitats, alters shore profiles, and prevents the establishment of plant communities. Shelter is also directly important to the growth of land plants and to the physical well-being of most living creatures, especially in winter when maintenance of body temperature at times of food scarcity may be a critical survival factor. It can be provided through land form design and through tree and shrub planting, related to prevailing wind conditions.

The ideal gravel pit wetland will have very extensive areas of water less than 1 m deep, fertile soils on banks, margins and shallows, and shelter from serious wind effects. The drier, terrestrial habitats will also benefit from wind shelter, but may require to be of lower fertility. This part of the manual describes broad principles of design and restoration, and gives prescriptions for the creation of the range of desirable habitats.

PHYSICAL FORM OF SAND AND GRAVEL EXCAVATIONS

Most of the sand and gravel exploited onshore is from thin, superficial deposits which, in the areas of greatest present and future production in the Midlands, East Anglia and the South-East, lie mostly at low altitude, often less than 100 m above sea level, and in areas of very low relief, dominated by gentle slopes and broad, shallow valleys. Streams and rivers in these areas are typically slow-moving and nearly all standing water bodies are man-made.

The extent of excavations is highly variable, but most workings or phases are now in the range 20–30 ha. Commonly the geological characteristics of a region lead to concentrations of sites being developed and thus in any single area the combined extent of adjacent exhausted workings may be hundreds or even thousands of hectares (Fig 3.1). This should permit a range of after-uses to be considered.

Original field boundaries, roads, footpaths and services such as pipelines nearly all affect the shape of individual workings. Increasingly recog-nition is taken of original features, such as streams or small areas of woodland, worthy of preservation. Operational aspects also play a role; for example, nearby houses or roads may dictate that certain areas will not be exploited because of noise or visual impact. Often, however, excavations extend to within a few metres of the boundary of the land holding, and this can be a severe limitation on the development of marginal or terrestrial habitats for wildlife, and in accommodating both people and birds within the same site.

The depth of an excavation is largely dependent on the geological nature of the deposit but also on the local hydrology, insofar as the latter affects practicalities of sand and gravel removal. A typical excavation extends to about 5 m in depth but the equivalent of about 1 m of the excavated material remains on site, comprising topsoil, subsoil, overburden and fines (silt and clay washings) (see Fig 3.2). If the watertable is high, the worked site may comprise both terrestrial and aquatic habitats together with a series of inter-

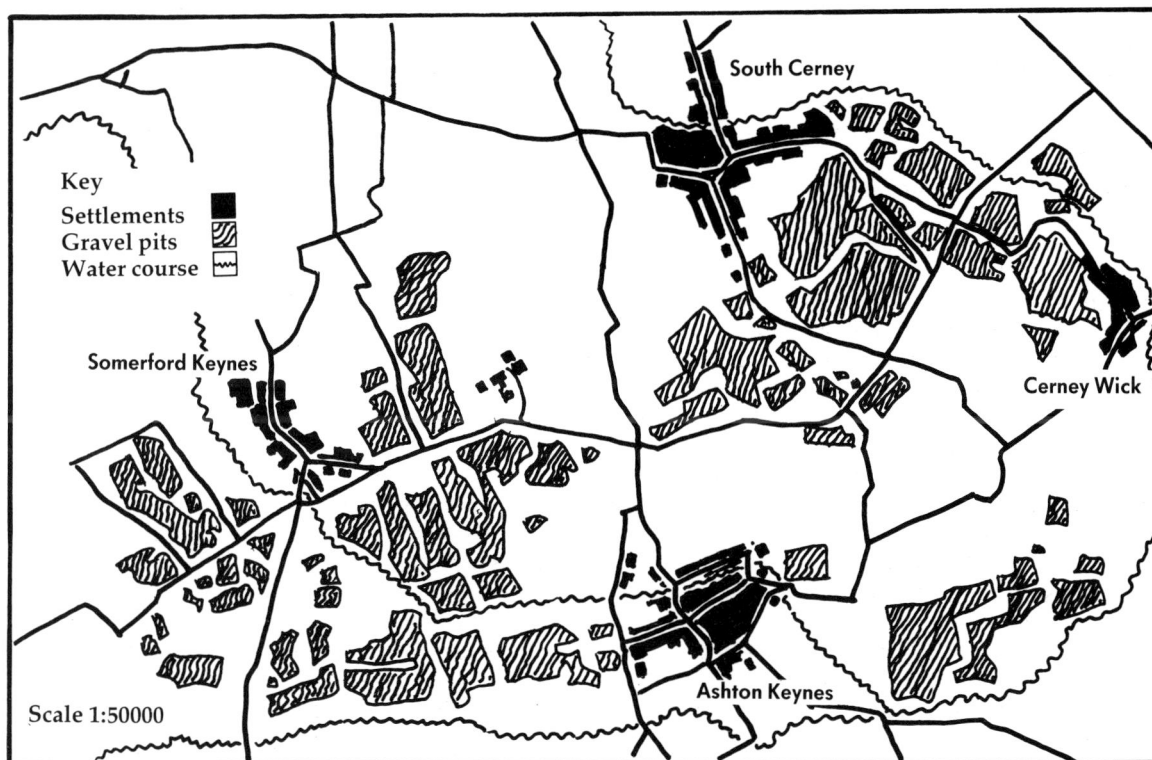

Fig 3.1 The Cotswold Water Park area. Extensive exhausted workings should permit a wide range of after-uses. Note how pit shapes are constrained by old field boundaries, water courses, buildings and roads.

93

Topsoil average 30 cm; may vary from 0 – >60 cm

Sub-soil average 60 cm; may be up to 1 m

Overburden variable in thickness; may be absent completely; rarely >5 m in economic sand and gravel deposits

Sand and Gravel economic deposits range from 2 – >10 m but average about 4 m.

Sub-gravel deposits may be sand and gravel with too great a proportion of fines; clay, chalk or almost any other rock types

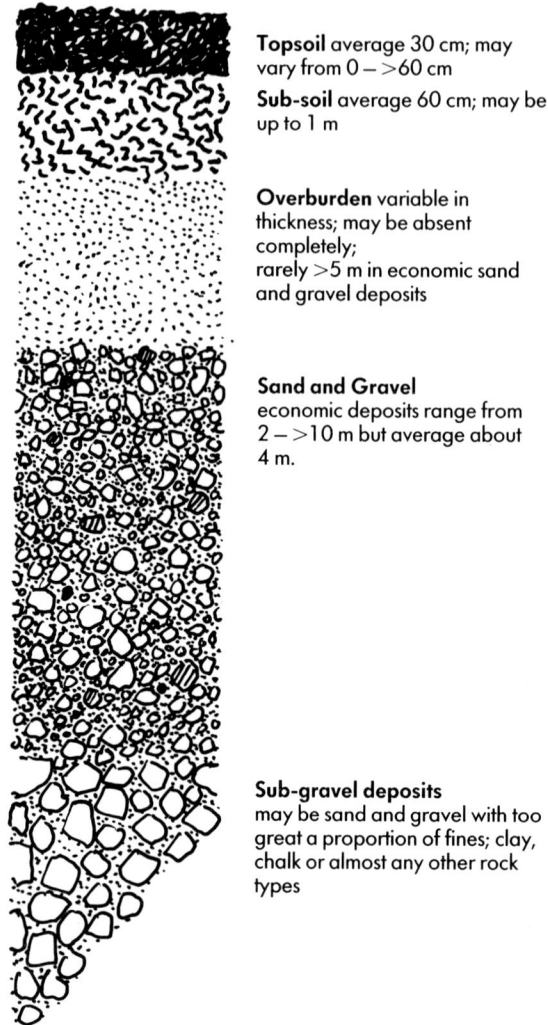

Fig 3.2 Typical vertical profile of sand and gravel deposits.

mediate marshland and shoreline habitats. The latter may undergo seasonal or irregular cycles of flooding or exposure dependent on the stability of the local water levels. In general, pits excavated so that the ultimate depth of flooding is greater than 2 m have limited conservation potential. Ideally, substantial areas should be less than 1 m deep. This requirement is a major problem which may be partly solved by careful preplanning of extraction and use of overburden in restoration.

The agreed site restoration scheme usually requires that topsoil, subsoil and overburden are removed by separate operations and stored separately for later use. For restoration to agriculture, this is recognised as particularly important and major efforts are made to protect soils from damage during stripping, storage and replacement: similar care is essential where wildlife conservation is an aim.

The margins of excavations are generally straight or gently curving; they are also normally fairly steep (about 45°) in order to maximise production from the site. Regrading or realignment of margins to meet restoration requirements may be carried out after extraction and, because of the importance of shallows for wildlife, is a crucial element of the work.

The floors of excavations are usually fairly level, their slope and contour being defined by the base of the sand and gravel deposit or by practicalities of the extraction process.

Most sand and gravel is washed, crushed and graded on site. The processes require that silt ponds be constructed to settle the fines out of the washing water before the water is either recirculated for further use or discharged to an agreed watercourse. Fines may be used in landform modelling or in creating specialised habitats.

WIND AND SHELTER

Summary

1. Most aquatic and terrestrial organisms and habitats benefit from wind shelter which results in increased warmth, decrease in physical stress and reduced wave erosion (see Table 2.1). Data on local wind patterns, and especially on the prevailing wind direction, are required.

2. High wind speeds and their effects can be reduced by planting tree shelterbelts, by reducing downwind dimensions (fetch) of lakes and by reducing water depths. These measures need consideration from the outset of extraction and restoration planning.

3. Shelterbelts should be planted at right angles to the prevailing wind direction and installed as early as possible in the development of a site. A structure with 50% permeability and a design height of 10–15 m will give effective shelter for 200–300 m downwind.

4. The proportion of a lake receiving wind shelter becomes greater as the length of lake along the shelterbelt shore is increased relative to its downwind dimension. Design values should be greater than 2:1 and preferably 3 or 4:1.

5. Installation of barriers between phases of excavation or of peninsulas, islands or submerged shallow banks all oriented at right angles to the prevailing wind direction will reduce potential fetch and hence erosion.

6. The downwind corners of excavations are very difficult to shelter; these areas might either not be excavated at all or infilled with overburden or spoil.

7. Design of the excavations and shelterbelts should make provision for areas of sheltered, sunlit land alongside the restored lake.

(See photographs 5, 6 and 8.)

The effects of wind

Most animals suffer from the effects of high wind which disrupts their activities, impedes movement and may cause chilling or physical harm. They typically use land forms or plant structures to gain shelter.

From the outset, restoration planning should take account of local weather conditions, primarily to predict and if necessary limit the effect of wind and hence waves on shorelines and islands, but also to provide shelter or exposure related to sun and/or wind for other purposes.

The effects of winds on the aquatic environment are to generate surface drift and waves. Drift of the surface layers of water is about 2% of the horizontal mean wind speed. Over the course of a day, under even the most gentle of winds, the total wind drift will exceed the downwind length of any gravel pit lake. This tends to concentrate plant and invertebrate flotsam at the exposed shore, attracting surface feeding waterfowl.

The physical characteristics of waves are related to two main variables – the wind speed and the length of open water, or fetch. In deeper lakes (over 2 m), fetch is the main factor controlling wave heights or lengths; at a constant wind speed, increasing the fetch from 150–600 m (the typical range in size of many sand and gravel pit lakes) almost doubles the wave heights and lengths, and hence increases their erosive effect on soft shores (see Table 3.1). However, as water becomes shallower (than about 2 m), depth has an increasing influence on waves and ultimately the stage is reached when wave characteristics depend only on wind speed and water depth and are independent of fetch.

Table 3.1

Influence of water depth and fetch on wave height and length			
(Data relate to a wind speed of 60 kph)			
Lake	A	B	C	D
Lake depth (m)	1·5	1·5	7·5	7·5
fetch (m)	150	600	150	600
Wave height (m)	0·20	0·33	0·20	0·39
Wave length (m)	2·8	4·7	2·8	5·5

The water particles beneath a wave have a roughly circular motion in the vertical plane and the depth of the wave-mixed layer is approximately half the wave length. In a long, shallow lake (eg column B in Table 3.1) the waves may be large enough to interact with the lake bed, picking up fine sediment particles and leading to turbid water, a condition which reduces light penetration through the water column and greatly reduces the growth rates of aquatic plants. Many aquatic animals are also adversely affected by turbid water. Thus the value of shallows created in a gravel pit lake and exposed to typical wave lengths will be significantly reduced.

As well as rotating, the water particles in a wave move in the direction of wave travel. Waves thus transport water in the downwind direction, the quantity and speed of movement being related to wind speed and fetch. The combined effect of wind drift and of waves is to mix the water in the lake and this plays an important role in the lake ecosystem, recycling nutrients and leading to increased productivity.

A third effect of waves is their impact on downwind shorelines. Although, as indicated in Table 3.1, the wave heights expected under the wind speeds, fetch and water depths of gravel pit lakes are rarely likely to exceed 40–50 cm, this is sufficient to erode sediments, change shoreline profiles and undermine marginal vegetation, thus removing the productive and accessible shallow-water zones important to many waterfowl, and destroying islands required for safe nesting.

In summary, the effect of wind and waves can be significant but the major variables are all capable of manipulation. For example, (a) wind speeds can be reduced by provision of shelter; (b) fetch can be reduced by limiting the downwind lengths of exposed water through provision of islands, shoal areas, peninsulas or complete barriers; (c) water depths can be engineered to inhibit wave development.

Shelterbelts

The physical effect of wind is related to its force, which is approximately proportional to the cube of its velocity. This means that reducing the wind speed by 20% almost halves its energy (see Table 3.2). A reduction of this order is worthwhile in most contexts.

Table 3.2

Wind speed/energy relationships	
Wind speed reduction %	Wind energy reduction %
10	27
20	49
30	65
40	78
50	87
60	94

Dense, impenetrable barriers direct almost the entire force of the wind over their tops, and the wind resumes its unhindered progress relatively quickly. Vigorous turbulence typically occurs to the leeward of a dense windbreak and vegetation in this area is commonly flattened to the ground (see Fig 3.3a). Woodland, which acts as an almost impermeable barrier, should not be planted where downwind shelter is required. In contrast, permeable windbreaks filter the wind, absorbing its energy so that the wind emerges on the leeward side at a slower speed, preventing the air forced over the top from sweeping down to the ground and resuming its normal pattern and speed until some considerable distance downwind (Fig 3.3b).

Fig 3.3a

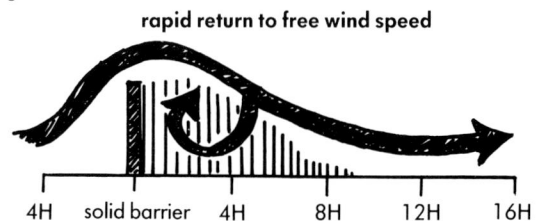

rapid return to free wind speed

4H   solid barrier   4H   8H   12H   16H

Zone with turbulence and downdraughts in strong winds.

Fig 3.3b

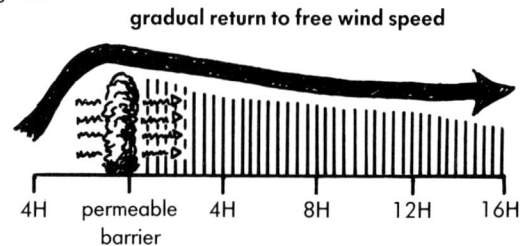

gradual return to free wind speed

4H   permeable barrier   4H   8H   12H   16H

Fig 3.3 Wind shelter by (a) solid and (b) permeable barriers (from Pollard et al 1974). Distance from barrier in H (height of hedge).

A moderately dense shelterbelt provides useful shelter for 2–4 times the shelterbelt height *upwind* and for 15–20 times its height *downwind*. The effect of the shelterbelt diminishes to zero at 30 times height (30H) in the downwind direction. Figure 3.4a shows clearly the upwind and downwind reduction of wind speed. Figure 3.4b converts the reduction of wind speed into terms of wind energy, providing a useful sense of the effectiveness of a moderately permeable shelterbelt.

Fig 3.4a

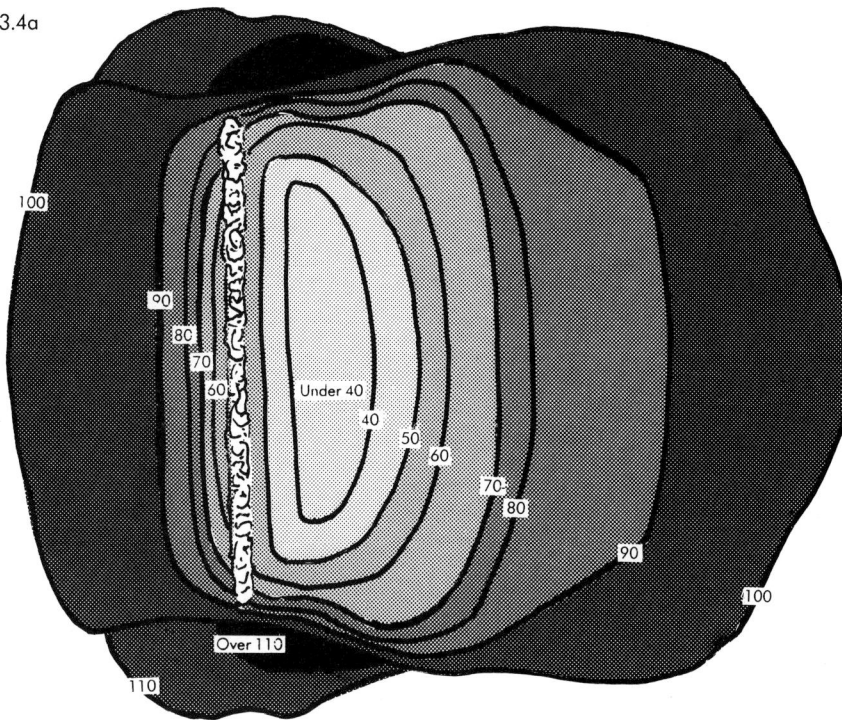

Wind direction

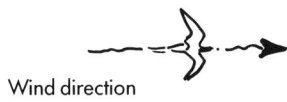

Fig 3.4b

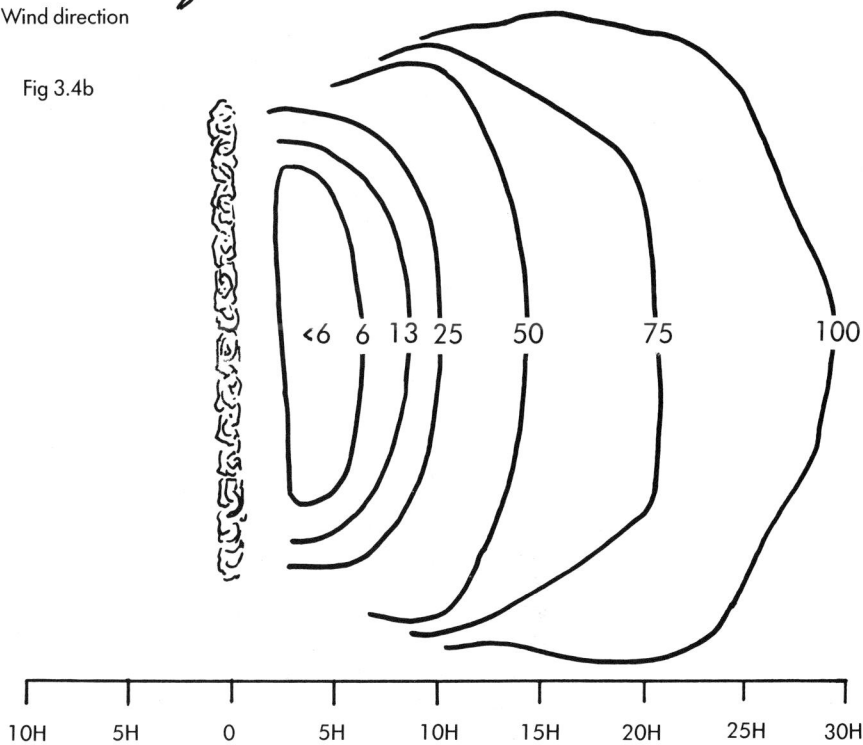

Fig 3.4 Changes in spatial distribution of (a) windspeed % (from Caborn, 1965) (b) wind energy % brought about by a moderately permeable (≈50%) shelterbelt.

Table 3.3

Wind reduction to leeward of 10 m high shelterbelts of different density				
Percentage wind speed reduction				
Density of Belt	Averaged over first 50 m (5H)	Averaged over first 100 m (10H)	Averaged over first 150 m (15H)	Averaged over first 300 m (30H)
Very open	18	24	25	18
Open	54	46	37	20
Medium	60	56	48	28
Dense	66	55	44	25
Very dense	66	48	37	20

(From Caborn, 1965)

If shelterbelts are planted so that their zones of shelter overlap (ie closer than 30 times their height), wind speeds will progressively reduce downwind. However, barriers need to be spaced closer than about 15–20 times their height for really significant cumulative effects to occur.

The effectiveness of a shelterbelt has been found to be largely independent of wind speed. The relative degree of shelter, expressed as a percentage reduction of the free wind speed, remains much the same provided that the permeability of the shelterbelt remains constant, as happens with artificial permeable screens for example. However, with hedges and shelterbelts comprising larger trees there is often an increase in permeability at high wind speeds as gaps are opened up through the bending of leaves, twigs and branches.

The optimum density for a shelterbelt has been found experimentally to be 50–60%, giving a permeability to the wind of 40–50%. The permeability should ideally be regularly distributed throughout the structure. For most purposes, however, it is better for a shelterbelt to be on the dense side towards the ground rather than vice versa. For artificial wind breaks, such as wooden lath screens or plastic mesh, the density can be determined precisely but for shrubs and tree screens this is much more difficult. Obviously, with deciduous shrubs and trees the permeability of a screen will vary seasonally but nevertheless there are methods of planting and types of plants with dense arrays of stems which can provide a surprisingly high screen density through the

leafless seasons. The wind reduction to the leeward of 10 m high tree and shrub shelterbelts of five different densities is given in Table 3·3.

If there is a need for the highest possible shelter over a short distance, a dense structure is to be preferred; but for more extensive shelter, a structure of medium density is best. Shelterbelt planting choices and methods are discussed at page 141. At the extremities of a shelterbelt occur areas where wind speeds are higher than the free wind speed: these are sites of excessive turbulence and

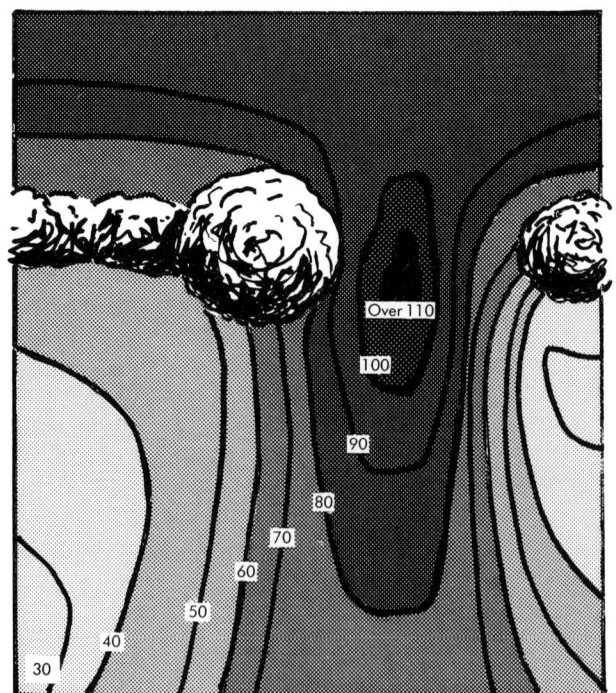

Fig 3.5 Wind acceleration in a shelterbelt gap (from Caborn 1965).

Wind speed in per cent of the free wind

potential damage (Fig 3.4). This can be reduced by gradually opening up the permeability of the barrier so that its effect is tapered off. This holds true both laterally and vertically. The ideal top to a permeable tree and shrub shelterbelt is not a solid mass of dense tree crowns all at the same height or a dense hedge top but, rather, an uneven feathery top with low density crowns extending above the main mass. In some instances, tall poplars have been successfully used to provide this structure.

Accelerated wind speeds will also occur where a shelterbelt is breached, for example, by an access road. Figure 3.5 shows the type of wind patterns associated with such a break. Ways of solving the problem include running the road through at an oblique angle or curving it within a broad shelterbelt, development of an overlap structure or baffle, and careful thinning of the structure adjacent to the required break, so that wind speeds build up gradually rather than abruptly and turbulence is reduced.

Normally the first priority is to obstruct the prevailing wind. Over much of the UK windbreaks are erected against SW–W winds. However, along river valleys where the wind may be channelled by the topography, it would be more appropriate to align the windbreaks at right angles to the axis of the valley. It may be, however, that a specific need dictates the windbreak orientation and siting; for example, NE winds, although infrequent, can occur in winter bringing very low air temperatures. To prevent winter waterfowl sites from freezing they may be protected from these winds but open to the south-west.

The annual percentage frequency of the force and direction of winds at selected stations in the UK and Eire is presented in Fig 3.6. The general dominance of the SW to W prevailing winds is clearly shown. Those stations with a major control by topography are also well shown (eg Dungeness where strong winds tend to be channelled along the coast, and Turnhouse where strong winds are channelled through the Clyde-Forth valleys). Clearly for any site an analysis of the local wind data is an essential step in planning the provision of any wind shelter.

It can be seen that, for many sites not significantly affected by topography, the prevailing wind blows not from a single direction but from a sector of almost 90°. One needs therefore to consider windbreaks to provide shelter from a prevailing wind which blows from a quadrant of directions.

Where a linear shelterbelt is used to provide shelter downwind for a rectangular gravel pit lake against prevailing winds blowing from a 90°

quadrant, only 25% of the site enjoys shelter at all times (Fig 3.7a), while the corner-to-corner angle of maximum wave fetch and potential erosion is not sheltered. In addition, the narrow area of potential shelter upwind of the shelterbelt is at times occupied by high velocity winds which shear along the barrier when the angle between the wind and the shelterbelt is significantly less than 90°.

To provide for a greater area of shelter from a 90° envelope of prevailing winds, the shelterbelt can be extended laterally, but site limitations may on occasion restrict this option. Figure 3.7b demonstrates the benefits, in terms of areas of water permanently receiving shelter from the envelope of prevailing winds, as the shelterbelt is progressively extended. For a square waterbody, the belt must be 2·4 times the length of the windward side to provide shelter at all times to 70% of the area.

A more practicable solution is likely to be to reduce the downwind length of an excavation (Fig 3.7c) or to site belts on two or three sides of a pit (Fig 3.7d).

Lake design to maximise shelter

It is generally advisable to use 20–25 times the height of the belt as the downwind extent of the most valuable wind shelter (the value of 30 times height has been used through much of this chapter to indicate the *maximum* extent of benefit achievable). Because of the time required to develop a shelterbelt of taller trees, it is advisable to use a design height of 10–15 m rather than say 20 m, even if the trees, in the long term, will reach this ultimate height. These two caveats would suggest designing for maximum downwind shelter distances of 200–300 m rather than the maximum of 600 m which is potentially possible. Clearly the planting of the major upwind shelterbelt should be carried out early, preceding active excavation whenever possible.

The effectiveness of a simple shelterbelt along the upwind margin of a pit, measured in terms of proportion of water area sheltered at all times from a 90° sector of prevailing winds, is dependent on the length to downwind width ratio of the pit; L:W ratios in excess of 2:1 and preferably as great as 3 or 4:1 should be aimed for. This shape will provide for a fairly high degree of wind shelter in a reasonable time as the shelterbelt height requirement will not be excessive. To obtain best effect from a shelterbelt, pits should be excavated with their long axes at right angles to the prevailing wind direction whenever possible.

A downwind sequence of gravel pit lakes, each

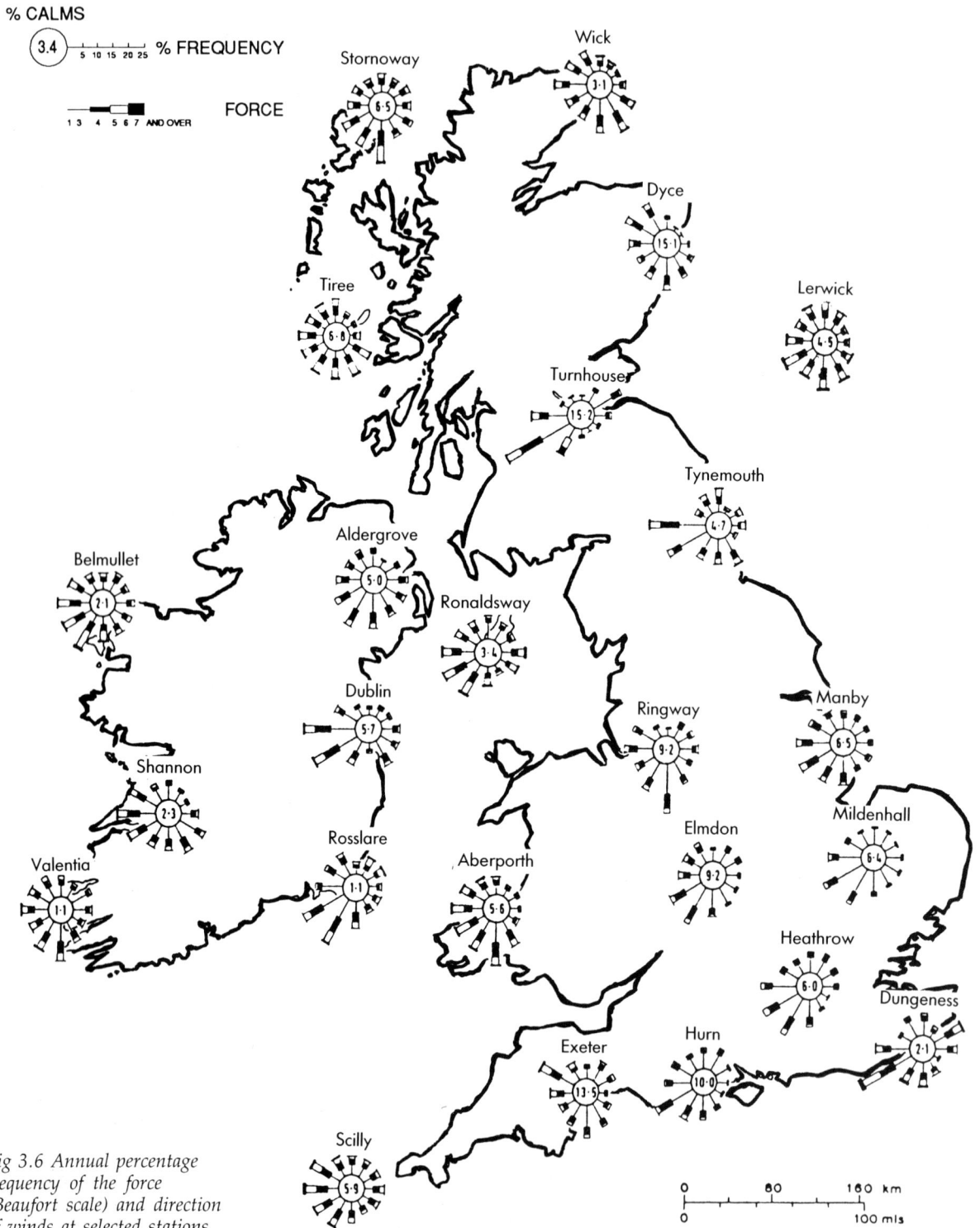

Fig 3.6 Annual percentage
frequency of the force
(Beaufort scale) and direction
of winds at selected stations
(from Chandler and Gregory,
1976, reproduced with
permission of the Royal
Meteorological Society).

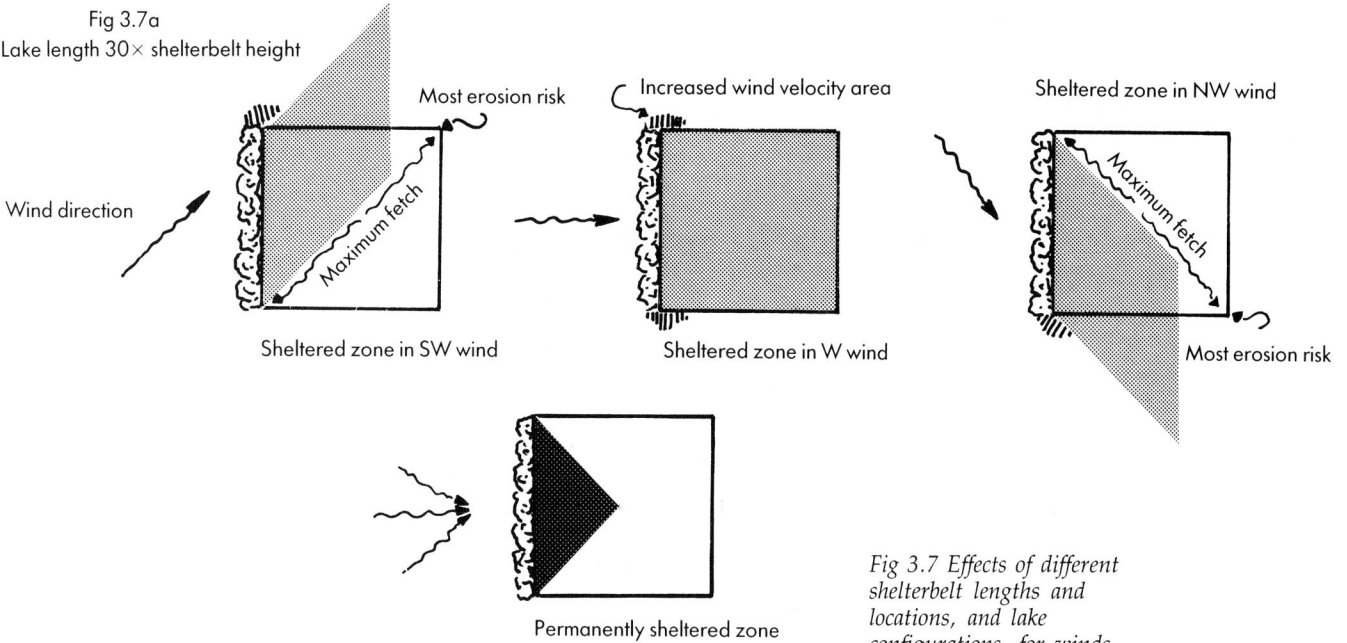

Fig 3.7a
Lake length 30× shelterbelt height

Wind direction

Most erosion risk

Maximum fetch

Sheltered zone in SW wind

Increased wind velocity area

Sheltered zone in W wind

Sheltered zone in NW wind

Maximum fetch

Most erosion risk

Permanently sheltered zone

Fig 3.7 Effects of different shelterbelt lengths and locations, and lake configurations, for winds from the NW-SW quadrant (a) for a square pit with a belt extending only to the ends of one bank, a 45° shift in wind direction permits exposure of the maximum fetch length, (b) extending the belt increases the area of permanent shelter and reduces potential fetch length, (c) restricting the down wind length of the pit improves shelter, (d) similar benefits are provided by belts on two or three sides of the pit there the belts have been set back to reduce shading of sheltered shores.

Fig 3.7b

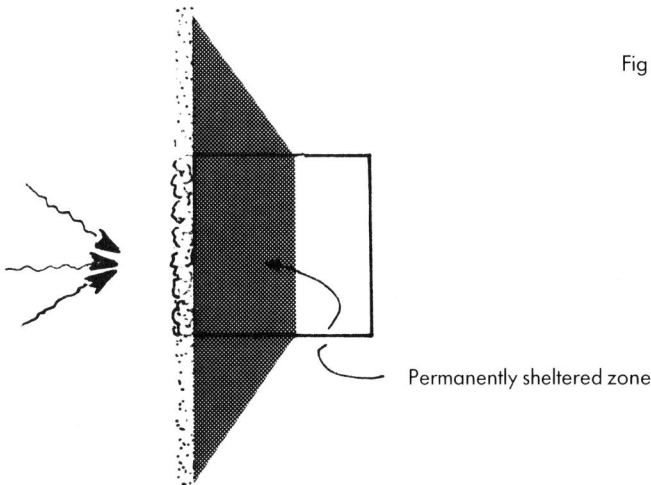

Permanently sheltered zone

Fig 3.7c

Permanently sheltered zone

Fig 3.7d

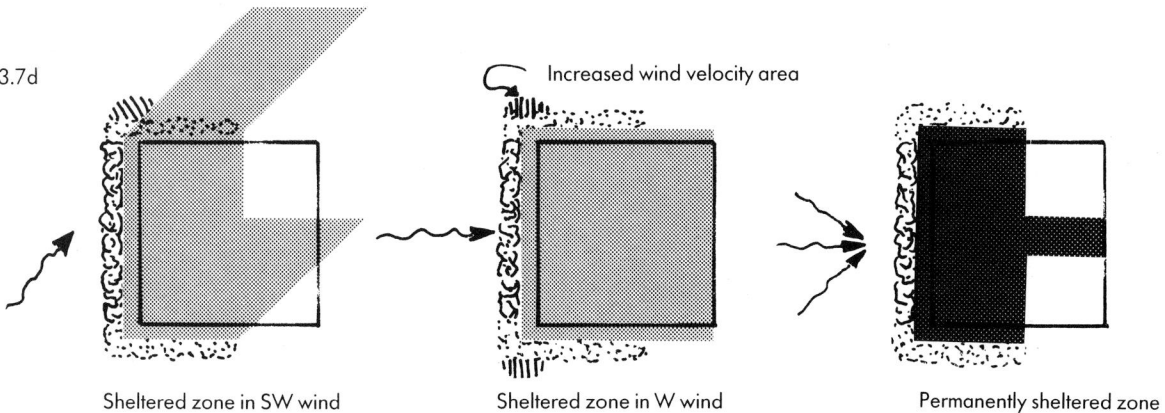

Increased wind velocity area

Sheltered zone in SW wind

Sheltered zone in W wind

Permanently sheltered zone

Habitat Management and Creation

sheltered as illustrated in Fig 3.7c, would have significant proportions of both water and land protected. If the design were such that, say, a distance of 20 times height was nowhere exceeded, then ground-level wind speeds would be progressively reduced across the site in the downwind direction, owing to the multiple shelterbelt effect. Alternatively, shelterbelts downwind could be progressively lower to achieve the same degree of protection over the whole site.

Where shelterbelts cannot be provided, limiting the downwind length of any excavation is of even greater importance to reduce wave lengths, water turbidity and shoreline erosion. The requirement to limit the downwind length of any single excavation can be met by excavating a series of pits as shown schematically in Fig 3.8, preferably starting at the upwind end of the site and working in sequence downwind. Barriers between the successive excavations may comprise unworked sand and gravel or they may be built of overburden and other spoil materials. If adequate rates and stability of tree growth can be assured then such barriers and shelterbelts may be used in combination.

An alternative way of effectively limiting the downwind length of gravel pits is by provision of peninsulas or islands: (i) peninsulas may overlap in the centre of the lake – a refinement might be to add curving extensions as these would afford good areas of sheltered water; (ii) islands should lie at right angles to the prevailing wind and provide overlap, in the downwind direction, so that maximum downwind length is everywhere reduced; (iii) the barrier between a pair of pits may be breached at either end, so that it is effectively an island, thus restricting access by humans and land-based predators, though foxes may swim to inshore islands.

The options are shown in Fig 3.8 combined in sequence on a site comprising six original phases of excavation (original phases shown by dashed lines). This layout is partly based on the proposition that one has been able progressively to reduce wind speeds across the site in the downwind direction; thus complete barriers can give way progressively to barrier islands, peninsulas

and islands. The more extensive and open water lies at the downwind end of the site.

Consideration of L:W ratios of excavations and of the design for windbreak extensions showed that the downwind corners of excavations would commonly be areas where it would be difficult to provide shelter from wind; in fact, such areas would often be subject to extreme wind speeds and turbulence. This conclusion suggests that these areas might either not be excavated at all or that they might be infilled with overburden or spoil.

Sunlight

In achieving shelter, care must be taken not to cause excessive shading from sunlight as this will

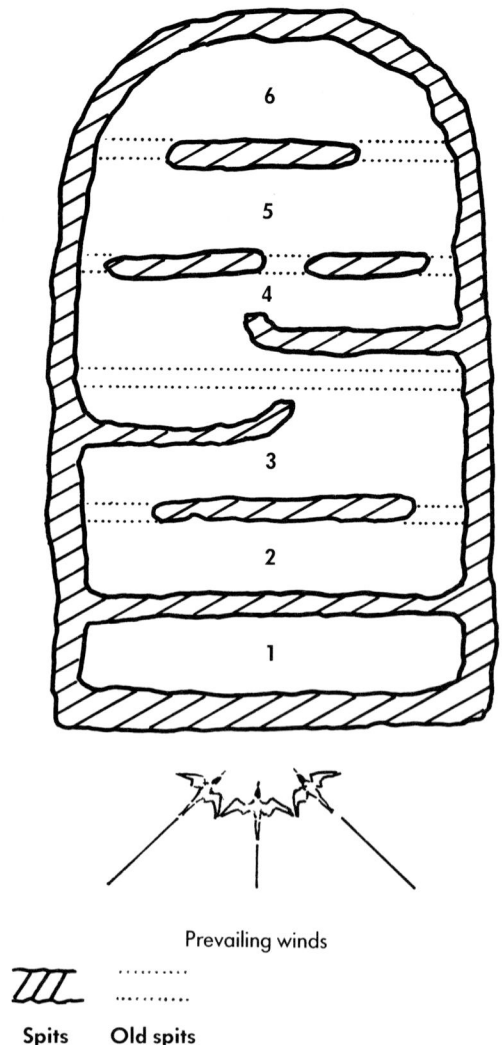

Fig 3.8 Barriers between pits will reduce wave fetch or may be used in the absence of shelterbelts or in combination with them. Peninsulas and islands also reduce fetch and provide shelter.

Table 3.4

Shelterbelt shadow extent			
Period	Sun elevation above horizon	Shadow (m) cast by W–E shelterbelt	
		10 m high	20 m high
Midsummer (midday)	62°	6	11
Equinox (midday)	26°	21	42
Midwinter (midday)	18°	31	62

affect plant growth and activity by invertebrates in both aquatic and terrestrial habitats.

Especially in winter, even a 10 m high shelterbelt aligned W–E will shade a substantial area (see Table 3.4; data for 52° latitude). Thus careful siting of W–E shelterbelts must be made. However, as the prevailing winds for much of the UK are westerly, major shelterbelts should be aligned N–S and thus will not cause major shade problems. Shelterbelt extensions to exclude winds with a southerly component, such as the one lying to the south of the lake in Fig 3.7c, need to balance the benefit of the shelter provided against the problem of the shade cast. In this example, the sheltered land to the north of the lake would be ideal, whereas the sheltered land along the southern shore would receive little sunlight. By setting the shelterbelt back from the shore by 1½ times its design height, a reasonable compromise will be struck in some cases but if the southern belt is moved back too far then all shelter effects on the northern shore may be lost.

If sheltered and sunlit conditions cannot be provided onshore, it may be that correctly sited islands may meet the requirements.

References

Caborn, J M, 1965, *Shelterbelts and windbreaks.* Faber & Faber, London, 288pp.

Chandler, T J & Gregory, S, (Eds), 1976, *The climate of the British Isles.* Longman, New York, 390pp.

Hutchinson, G E, 1957, *A treatise on limnology.* Vol. 1. Wiley, New York, 1015pp.

Pollard, E, Hooper, M D, & Moore, N W, 1974, *Hedges.* New Naturalist Series, Collins, London. 256pp.

Pollock, M R, 1984, *Shelter hedges and trees.* 42pp. Leaflet No 2, Rosewarne Experimental Horticultural Station (MAFF-ADAS) 4th Edition.

Shepherd, F W, 1979, *Hedges and Screens,* Wisley Handbook 17, Royal Horticultural Society, London 47pp.

Smith, I R, and Sinclair, I J, 1972, Deep water waves in lakes. *Freshwater Biology 2,* 387–99.

WATER DEPTH AND THE WATERTABLE

Summary

1. The relationship of water level to ground surface is the primary environmental factor controlling numbers and variety of plants and animals in wetland habitats. Shallow-water areas less than 1 m deep are very productive and are colonised by a wide variety of plants, support many breeding invertebrates and fish and are the favourite or essential feeding area for many waterfowl and their young. Marshland and seasonally-flooded wet grassland also have considerable value for specialised plants and animals. Deep water is least useful.

2. The inter-relationships of topography to ground watertable and hydraulic gradient need to be determined from topographical, geological and piezometer survey data. Final water levels on site need to be estimated as precisely as possible.

3. Sites with a strong hydraulic gradient should have shallow-water areas designed for up-gradient positions. Excavation sequence of such sites will be dictated by hydraulic gradient rather than sequential provision of shelter. Shelter versus water-depth development will depend on relative directions of any hydraulic gradient and the prevailing wind.

4. Shallow water, marginal habitats, marsh or wet grassland, pond sides, islands and shoals will need precise grading after excavation and de-watering have ceased and the watertable has stabilised. Access for requisite machinery must be maintained. Slopes of designed shallow areas around the main lake or islands or peninsulas should be 1:15 or less; for certain marsh and flooded grassland habitats, slopes of 1:50 to 1:100 are required.

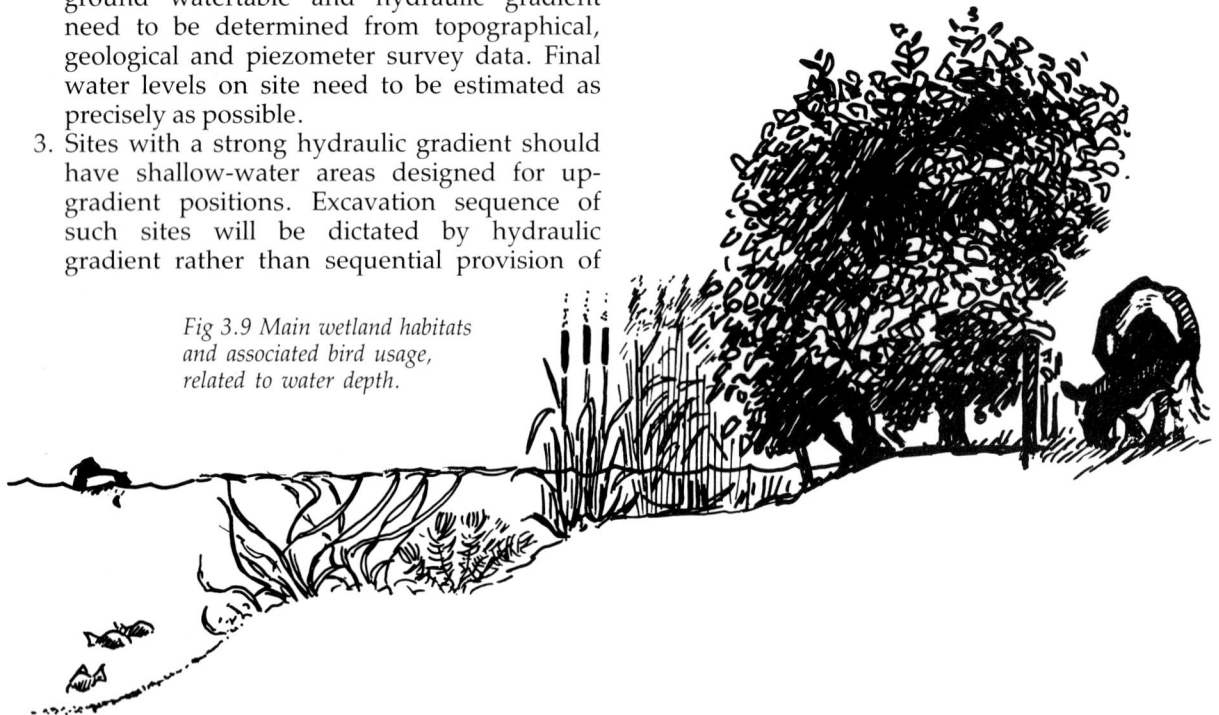

Fig 3.9 Main wetland habitats and associated bird usage, related to water depth.

Water depth >2 m	Water depth 0·5 – 2m	Water depth <0·5 m	Seasonally flooded
Reduced light penetration	Good light penetration	(a) colonisation by emergent plants	(a) Willow carr
Limited/no plant growth	Vigorous plant growth	Main bird usage – nesting habitat	Main bird usage – nesting habitat, songbird feeding
Main bird usage – fish-eating birds (cormorant, grebes)	Abundant invertebrates	(b) open water	(b) Wet grassland
Wildfowl roosting	Main bird usage – feeding by diving ducks, grebes	Main bird usage – feeding by dabbling ducks, ducklings and waders	Main bird usage – wader feeding and nesting habitat, feeding by grazing and dabbling wildfowl, wader feeding and nesting habitat
		(c) exposed mud	
		Main bird usage – feeding by some ducks and waders	

5. Control of water levels is highly desirable for a number of specific management purposes, notably the provision of ideal feeding conditions for dabbling ducks and waders. It may be achieved by the provision of sluices to permit partial or complete draw-down, to restore levels and, ideally, to flood areas at will.

6. Ability to completely drain down a lake is valuable, especially to help with the removal of unwanted fish.

7. Where it is not possible to manipulate water levels, extensive low angle lake margins which are flooded whether the lake is at high or low water level should be made.

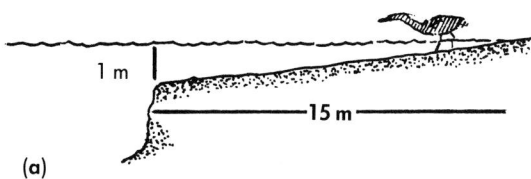

(a)

Winter water level: extent of shallows 15 m

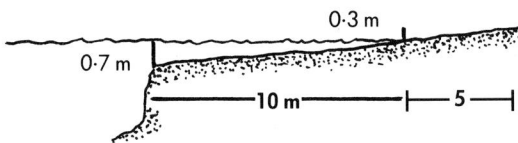

(b)

Summer water level down 0·3 m, extent of shallows 10 m

In (b) the extent of accessible feeding area is reduced by one-third.

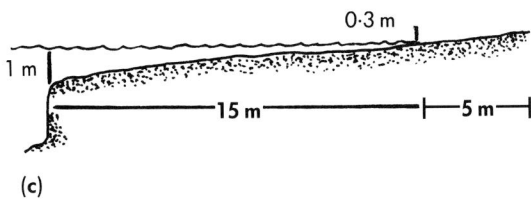

(c)

Summer water level down 0·3 m, extent of shallows 15 m

In (c) by taking the shallow shelf to a winter depth of 1·3 m, the main accessible feeding area is not reduced in summer.

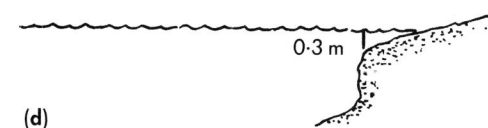

(d)

Bad restoration design, with shallows lost when levels fall in summer.

The influence of water levels

In wetlands, depth of water is the primary environmental factor controlling the numbers and variety of plants and animals. With the passage of time, all water bodies tend to infill with mineral and/or organic sediments so that depth is progressively reduced. Even where there is no inflow bearing material to be deposited, the growth and decay of plants gradually builds up the lake bed. In waters with shallow margins, encroachment by emergent plants may be rapid. When the lake bed rises to a point where it is at least seasonally above water, colonisation by willows can occur and ultimately the site becomes sufficiently raised and dry for other tree species to grow. These transitional marginal habitats differ little in their water-depth or watertable requirements but show major differences in the plant and animal communities which they support (see Fig 3.9).

In a gravel-pit restoration it is possible to design for deep water, shallows, marsh or wet grassland.

Deep water and shallows

Water over 1.5 m deep is the least valuable habitat for most wetland wildlife. Most modern workings go below this depth and the aim in conservation restorations should be to reduce the extent of deep-water areas as much as possible.

A great variety of plants grows in permanent shallow water, helped by good light penetration and rapid warming in spring. Both submerged and marginal species can flourish there. Shallows provide the breeding habitat for most dragonflies, many coarse fish and, where fish are excluded, for amphibians. The luxuriant plant growth and abundant populations of aquatic animals make this the favourite feeding zone for many waterfowl. Indeed, most species, including mute swan and dabbling ducks and waders, make little or no use of deeper water. Although diving ducks and grebes will use deeper water, they feed with least expenditure of energy in shallows, while the survival of ducklings and the young of many other waterfowl depends on the availability of large areas of sheltered, warm shallows containing abundant and accessible food.

In many gravel workings, the shallow-water zone is limited to a strip about 1 m wide around the pit margins and is inadequate to support large

Fig 3.10 Effect of summer draw-down on extent of shallows.

Habitat Management and Creation

numbers of birds at any season, while breeding success is extremely low, many ducklings and cygnets dying of starvation in the first weeks of life. In such sites, natural wave erosion may create a wave shelf on exposed shores but its value will be limited by exposure, as wave action will continue to cause turbidity (reducing light penetration) and to damage or uproot plants. The time scale for the development of extensive areas of productive marginal habitats on sheltered shores, as a result of sediment accretion, may be measured in centuries. Therefore, because of their very high wildlife value, extensive shallows should be designed into the restoration and, ideally, they should be created on shores in the lee of the prevailing wind and/or protected by shelter belts. Where this is not possible, marginal habitats are likely to require physical protection by islands, booms or bunding. Subsequent management is likely to be needed to maintain the desired proportions of open water, stands of emergent plants and areas of bare mud.

In the UK, precipitation is fairly regularly distributed through the year, whereas evapotranspiration losses are negligible in winter but high in summer. Surface and shallow groundwater levels thus vary seasonally, being typically high in winter and early spring, and low in summer and early autumn. However, drought years may lead to desiccation of habitats dependent on shallow-water conditions or a high soil watertable (eg marshlands) with consequent destruction of wildlife. It is therefore important to have the best possible predictive information on final water levels and their fluctuations before planning land-forms. Thus, an area of shallows with a 1:15 slope to a depth of 1 m will be 15 m wide: to provide the same extent of feeding habitat after summer draw-down of 0·3 m, the area of shallows would need to extend to 20 m, to a maximum depth of 1·3 m (see Fig 3.10).

Marshland and wet grassland

Where the ground surface lies within the zone of watertable variation, being shallowly flooded in winter and only a little above the summer water level, it is usually colonised by marsh plants. If shores slope steeply, marsh conditions are confined to a narrow marginal band but extensive areas may develop on silt lagoons, where soil compaction impedes surface drainage, or by design. However, marsh is a difficult habitat to retain because of the rapid rate of willow invasion, so it is probably best omitted from a restoration plan except where year-round control

of water level will be possible and deliberate flooding can be carried out at the correct seasons to control or set-back changes in the vegetation.

Alternatively, where summer grazing or mowing is practicable, wet grassland can be created for shallow flooding (up to 15 cm) in the winter months. Grazing will prevent development of scrub or woodland and, although the sward may be mainly composed of grasses, a variety of wetland plants will invade it naturally. The flooding will make plant seeds and invertebrates available for feeding by wildfowl and waders, and is particularly valuable if it can be timed for mid to late winter when food resources in the shallows will be much reduced. If the flooding regime cannot be controlled, it is important to set the soil surface at the predicted level of the water in mid March. If grass is not free of flooding by the time it starts to grow vigorously (usually end March in southern England), it will be killed. The habitat will also be valuable for breeding waders – lapwing, redshank or snipe – provided grazing is delayed until late June so that nests are not trampled.

Because of the practical management problems posed by both marsh and wet grassland, in most sites it will be wiser to concentrate on creating the largest possible areas of shallow water.

Ponds

Ponds can provide conditions which are particularly favourable to invertebrates and amphibians. They warm up quickly in spring, being small, shallow and often sheltered by marginal vegetation and they tend quickly to accumulate a bed layer of organic detritus which supports a large detritus-feeding invertebrate population on which other invertebrates, such as damselfly larvae, can feed in turn. In addition, the combination of warmth, good light penetration and ample organic material means that ponds develop rich communities of aquatic plants, providing the cover and feeding habitat for predatory invertebrates and newts. Finally, they tend to be less affected than larger waters by fish, which, depending on species, may reduce plant cover or eat invertebrates and tadpoles.

Pond siting will depend on the management aim. If located on the watertable, summer draw-down may be used to expose margins for feeding by waders or wildfowl. However, the ideal site for amphibians is one which dries out completely about one year in five, so destroying any fish populations which may have colonised during floods or as a result of human intervention: the urge to put fish in ponds is almost irresistible to some people. Ponds may be placed above the watertable where soil compaction impedes drainage but such sites are likely to dry out too regularly to develop much value unless they receive abundant surface run-off. Alternatively, puddled clay or a liner may be used to site a pond in an otherwise dry area. Liners are liable to puncture unless deeply sandwiched between layers of stone-free material.

Ponds should be less than a metre deep and be excavated with variable though generally shallow gradient margins. The length of the margin should be maximised by making the pond elongated or of irregular shape. Excavated surfaces should be left uneven rather than smoothly graded. If a substrate such as a layer of topsoil is to be added to the excavation the initial form/ depth should take account of this. If a series of ponds is being made, they should be variable in size, shape, nature of margins, water depth, nature of substrate (muddy, sandy, stony, topsoil-lined, detritus-enriched) and degree of shading.

Site factors and land-forming

The initial and final physical form of a site are defined from:
(a) the initial site survey which provides a detailed topographic map;
(b) site drilling to determine depth and distribution of the economic sand and gravel deposit; the data are used to produce an isopach map and a map of the sub-deposit topography;
(c) a piezometer survey to provide data on the watertable level and its seasonal variation; these data will indicate the hydraulic gradient across the site.

However, during the working of most sites, areas are actively dewatered and any standing water levels are consequently disturbed. Stable water levels cannot be defined until active working and dewatering have ceased. Although the final standing water level should be predictable from the piezometer survey, in practice it is found that it is usually lower than the original watertable level at the site, but by not more than 0·3 m.

Sites with a considerable hydraulic gradient across the area to be excavated can present special problems. An elongated site stretching along the axis of a reasonably steep river valley is likely to fall into this category. The problem is exacerbated where the deposit being excavated is fairly thin. Figure 3.11 (a) indicates schematically a typical relationship for such a site, the ground surface, overburden and sand and gravel layers all sloping

up the valley, with the ground water table approximately paralleling the general valley slope. After excavation the water level relationships will be as shown in Figure 3.11 (b).

In such a situation, one should clearly design the restoration to take advantage of those relationships, ie locate the areas designed for deeper water in the downslope part of the site and locate marsh, reedbed or shallow water habitats at the upslope end.

It is possible to limit the upgradient extent of any single lake by constructing a reasonably impermeable clay/silt bund as indicated schematically in Figure 3.11 (c). Habitats will then be developed in response to each of the lakes and its standing water level. This approach can be used to increase the area of water with a depth most suitable for feeding by diving ducks. It may also permit seasonal drawdown through a series of sluices built into the bunds, thus enabling areas of fresh mud to be exposed for feeding by passage waders or wintering wildfowl.

Compromise may be required in the restoration design for sites with strong hydraulic gradients. The excavation sequence provides the deep-water part of the lake first and the extensive, shallow-water environments later. This temporal and spatial sequence needs consideration with respect to the prevailing wind direction and to the provision of shelter for the lake. Using Figure 3.11 (a) as an example: here, the hydraulic gradient falls from left to right and the excavation sequence would normally move uphill from right to left; if the prevailing wind were from right to left then a shelterbelt would be required on the right-hand or upwind edge of the site and the area finally receiving most shelter would be the deeper water area of the lake. There would be a strong case here for the provision of linear islands topped with low tree or shrub plantings, to be sited near the downwind end of the lake, to provide shelter for the shallow-water downwind areas (Fig 3.11 (d)). If the prevailing wind were from left to right, then a shelterbelt could be installed at the left side of the site and on completion of excavation it would be the shallow-water end of the site which would receive most shelter. This is the preferred option wherever it can be achieved.

Areas designated as shallow-water habitat, as marsh, grassland for seasonal flooding or as pond sites, are likely to need detailed grading in the final stages of restoration in response to the stabilised water level, which cannot be predicted with certainty. This will also apply to islands with low gradient shorelines. Access for earth-moving plant to any of these sites in need of final grading must be maintained. This would argue strongly

Habitat Management and Creation

for proposed islands to remain as peninsulas until the final stages of grading are complete. Allowance should be made for the application of topsoil, ideally to a thickness of 30 cm to provide a growing medium for submerged and marginal plants.

The very shallow water, marsh and floodable grassland habitats obviously require grading fairly precisely and the preferred slopes of such surfaces are extremely low (around 1:100). In many instances rather than try to grade a simple, continuous, low-angle slope it may be both easier

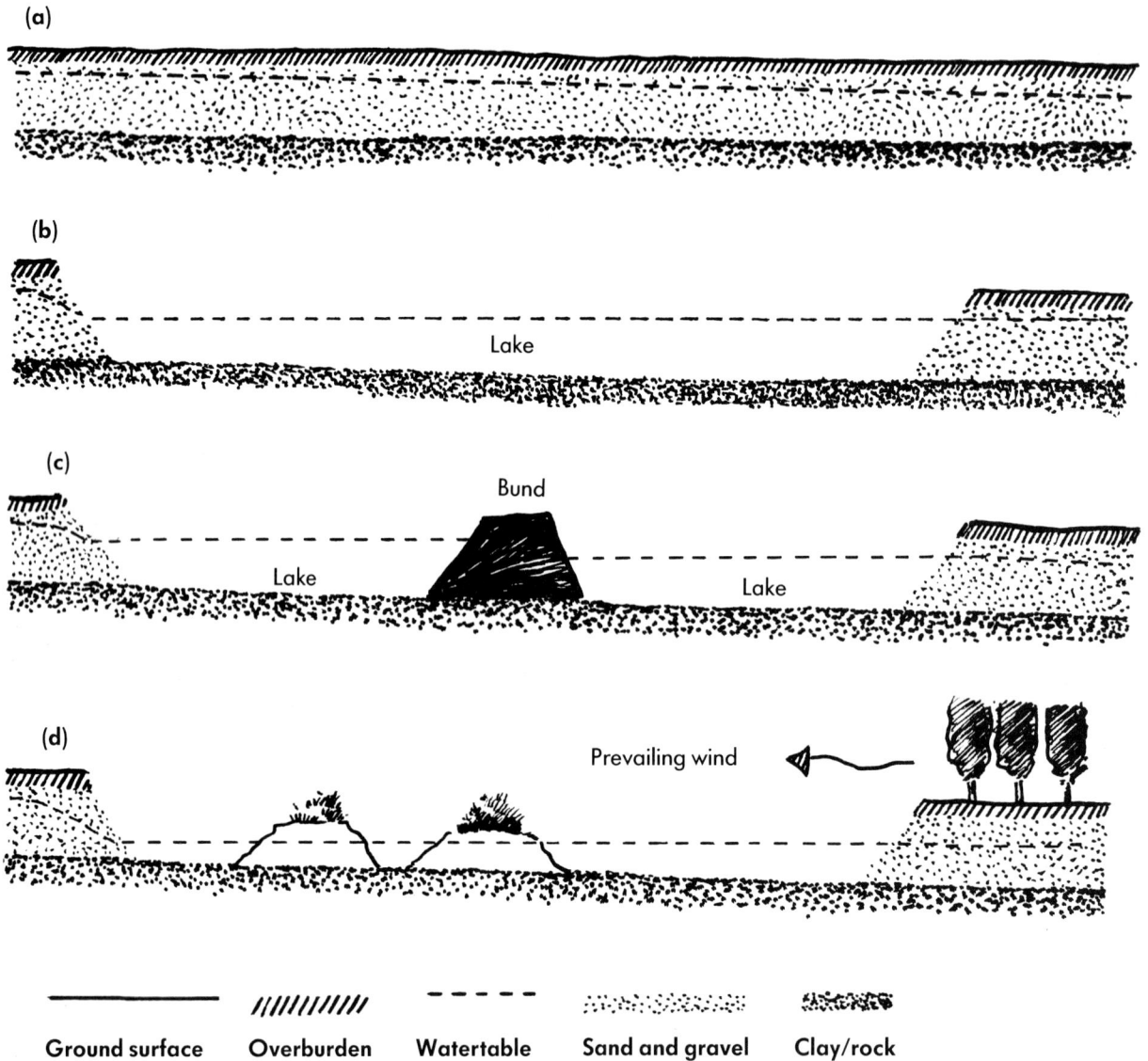

(a)

(b)

Lake

(c)

Bund

Lake

Lake

(d)

Prevailing wind

| Ground surface | Overburden | Watertable | Sand and gravel | Clay/rock |

Fig 3.11 Treatments for a site with a strong hydraulic gradient.

(a) Pre-excavation watertable.

(b) After excavation, with shallows or dry ground at the up-gradient end.

(c) Correctly sited cross-bunds create desired water depths: if sluices are incorporated the up-gradient lake may be drawn down, eg to expose shallows.

(d) Depending on orientation, islands or spits may be essential to shelter shallow water habitats.

and preferable to develop a very gently undulating surface which will have pockets which flood slightly more deeply and elevations which remain less deeply flooded or unflooded. This variety of microtopography (5–10 cm in tens of metres) will add considerable diversity to habitat development. Shallows may be created by excavating back from the margin of the worked pit, or by depositing material within it: this may include over-burden, silt from washings or inert material imported onto site (for which a tipping licence will be required and income may be gained). Account should be taken of the topography of the excavated site, to take advantage of less deep areas if reasonable shelter can be contrived for them, and no material should be wasted in reducing depths of water where the end result will be more than 1·5 m deep.

For all practical purposes, the area of shallows cannot be too large. It is better to create one broad area on a sheltered and disturbance-free shore than to produce a narrow 'bench' of shallows around the whole perimeter of the pit, as the broad sheltered area will be more productive of plant and animal life. In sheltered locations, the slope may be as slight as can be contrived. An unsheltered slope of steeper than 1:15 to a depth of 1 m is particularly likely to suffer wave erosion, whereas extensive, gently-shelving shores tend to reduce wave height and energy progressively without suffering significant erosion.

Because of their fine character, it may be best to isolate washings in lagoons, separated from the main area of a waterbody by off-shore bunds built from overburden or inert waste. Silt may be pumped into these to create shallows sloping to a central maximum depth of 1·3–1·5 m.

Many emergent plants can grow in water depths down to a metre or somewhat more, though they must initially become established in very shallow conditions or even on land just above the watertable. It may therefore be advantageous to separate areas of shallows by leads of water 2 m wide and more than 2 m deep as a means of inhibiting the spread of beds of emergent plants onto the open areas required for submerged plants, waterfowl feeding etc.

The shoreline itself can be modelled to aid the provision of shelter and of seclusion, which are important for some breeding waterfowl. Fine-scale modelling is likely to erode, but a pattern of spits and bays approximately 10×10 m is ideal (Fig 3.12).

If it is not practical to create shallows within a worked pit, consider excavating shallow pools on adjoining land. Even if they are too small or too

Shorelines

(a) **Poor:** minimal length

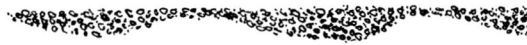

(b) **Fair**

(c) **Good**
Bay dimensions about 2×2 m

(d) **Excellent**
Bay dimensions about 10×10 m. Total length same as (c) but more resistant to erosion, and giving better shelter and cover for wildfowl and waders.

Fig 3.12 Shorelines.

easily disturbed to support many wildfowl, they may be ideal for dragonflies and amphibians. Ideally, a site will contain separate small pools from which fish can be excluded as well as shallows within the flooded pits.

Water level control

Experience of many wetland habitats has demonstrated that it is of prime value to be able to manipulate water levels. Where water supply and freeboard permit, water-level manipulation can be used to achieve a variety of management objectives such as:
(a) control of vegetation by drowning invasive emergents;
(b) rejuvenation of wetlands to maintain an early stage in plant succession;
(c) compensation for irregularities in rainfall;
(d) managing the invertebrate and fish fauna;
(e) reducing competition for food between ducks and fish;
(f) providing access to invertebrate-rich substrates for waders on migration;
(g) floating-out seeds shed from marginal plants to provide a food resource for winter dabbling ducks.

Habitat Management and Creation

Winter: high level (<1 m): used by dabbling and diving ducks.

Spring: progressive drawdown: used by dabbling ducks, ducklings, waders.

Summer: dry: flush of wetland annual plants or part shallow flooding maintained.

Autumn: progressive flooding: used by passage waders and dabbling ducks.

The annual production of plant material recharges the system for feeding by wildfowl and waders. Note uneven bed, creating a mosaic of shallow water and damp ground when the level is drawn down.

Fig 3.13 Wildlife benefits of a water-level control regime.

Most of these objectives can be achieved by installing sluices to control water levels over a vertical extent of only about 50 cm from the mean. However, there may be certain requirements, such as complete removal of fish from a lake, where to be able to drain down completely would be ideal.

Figure 3.13 illustrates a water-level control regime applied to a small waterbody to provide good feeding conditions for wildfowl, especially teal and shoveler, and for migrant waders. Where a large gravel pit lake can be controlled similarly, the margins could be shaped in this way to create extensive shelves of wet mud and shallow pools when the level is drawn down in spring and raised afresh in autumn.

For some sand and gravel pit lakes it may prove difficult to manipulate water levels at all and the best one can then do is to ensure that low angle lake margins are as extensive as reasonably possible so that some part of these shallow areas is always flooded, whether the lake is at high or low level (Fig 3.10).

References

Scott, D A (Ed.), 1982, *Managing wetlands and their birds.* Int. Waterfowl research Bureau, Slimbridge, 368p.

Street, M, 1989, *Ponds and lakes for wildfowl.* Game Conservancy. Fordingbridge, 184pp.

SOIL, PLANTS AND PRODUCTIVITY

Summary

1. Most management for wildlife is the management of plant communities because plants form the base of food chains for all wildlife, as well as providing physical shelter and concealment. Plant development depends on the nature of the soil, so soil management is of vital importance.

2. Soil is a dynamic physical, chemical and biological entity, where nutrient elements are progressively released and taken up by plant roots. Its value for plant growth can be destroyed by incorrect handling.

3. During removal, storage and reinstatement, the attributes of soils should be maintained as close to their original condition as possible. Topsoil, subsoil and overburden should be stripped and stored separately and ideally should be used quickly during progressive restoration. Stockpiling topsoil reduces its value for plant growth.

4. If handled when wet, soils, especially clays, are severely damaged and this impairs subsequent plant establishment. Damage to soil structure should be minimised by limiting stripping and handling to the drier months (normally May-September) and to dry conditions.

5. Compaction may result from vehicle movements during or after restoration. It impairs root development and causes water-logging but can be avoided by correct techniques. Subsoiling may be successful in relieving compaction.

6. Silt washings are most usefully contained within a settlement lagoon and the area used for development of shallow water or marsh habitats.

7. Excess sand and overburden can be used for development of restored landform contours. Large stones are useful for protection of exposed shorelines.

8. Reasonably well-drained soils with adequate nutrient supplies are required for tree and herb growth. Topsoil should be redistributed on site for shelterbelt planting, for shallow lake margins and marshland areas and for deeper lake floor areas. Subsoil is preferable for all other tree and shrub areas and most other terrestrial environments. Additional nutrients may sometimes be required, either as artificial fertilisers, organic manures or sewage sludge cake.

9. Nutrient concentrations in many gravel pit lakes are likely to support fairly dense algal populations and submerged plant communities may be poorly developed as a result of low light penetration. For good aquatic weed development, low to moderate nutrient levels are required.

10. Analysis of lake water should be carried out before any decision on nutrient or other chemical adjustment is considered.

The importance of soils

In all habitats plants are the primary producers of the organic materials which are essential to animals for their respiration, growth and reproduction. Plant and animal tissues are ultimately recycled by decomposers, the bacteria and fungi which consume non-living organic materials, releasing elements in forms which are available for uptake by plants: the interdependence of plants, animals and the decomposers comprises the so-called food chain. Plants are also essential to provide animals with concealment and shelter from weather, and as different plant species have different physical qualities many creatures have preferences or even absolute needs for particular vegetation types.

Plants colonise gravel pits even during the extraction phase, growing on heaps of topsoil and overburden, on bare sand and gravel areas and in temporary ponds and silt lagoons. Many of the initial colonisers are opportunistic species such as birch, gorse or coltsfoot which can thrive under conditions of poor soil development and low nutrient supply. Abandoned workings ultimately support deciduous woodland, though this may take many decades to develop. Meanwhile, the lakes are colonised by emergent vegetation in shallow water and, in deeper water, by floating or submerged aquatic plants.

However, to maximise the wildlife benefit of a gravel pit, certain plant species will prove particularly beneficial and the planting of selected trees, shrubs and other plants in planned locations will greatly speed the required development of a site. Active management of some types of vegetation may be needed to maintain maximum habitat quality.

Table 3.5
Soils – Particle sizes and related characteristics

International system	Approximate number of particles per gram	Approximate surface area, cm^2 per gram	Visibility of individual particles	Physical character	Mineralogical composition
Coarse sand	$5 \cdot 4 \times 10^2$	21	Visible to naked eye	Loose and single-grained; not sticky or plastic	Mainly quartz with some rock fragments
Fine sand	$5 \cdot 4 \times 10^5$	210	Visible to naked eye	Loose and single-grained; not sticky or plastic	Mainly quartz and feldspar with some ferromagnesians
Silt	$5 \cdot 4 \times 10^8$	2,100	Visible under microscope	Smooth and floury; only slightly cohesive	Mainly quartz and feldspar with some ferromagnesians, mica, and clay minerals
Clay	$7 \cdot 2 \times 10^{11}$	23,000	Invisible under microscope except in upper range; many particles resolved by electron microscope	Sticky and plastic when moist; hard and cohesive when dry	Mainly clay minerals with some quartz

Coarse sand, diameter of particles, 2·0–0·2 mm. Fine sand 0·2–0·02. Silt 0·02–0·002. Clay 0·002–0·000.
(After Bradshaw & Chadwick, 1980)

Reasonably well-drained and aerated soils are needed by most plants, though the plants of marshland and shoreline have developed a tolerance to waterlogging and low oxygen levels. An adequate depth of soil and a good soil structure permit development of extensive root systems which help to anchor the plant and tap into the element resources of a relatively large soil volume. Supplies of essential nutrients are derived both from the mineral and the organic matter fractions of the soil.

The original topsoil of a site is a major source of plant nutrients and of plant seeds, and many of the types of plants and their rate of growth will reflect what is done with the topsoil in the restoration process.

Soil composition and function

Typically, topsoil is a mixture of 55% mineral particles, 25% water, 15% gases and 5% organic matter, and is home to many animals, bacteria and fungi. It provides anchorage and all the chemical components needed by the plant, except for carbon dioxide which is derived from the atmosphere.

The mineral particles in soils are derived mostly from the breakdown or weathering of rocks and occur in a range of sizes with attributes shown in Table 3.5. The relative proportions of sand, silt and clay in a soil comprise the soil texture, an attribute which is very difficult to change except by massive additions of a particular particle size. Soils with a high clay component are very susceptible to damage if handled when wet, severely impairing subsequent plant establishment.

Dead organic matter derived from plants, animals and micro-organisms has several important functions in soils; for example, the partially broken down, fibrous, organic materials are very water retentive. As breakdown proceeds, humus is formed, significantly improving the structure of soils by binding particles together into aggregates or crumbs. Organic matter is also a major source of nutrients for plant growth. In storage, the organic component can be destroyed unless appropriate precautions are taken.

The spaces between the mineral and organic soil particles are filled with soil water and/or air. Plant roots and the spectrum of animals and micro-organisms within the soil all respire, absorbing oxygen and releasing carbon-dioxide, the source of the oxygen being air which has penetrated into the soil pore spaces. The movement of gases and elements through the soil is achieved predominantly in solution by the physical movement of soil water upwards, downwards or laterally. Thus, as well as being the major component used by plants, water performs other essential roles within the soil system.

The roots of plants extensively penetrate the soil for anchorage and for the uptake of essential water and nutrients; in addition, the roots are respiring at all times, taking up oxygen from and releasing carbon-dioxide into the soil solution and soil atmosphere. Earthworms actively burrow through the soil, ingesting soil particles. In the process, organic matter is broken down, and gases and water can more readily circulate. Vast numbers of other organisms also live within the soil: nematodes, protozoa, bacteria and fungi all metabolise organic materials and ultimately play a part in the release of the constituent nutrient elements. Many of these important soil organisms can be destroyed by incorrect stripping, storage or compaction on restoration.

Soil handling and storage

During the removal, storage and reinstatement of soil the objective should be to maintain its physical, chemical and biological attributes as close to their original condition as possible. Bulky surface vegetation should first be removed and topsoil, subsoil and overburden should each be stripped and stored separately. If soils or overburden vary significantly across the site, material of differing characteristics should be stripped and stored separately. Topsoil should be stripped from areas to be used for storage of subsoil or overburden.

Any topsoil stored for more than a month should be seeded with a low-maintenance grass seed mixture or with white clover to stabilise the surface and protect against erosion and loss. Most earthworms survive only in the top 30 cm of stored soil so, if stockpiling is essential, low and wide mounds are best. Surviving worms are likely to be killed by soil cultivation after spreading, so restorations which do not create compaction requiring cultivation are to be preferred.

Soil structure is particularly prone to damage during stripping or reinstatement operations. The two principal causes of damage are compaction and smearing, both of which are related to moisture content. Damage can be caused readily when soils are wet and so handling should be restricted to the drier periods of the year (predominantly May to September) and operations should be halted during rain and for up to 48 hours afterwards. As a rough guide, do not move soils or permit vehicular traffic over them unless the soil is sufficiently dry to crumble when rolled between the fingers. Guidance based on rainfall criteria is given at Table 3.6, for stripping or replacement of soils by earthscraper, or by backacter and dump-truck.

Soils and overburden for reinstatement should

Table 3.6
Soil handling criteria based on rainfall

Earthscrapers	Rainfall	Loader and Dump Truck
For readings taken at 07.30		
May be ignored	0–3 mm	
	0–4 mm	May be ignored
Soil operations may start at mid-day	3·1–5 mm	
	4·1–7 mm	Soil operations may start at mid-day
Soil operations may start next day	5·1–10 mm	
	7·1–10 mm	Soil operations may start next day
Soil operations may start after 48 hours	10·1 or more	
	10·1–15 mm	Soil operations may start mid-day next day
	15·1 or more	Soil operations may start after 48 hours
For readings taken at 18.00		
May be ignored	0–4 mm	
	0–5 mm	May be ignored
Soil operations may start mid-day next day	4·1–10 mm	
	5·1–12 mm	Soil operations may start at mid-day next day
Soil operations may start after 48 hours	10·1 or more	
	12·1 or more	Soil operations may start after 48 hours

NB. These criteria should be applied with caution as factors including soil characteristics, humidity and wind speed will alter individual cases.
(From A Practical Guide to Restoration, RMC, 1986.)

be stored close to where they will be respread. Ideally they should be moved directly from the area being stripped to the area being restored, as this saves double handling and also reduces deterioration of soils in stockpiles. The first topsoil to be stripped could be spread for establishment of a shelterbelt on the upwind margin of a site. Then, as the more extensive shallow-water areas are preferably developed toward the protected upwind end of the site, soils and overburden from successively downwind and later parts of the excavation could be used to develop the physical form of the immediately preceding, upwind areas. Some topsoil should be stored in small piles around the site for final spreading after the detailed grading of the marsh and other shallow water and shoreline areas is carried out.

Compaction

Both poor soil drainage and check in tree growth are the most common problems associated with restored land and are often caused by soil compaction. Some degree of compaction during soil handling is almost inevitable but it can be minimised by use of a backacter to spread subsoil and topsoil in successive 'panels' which can be worked without tracking over them at any stage (Fig 3.14). If compaction occurs, it can be relieved by subsoiling. Normal agricultural cultivation is likely to be inadequate except on original surfaces which have been compacted by light vehicle traffic only. Once spread and treated, the surface should not be driven over when wet, even after vegetation cover has developed.

Although for agricultural restoration the installation of piped drainage is often necessary, in restoration for nature conservation such additional drainage is rarely required.

Soil compaction may be an asset in conservation management as impeded drainage may be used to create 'perched' wetlands especially at sites which will receive drainage from a surrounding catchment.

Other materials on site

The clay, silt and finer sand-sized particles removed during the crushing, grading and washing processes are normally separated by settlement in silt ponds, the water being recirculated for further use or discharged to a surface watercourse. Silt deposits may be used in development of restored landform contours. Alternatively, if the silt pond infilling can be developed

close to the final restored water level the low-angled surface can be used for a shallow water and marsh sequence of habitats. It will require wind shelter to prevent wave action causing severe erosion and water turbidity.

Some deposits contain a higher sand content than is desirable for certain aggregate uses. Such material can be used on site in the same way as overburden for the development of restored landforms. Its free-draining qualities will make it unsuitable as a basis for some types of plant community.

Occasionally, a deposit will contain larger stones which are separated out during the screening process. These should be stored and used during restoration for protection of downwind shorelines against erosion, for development of shingle islands or for capping shoal banks out in the lake. Piles of large stones can also be strategically placed around the restored site, some in shaded areas, some in open and sunlit areas where they will provide habitat for amphibians, reptiles, and other small animals; giving shelter from weather, desiccation and predators.

Plant nutrients and water

Over 90% of plant tissues (except the wood of trees) is water. The remainder is largely oxygen and carbon, in roughly equal proportions, plus a much smaller quantity of hydrogen. Next in abundance is a group of six macro-elements (nitrogen, potassium, calcium, magnesium, phosphorus, sulphur). Trace elements are present in smaller concentrations. Oxygen, hydrogen and, normally, carbon are never in short supply. The trace element requirements of plants can be met by most soils. Similarly, sulphur, calcium and magnesium are usually adequately available but the other three macro-elements are often inadequate and can limit plant growth. The deliberate restriction of nutrients is a useful mechanism for controlling the plant community, though in other cases abundant nutrient supply may be desired.

Most **nitrogen** in soils is originally derived through the activities of nitrogen-fixing bacteria, associated with the roots of leguminous plants such as clover. The quantity released annually from the organic matter store (typically 100 kg/ha/yr) is insufficient to support potential plant growth and addition of nitrogen will normally stimulate growth, where this is a desirable conservation aim.

In high rainfall areas or in very open, porous soils, losses of nitrogen can be severe with

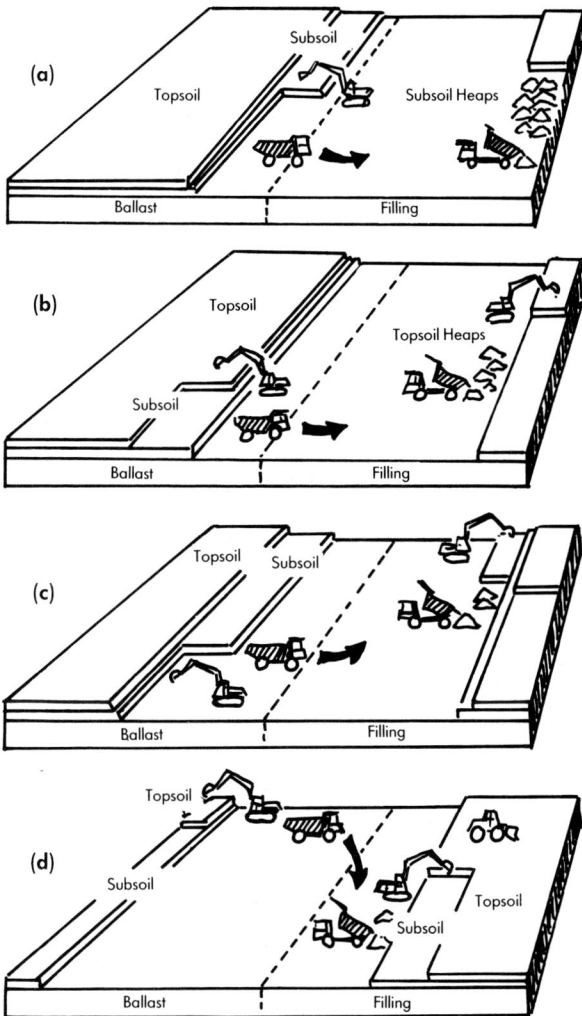

The dump truck and loader techniques:
(a) Subsoil removal and reinstatement;
(b) Topsoil removal and spreading;
(c) Subsoil removal and reinstatement;
(d) Completion of operations including grading of topsoil.

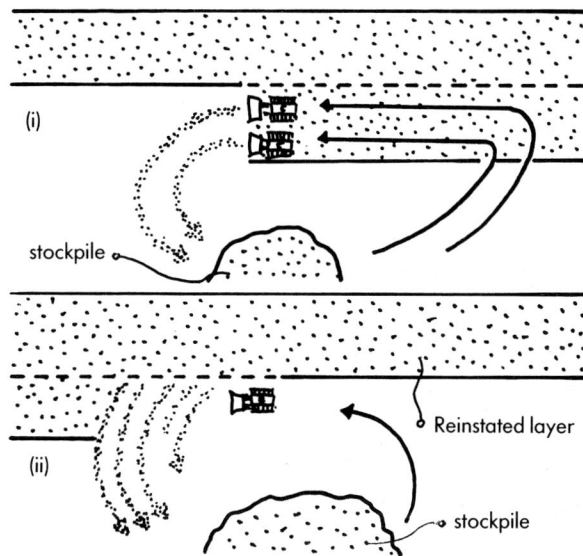

Soil replacement with earthscraper: (i) Indiscriminate running over soils; (ii) Bed system with no running over replaced soils.

Fig 3.14 Soil handling techniques (from RMC, 1986).

nitrogen being washed out of the soil profile, especially in winter and early spring.

Phosphorus is present in many soil mineral particles from which it is slowly released. Soil organic matter comprises the main source of supply for plant growth. During the active growing season, phosphorus is often rapidly depleted, the plants taking it up faster than the resupply processes can make more available. The relatively immobile nature of phosphorus within soils thus favours those plants with extensive root systems, capable of tapping a large volume of soil and its associated soil solution.

Potassium in soil solution is derived almost entirely from mineral sources, particularly those associated with clay soils. It is most important in stimulating or controlling water uptake and use within the plant.

Plants take up large amounts of **water** via their roots, in order to obtain soil-derived nutrient elements. Nearly all of this water is lost through transpiration from leaf surfaces. For example, to produce 1 kg of dry plant matter typically requires at least 250 kg of water. In fact, the evaporation loss of water from a vegetated soil surface is grossly similar to that from an open, exposed water surface. In summer, when leaf development

115

and seasonal temperatures are both at their maximum, a moisture deficit may develop within the soil, particularly in the south and east of the country.

The availability of water and nutrients to a plant is related to the volume and nature of the soil penetrated by its roots. Soil depth is obviously important, most herbaceous plant roots extending to at least 60 cm depth and tree roots often extending to a depth of several metres. Thus compaction of surfaces prior to addition to topsoil can check or even prevent plant development. It can be used as a device for that purpose but is much more commonly an obstacle to growth.

The texture of a soil is a fundamental characteristic of its potential water-holding capacity, sandy soils having a lower potential water content than clay soils. However, by no means all of the water present in a soil may be available to plants; for example, some water is tightly bound, particularly in clay soils, and plants are unable to gain access to such water. In fact, clay soils may have a relatively high water content (as much as 20%) even when plants rooted in them start to wilt. The presence of organic matter in soils can greatly increase their available water capacity. Whereas texture cannot be directly modified on a large scale except at disproportionate cost, organic matter can be readily supplied.

The majority of plants grow best when the soil is just slightly acid (pH 6·5), although many plants grow fairly well under much more acid conditions (pH 5 and even lower), while others favour more alkaline conditions (pH 8). Many processes affect the soil pH, from the input of rain (pH 4–5), through the mineral-water reactions which mostly tend to raise the pH, to many biological processes which generally lower the pH. The pH of the soil affects the release rates of elements from sources within the soil and controls the chemical forms in which certain soil elements occur, thereby affecting their availability for uptake by plant roots. In most gravel workings, the soil pH is satisfactory to develop a rich and diverse plant community.

Soil types in gravel pits

There are four major soil types, any of which may be encountered forming the topsoil of gravel workings. Sometimes the original field boundaries will be found to separate areas with substantially different soils and it would certainly be desirable, where possible, not to mix loam with other types because this will reduce its value. After restoration, sandy soils are likely to pre-

dominate over large areas, although clays may dominate at some sites.

Sandy soils are composed of relatively large mineral grains with large pore spaces between the grains. Well drained and well aerated, they are easy to cultivate and quick to warm up in spring but drain readily, retain nutrients poorly, and usually have a low organic content. A limited herb community will usually develop fairly quickly and some pioneer tree species such as birch and Scots pine readily colonise these soils.

Clay soils comprise very small, flattened, mineral particles with minute spaces between the grains. They hold large quantities of water but drain poorly and only a limited part of the water is freely available to plant roots. Poorly aerated, heavy and difficult to cultivate, they are slow to warm up in spring but hold on to nutrients well, and are slow to dry out, though on drying they shrink and crack badly and can be difficult to rewet. They are very suitable for topsoiling shallows and marshes. Tree growth is usually good.

Silty soils tend to combine the worst qualities of both the above; poorly drained and aerated, low in plant nutrients and difficult to cultivate. Do not restore with them where vigorous plant growth is required.

Loams are mixtures of sand, silt and clay and their performance depends on which grain size particle dominates. In general they have fairly good drainage, aeration, nutrient retention and availability plus reasonable organic content so that they make by far the most fertile soils.

Aquatic plants: their nutrient supplies

Aquatic plants comprise algae and the so-called higher plants or macrophytes. Some kinds of algae float in the water column and others are attached to higher plants or to other substrates. They are a very important food for the innumerable microscopic organisms which in turn fuel creatures higher up the food chain.

The composition of aquatic algae and higher plants is essentially similar to that of terrestrial plants. Algae gain all their nutrient elements from the surrounding water. Only rarely does carbon become temporarily limiting for algal growth. Nitrogen exists in lake waters in several forms capable of being used by algae and much of this is derived from agricultural sources. The element generally in most limited supply in freshwaters is phosphorus; it is derived initially from the rocks and soils in the catchment of a lake,

116

though these days a large proportion in many freshwaters is a pollutant of man-made origin. In lakes where phosphorus is relatively abundant, large crops of blue-green algae, fixing atmospheric nitrogen, may develop. The other elements required for algal growth are almost never in short supply.

Silicon is an essential element for the growth of diatoms, which are an important food resource for some chironomids, in turn supporting fish and waterfowl. It is plentiful in gravel-pit lakes.

Higher plants not rooted into the lake sediments obtain all their nutrients, as do algae, from the surrounding water. However, aquatic plants with root systems, even if apparently rudimentary, gain essentially all their requirements from the sediments.

Rooted aquatic plants, whether their upper parts are submerged or are emergent, are very often rooted in anaerobic sediment but have developed mechanisms of overcoming the physiological problems of low oxygen levels around their roots.

In new gravel-pit lakes, an organic sediment layer will be absent. Topsoil can be used to encourage the start of plant growth by aiding rooting and providing an initial supply of nutrients. In lowland situations where most groundwaters have high nutrient loadings from agricultural fertilisers and sewage effluent, the levels of nutrient input will be adequate to sustain subsequent growth and may lead to algal blooms.

A fundamental need for all plant photosynthesis is an adequate supply of light and for aquatic plants this can be a major limitation. In temperate lakes, the water is usually fairly transparent during the winter and early spring unless affected by turbid river-water or lake-bottom muds temporarily stirred up by stormy conditions. However, as spring progresses, temperatures and light levels increase and algae start to grow more rapidly within the well-lit part of the water column; where nutrients do not limit them, they will become sufficiently abundant to colour the water green and severely limit light penetration, thus inhibiting their own further productivity and also impairing growth by macrophytes. For higher aquatic plants, particularly those rooted in the sediments, light penetration is a major influence on growth. In general, the depth of macrophyte colonisation is inversely proportional to the algal standing crop and thus to the nutrient loading. In fertile lakes with dense algal populations, the submerged plant communities are rather restricted, though often the emergent macrophyte vegetation may be prolific at the lake margins.

Soil and nutrient distribution

Before excavation, many sand and gravel sites are covered by a nutrient-rich topsoil layer. However, a wet restoration will include a diversity of habitats, some of which may benefit from soil of low nutrient status. For example, to establish a herb-rich grass sward, a soil of low fertility is ideal because high fertility favours a vigorous growth of grasses which tends to cut off light from the desired herbs and thus suppress them. But a fairly rapid growth-rate would be wanted for hedges and shelterbelt shrubs and trees and, for these, a higher nutrient soil may be preferred. The aquatic environment, unless there is nutrient input via a surface stream, is very likely to become seasonally depleted in plant nutrients and thus a source of nutrients would generally be beneficial to sustaining high aquatic productivity. (The release of nutrient elements from lake-floor sediments proceeds in a similar way to that previously discussed for soils, the nutrient elements being released to the sediment-pore waters, either then to be taken up by aquatic macrophyte roots or to escape into the lake and become available for planktonic algae and non-rooted macrophytes).

These considerations may be met by redistribution of original topsoil during restoration:

(a) for margins, shallows and marshland areas, provide 30 cm of topsoil, if available, to create the initial high nutrient conditions required;
(b) for deeper water areas, a 15 cm topsoil layer spread out over the bottom will slowly release nutrients and provide an organic substrate for colonisation by Chironomids, which are an important food resource for some fish and waterfowl. However, as nutrient inputs from groundwater are likely to be high in almost all gravel pits, this may increase the risk of severe algal blooms, especially in prolonged hot weather;
(c) for shelterbelt areas, a thick (20–30 cm) topsoil and good cultivation may be used, but will lead to strong growth of weeds competing with newly-planted trees and shrubs and this will require control (see page 140). A well-drained subsoil will present fewer maintenance needs. In any event, additional supplies of nitrogen fertiliser will be beneficial;
(d) for most other terrestrial areas, supply little topsoil or mix some topsoil with subsoil;
(e) for non-shelterbelt tree and shrub planting, subsoil is preferred as this will not generate competitive weed growth;

Habitat Management and Creation

(f) for herb-rich seedings, no topsoil should be provided.

Not all sites will have a nutrient-rich topsoil available for redistribution. Bradshaw and Chadwick (1980) suggest that for a low maintenance end-use a self-sustaining ecosystem requires a nitrogen store of at least 1,000 kg/ha. Should additional nutrients and other soil conditioners be required, they may be added in various ways:

(a) by artificial fertilisers, adding balanced fertiliser or sources of specific elements to make up the known deficiencies;

(b) by farmyard or other manures, mushroom compost, etc. Although the nutrient content of most such materials is generally rather low, the addition of the organic matter may significantly improve the fertility of the soil;

(c) by sewage sludge, to land or water, preferably as de-watered sewage sludge cake. The suggested level of 1,000 kg/ha of nitrogen could be supplied by 130 tonnes/ha of de-watered sludge cake (33 tonnes of dried solids/ha). Sewage sludge contains significant quantities of mainly organically-bound nitrogen and phosphorus and has a fairly high organic content. Much of the nitrogen is released in the first year, whereas the phosphorus is released more slowly. The nitrogen is taken up by the algae and aquatic plants and animals, and ultimately recycled within the lake so that the initial input provides a nitrogen store for several years. Nutrients should not be added to the aquatic environment without first determining the water chemistry of the site.

Water chemistry analysis

A knowledge of the likely water chemistry of a new gravel-pit lake is an essential prerequisite to any restoration. National Rivers Authority data may be available for surface or ground waters which are likely to feed the lake and these data should be examined before any new analyses are undertaken. If no data are available, a minimum of three water samples from likely input sources should be taken and analysed. At a later date, when the lake has filled, a surface water sample taken well out from the shore in late winter (February) is likely to be the most useful, as experience has shown that element concentrations at that time tend to be close to the annual average.

The laboratory analysis should include major elements, nutrients and pH. These data will form the basis for any water chemistry adjustment or management. For example, a low pH (below 5) is likely to be caused by oxidation of natural iron sulphides exposed during the excavation process and under such acidic conditions only rather limited aquatic plant and animal species will survive; advice would need to be taken on how best to resolve such a problem. Similarly, nutrient concentrations and ratios will give good guidance on the likely algal productivity levels of the lake. Addition of nutrients should not be made to lakes until water chemistry data have been evaluated and the need clearly identified.

References

Bradshaw, A D, & Chadwick, M J, 1980, *The restoration of land*. Blackwell, London. 317pp.

Hall, J E, Daw, A P, & Bayes, C D, 1986, *The use of sewage sludge in land reclamation*. Water Research Centre Report. 146pp.

Jollans, J L, 1985, *Fertilisers in UK farming*. Centre for Agric. Strategy. Univ. Reading. Report No. 9. 215pp.

Le Cren, E D, & Lowe-McConnell, R H, (Eds.), 1980, *The functioning of freshwater ecosystems*. (Int. Biol. Prog. 22). Cambridge University Press. 588pp.

Moss, B, 1980, *Ecology of freshwaters*. Blackwell, London. 332pp.

RMC Group, 1986, *A practical guide to restoration*. RMC Group Pub. Feltham, 83pp.

Svedarsky, W D, & Crawford, R D, 1982, *Wildlife values of gravel pits*. Misc. Pub. 17 Agric. Exp. Station, Univ. Minnesota. 249pp.

AQUATIC AND WATERSIDE PLANTS

Summary

1. Wetland plants include algae and submerged, floating, emergent and waterside or marsh-land species of higher plants. Submerged plants are typically found at depths down to 2 m – more where water clarity is good and there is high light penetration but much less where high nutrient levels cause algal blooms which limit available light. Emergent plants grow on wet ground or down to water depths of about 1 m.

2. Abundant and diverse wetland plant growth is essential to fuel the food-chains on which all aquatic wildlife depends. As well as providing a direct food resource for many species, it creates the necessary physical structure in which innumerable micro-organisms, invertebrates and fish-fry find shelter.

3. Gravel pits in flood plains will probably be colonised naturally by the local wetland plant community. Where this is unlikely to occur, early introductions should take place.

4. Plant material can be obtained from a variety of sources including established gravel pits. Only native plant material appropriate to the locality, nutrient status and pH of the site should be introduced.

5. Receptor sites for marginals should ideally shelve at 1:15 or less, to a maximum summer depth of 1 m, and be sheltered from wave action: those for submerged plants should be 0·3–2 m deep. Top-soiling is desirable to speed plant growth, particularly on nutrient-poor gravels or compacted substrates.

6. Wetland plants should not be allowed to dry out in transit. Submerged species can be weighted with clay or stones and dropped into the water. Marginals and waterside plants can be planted in clumps, well firmed into the substrate (but reed rhizomes are damaged by trampling).

7. Introduce plants at the start of the spring growing season: if necessary, net or fence emergents and waterside species to protect them from grazing (eg by wildfowl) or tramp-ling by livestock.

8. Plant large beds of single species. Keep less vigorous growers away from species such as reed-mace, to prevent them from being over-whelmed before they get established properly.

9. Emergents will need management to con-trol spread and litter build-up. Clearance of small areas on rotation is desirable.

10. Large-scale herbicide use in small sites may lead to sudden nutrient release due to vegeta-tional decay, in turn creating algal blooms, the death of submerged vegetation, invertebrates and fish.

(See photographs 10, 11 and 12)

General

Wetland plants are very diverse. They include both unicellular algae and the so-called macro-phytes (large plants). Some are free-floating in the water column (eg algae) or at the surface (eg duckweed). Some are rooted and almost wholly submerged though they may put up flowers above the surface (eg milfoil). Some are rooted and have almost all their foliage on the surface (eg white waterlily) or held above it (eg reeds). The plants with foliage which emerges above the water can grow only in shallows and so tend to be distributed at the margins of waterbodies or even right away from standing water where the ground is waterlogged. Waterside plants also require wet soil but cannot colonise the water itself.

The majority of submerged aquatic plants are to be found in water depths between 0·3 m and 2 m. If the waters are clear, submerged plants may occur to 10 m or more, but if the water is deeply coloured (for example, by peat), if high turbulence suspends fine sediment particles in the water column, or if plant growth itself is abundant and creates shade, then vegetation will occur only to a more limited depth. The more nutrient-rich waters will tend to produce a larger crop of planktonic algae over spring and summer, the water will become noticeably green, and light penetration will be greatly retarded; under such conditions submerged plants are typically limited to less than 2 m of water depth.

Floating-leaved vegetation is a characteristic feature of more sheltered waters. The rooted plants of this group, including waterlilies, are generally to be found growing in rather muddy, often organically rich, unconsolidated substrates, such materials typically accumulating in shel-tered areas. Leaves usually float on or just below the surface and flowers appear either at the surface or project slightly above. Summer water depths must usually exceed 30 cm and the plants may extend into about 2 m of water. Beds are often of a single species and occur commonly beyond the shoreline fringe of emergent plants.

Habitat Management and Creation

Emergent and waterside or marshland plants form a large group of species which need to be rooted in wet ground. They will form stands wherever the watertable is close to the soil surface and also tend to form a fringe at the margins of waterbodies: hence they are often referred to as 'marginals'. The emergent species can grow in shallow water, some tolerating depths of a metre or more. Some are narrow-leaved, including for example the common reed, greater reedmace and bulrush. Others, such as water mint and watercress, have broader leaves. The flowers are always held above the water surface. A number confined to moist ground include some showy flowering plants such as purple loosestrife and greater willowherb.

Thus for all wetland plants, the water depth or watertable is a critical factor controlling plant establishment and growth in general, though nutrient status, substrate sediments and the water pH are, predictably, important influences on the success of particular plant species.

Importance

Submerged plants play several important wildlife roles, the most crucial being that they serve as the basis of the aquatic food-chain and, together with washed and blown-in terrestrial vegetation, provide the food resources on which the whole range of aquatic animals depends. Some serve directly as food; many waterfowl are vegetarian, eating stems, leaves, rhizomes and tubers or seeds. Plants also provide organic detritus which is consumed by many chironomids and other invertebrates. Of equal importance, submerged plants create a physical structure within which large populations of attached algae, other micro-organisms, insects, fish and other animals live, either attached to the plant surfaces or finding food and cover within this rich and sheltered foraging habitat. This leads to stands of plants being favoured feeding habitat of many larger creatures, for example fish and waterfowl.

Aquatic plants help to stabilise the substrate, thereby preventing resuspension of fine sediment particles during rough weather conditions (a lake which is often turbid typically has few aquatic plants and a generally low wildlife value). Large beds of floating-leaved plants are also effective wave dampeners and help to protect reedbeds and other shoreline habitats, though if a site is very exposed to the wind and waves it is unlikely that floating-leaved plants will ever become established or survive.

Marginal plants have many values in restoration for wildlife. Once established, their stems and root systems provide a measure of physical protection for shorelines. They tend to trap sediments and themselves generate organic material in which detritus-feeders such as chironomids can live. Below water, they offer cover for fish-fry and above the surface the tall stems make sheltered hunting habitat for damselflies. When in flower, some species such as water figwort are valuable nectar sources for bees, hoverflies and butterflies.

Waterfowl feed on many kinds of marginal plants, some grazing the leaves and others exploiting those with nutritious seeds. Grebes and pochard prefer to construct their nests in beds of emergents where they are surrounded by water and have overhead cover: thereby they gain some protection from both terrestrial and aerial predators. Otters use drier areas, for example, in stands of willowherb or reedbeds, for lying-up.

A number of emergent plants form large single-species stands. Extensive reedbeds (>1 ha) are now a scarce habitat in England and Wales and may be colonised by the rare bearded tit or support big colonies of reed warblers.

Wet grassland is a distinctive wetland plant habitat which, depending on the mowing or grazing regime adopted and on the variation in water table, may have great value for scarce plants, breeding waders (see pages 73–75) and other wildlife.

Site selection and preparation

Marginal or marshland plants will grow in soils up to about 15 cm above the watertable with emergents extending into water depths down to about 1 m. Contouring of the restoration should therefore provide broad, gently sloping (<1:15) marginal shelves wherever possible, and peninsulas, islands and shoal banks out in the lake should also be formed with similarly shelving margins. Note that it is difficult to establish marginals where there is likely to be a substantial rise and/or fall of water, though, once established, most species can tolerate normal seasonal patterns of drying and flooding.

Submerged plants may be accommodated by extending marginal slopes to 2 m depth or by levelling areas of the lake bed at between 0·3 and 2 m depth.

Levels should be determined relative to the lowest seasonal water-level (usually summer), allowance having been made if necessary for the addition of up to 30 cm of topsoil. This can provide a valuable, nutrient-rich substrate increasing the rate of growth and spread by both submerged and marginal plants, particularly where the new, shallow lake floor or margins are of coarse gravel or rather compacted. In an acid or nutrient-poor lake there are the options of neutralising the acidity and/or adding additional nutrients (topsoil, sewage sludge or soluble fertiliser). Specialist advice should be sought if these options are to be considered. Bear in mind that such lakes are now uncommon and may have special value in the conservation of certain scarce plants and invertebrates which require such conditions.

An important long-term management consideration is to inhibit the rate of spread by marginals into any areas which it is desired to keep as open shores, for instance for use by feeding waders or ducklings. Colonisation into such areas through the spread of runners or rhizomes may be discouraged by separating them with stretches of water more than 2 m deep and 2 m wide. These trenches should be dug in advance of planting. In the long-term, colonisation by marginals is inevitable however, and physical or chemical control will be necessary.

Plant selection, sources and establishment

To maximise the conservation value of a lake, a reasonably diverse plant community should be the aim of the restoration. Some marginal plants, especially those with wind-borne seeds such as great reedmace and great willowherb, will quickly colonise wet ground in gravel workings. Excavations in river valleys which are seasonally flooded will also be colonised by plants from the locality, in the form of floating seeds, stem fragments or root material. In excavations not subject to such flooding, waterfowl may bring seeds or small pieces of plant tissue into the new lake. It is surprising, also, the extent to which members of the public will – quite uninvited – introduce plants, fish and other animals to new waterbodies.

Where natural colonisation is unlikely to occur rapidly, deliberate introduction may be necessary. This should take place soon after flooding as, once bottom-feeding coarse fish or herbivorous waterfowl (swans, gadwall, coots etc) colonise the lake, establishment of plant material may be difficult.

A wider benefit of the early introduction of aquatic plants will be the colonisation of associated invertebrate animals, normally in the form of attached eggs or larvae living in the vegetation. Many other invertebrates such as water beetles and dragonflies will colonise naturally, having winged adult stages which range widely in search

of new sites. Deliberate introduction of invertebrates other than those present in plant material is unnecessary.

Most aquatic plants will grow in medium to fine substrates with moderate to rich nutrient levels. A few favour or avoid waters with a high pH. Not enough is known of the precise requirements of many of the possible species which may be introduced so the practical solution is to plant a range of species, accepting that some may fail to become established. Particular wildlife objectives will also play a part in the final plant selection. Table 3.7 lists the commoner submerged, floating and marginal plants with some comments on their value for other wildlife.

As a general guideline, one should always use native plant materials, preferably those available close to the site. Do not introduce exotics.

Commercial suppliers of native aquatic plants do exist but prices and availability of material are likely to prove serious obstacles for any large-scale restoration project. Natural sources need consideration from the outset. If there are wetland areas within the site before excavation starts then these plant materials should be carefully protected and moved into the early phases of the restoration. If such plant sources are not available, possible alternatives include:

(a) Other wetland restorations.
(b) Farmers clearing out farm ditches and ponds.
(c) County Wildlife Trusts for materials derived from their wetland management activities.
(d) Internal Drainage Boards or the National River Authority for materials derived from watercourses.

As many aquatic plants grow and propagate themselves vigorously, the initial introduction of plant material may not need to be vast, and early-planted material may be thinned for planting later restoration stages.

Wild plants are protected under the Wildlife and Countryside Act 1981, and it is necessary to obtain the permission of the landowner before collecting any material. Some plants are specially protected under the Act and these must not be removed. If there is any doubt, the Nature Conservancy Council should be consulted.

Aquatic plants should not be allowed to dry out at all between being collected and being planted. Plants should be covered with polythene sheeting or bagged up during transit. The selected planting sites should not be heavily shaded by overhanging trees or subject to prolific autumn leaf fall. The substrate should be muddy or sandy and unconsolidated.

Tuberous or rooted submerged plants should

121

Habitat Management and Creation

be inserted into the bottom sediment at water depths of 30 cm–1 m, and allowed to extend into deeper water as they become well established. For planting in deeper water, plant material should be weighted, eg with roots or stem bases in clay balls, or firmly tied in clumps to stones, and dropped into the water. For some species, small lengths of stem can be used as cuttings and the take rate is generally high.

It is preferable to establish relatively large areas of a single species (eg 10–20 m length parallel to the shore) as this provides a large stretch of a single habitat type, which can then support an appropriate community of invertebrates and other organisms. In particular, avoid mixing the more vigorous species with those which are slower to become established. By having separate blocks of species the plants in each can become

Table 3.7

Common wetland plants

The following are species widely distributed in still waters throughout southern and central England. They are therefore suitable for introduction into any gravel pit in those areas. Most of these plants are also common elsewhere in the United Kingdom, though other species may be more appropriate. Ideally, stick to the rule of using material from sites in your own locality.

Unless otherwise stated, the plants are suitable for any site with a medium or rich nutrient status, medium to fine substrate, moderate to high pH. The great majority of lowland gravel workings will fall into this category.

All submerged plants and most floating and marginal species are used by a variety of invertebrates and may be assumed to be of general value. Only those which are known to be particularly favoured are indicated as such.

Where appropriate, the average preferred water depth is given with maximum depths in brackets.

Information on the wildlife value of plants is largely derived from Street, M. *Ponds and Lakes for Wildfowl*. Game Conservancy, 1989.

Species	Depth	Comments
Submerged plants		
Stoneworts (*Chara* sp.)	To 2 m	Good invertebrate habitat. Main food of pochard.
Water crowfoot *Ranunculus aquatilis*	To 1 m	Seeds used by wildfowl.
Rigid hornwort *Ceratophyllum demersum*	1 m (8·5 m)	Unrooted. Good invertebrate habitat.
Spiked water-milfoil *Myriophyllum spicatum*	0·7 m (2 m)	Favours lime-rich waters. Excellent invertebrate habitat.
Mare's-tail *Hippuris vulgaris*	To 1 m	Favours lime. Good invertebrate habitat. Seeds eaten by wildfowl. Cover for duckling broods.
Common water starwort *Callitriche stagnalis*	To 1 m	Good invertebrate habitat.
Canadian pondweed *Elodea canadensis*	0·5 m (3 m)	Introduced but widely naturalised. Excellent invertebrate habitat.
Shining pondweed *Potamogeton lucens*	To 4 m	Often in lime-rich waters. Seeds eaten by wildfowl.
Perfoliate pondweed *Potamogeton perfoliatus*	To 2 m	Seeds eaten by wildfowl.
Curled pondweed *Potamogeton crispus*	To 2 m	Seeds eaten by wildfowl.
Fennel pondweed *Potamogeton pectinatus*	0·5–2·5 m	Tolerates heavily polluted and turbid water. Seeds and tubers eaten by wildfowl.
Horned pondweed *Zannichellia palustris*	To 2 m	Seeds eaten by wildfowl.

122

Table 3.7 (continued)

Species	Depth	Comments
Floating-leaved plants		
White waterlily *Nymphaea alba*	To 3 m	Duckling broods forage among leaves.
Yellow waterlily *Nuphar lutea*	1–5 m	Duckling broods forage among leaves.
Amphibious bistort *Polygonum amphibium*	To 2 m (also on damp ground)	Good invertebrate habitat. Good seed production taken by wildfowl. Good duckling foraging habitat.
Frogbit *Hydrocharis morsus-ranae*	Free-floating	Overwintering buds eaten by wildfowl
Broad-leaved pondweed *Potamogeton natans*	To 3 m	Good seed production.
Duckweeds *Lemna* spp.	Free-floating	Plants eaten by wildfowl.
Emergent/marginal plants		
Marsh marigold *Caltha palustris*	Damp ground To 0·3 m	
Watercress *Rorippa nasturtium-aquaticum*	To 0·3 m	Favours chalk and limestone.
Great yellow-cress *Rorippa amphibia*	Damp ground To 0·3 m	
Fool's watercress *Apium nodiflorum*	To 0·3 m	Favours chalk and limestone.
Great water dock *Rumex hydrolapathum*	Damp margins To 0·5 m	Seeds eaten by wildfowl.
Water forget-me-not *Myosotis scorpioides*	Damp ground To 0·2 m	
Brooklime *Veronica beccabunga*	Damp ground and shallows	
Water mint *Mentha aquatica*	Damp ground and shallows	
Water-plantain *Alisma plantago-aquatica*	To 0·75 m	
Arrowhead *Sagittaria sagittifolia*	0·3 m	Plant eaten by wildfowl. Brood foraging habitat.
Flowering-rush *Butomus umbellatus*	Damp ground and shallows	
Juncus spp.	Damp ground	Seeds eaten by wildfowl.
Yellow flag *Iris pseudacorus*	Damp ground	
Sweet flag *Acorus calamus*	Damp ground To 0·5 m	
Bur-reeds *Sparganium* sp.	To 1 m	Good invertebrate habitat and seed production.
Great reedmace *Typha latifolia*	To 1 m	Winter cover for wildfowl.
Common spike-rush *Eleocharis palustris*	Damp ground To 0·3 m	Very good seed producer. Used by duckling broods.

Table 3.7 (continued)

Species	Depth	Comments
Sedges *Carex* spp.	Damp ground, some species to 0·5 m	Very good seed producers. Nesting cover for wildfowl.
Reed *Phragmites australis*	To 1·5 m	Prime habitat of reed warbler. Winter cover for wildfowl.
Reed sweet-grass *Glyceria maxima*	To 0·5 m	Highly invasive and limited value.
Reed canary-grass *Phalaris arundinacea*	To 1 m	
Purple loosestrife *Lythrum salicaria*	Damp ground	
Meadowsweet *Filipendula ulmaris*	Damp ground	
Great willowherb *Epilobium hirsutum*	Damp ground	
Water figwort *Scrophularia aquatica*	Damp ground	Good nectar and seed producer.

established before there is competition from adjacent stands. If some plants are not available in enough quantity to create large stands, try to group them near species of similar size and rate of spread. Planting in separate blocks also allows rates of colonisation to be monitored and appropriate action to be taken in case of failure. Although the initial effect may appear somewhat unnatural, this will remedy itself as the vegetation becomes established.

Marginals may be planted individually or as clumps of material either by spade or by back-acter. An advantage of using larger pieces of material is that cohesive chunks are less likely to be washed out or broken up before the root system gains anchorage. Smaller, more fragile marginal plants, such as brooklime or water forget-me-not, naturally need more care than strong emergents such as reedmace.

In most instances, it is easiest to put marginal plant material into soft soil just on the waterline, when it can spread into the shallows. Where possible, it should be firmed into the ground to prevent it washing out before it has gained a hold. The new shoots of reeds, however, are particularly sensitive to pressure and should not be firmed in.

Where a shoreline is subject to wave action, planting may have to be protected, either by a boom moored off shore or by use of artificial fabrics such as Enkamat. Once established, emergent vegetation may absorb moderate wave energy and prevent further erosion.

Planting should take place in late spring when the plants have started into active growth, and light levels and water temperatures are high; the new plants then have the remainder of the growing season in which to establish themselves. During this time, if fish, grazing birds or mammals remove parts of a plant, it has the capacity to replace the loss and is likely to survive. If planted in the autumn, plants have little time to become established before winter and are much less likely to withstand any physical onslaught.

In an established site where grazing pressure may be high, new plantings at any season may require physical protection by netting. Livestock, cattle in particular, will also graze marginal vegetation and may break down stands of it by trampling. Fencing may therefore be necessary. However, once plants are well established, these effects can be beneficial provided that they only occur on a limited scale, because they open up solid beds of vegetation, creating patches of bare mud where smaller or less vigorous plants may colonise and where waders and wildfowl will feed.

Management

Many aquatic plants can be very invasive and effectively take over large parts of a waterbody. For example, on very sheltered, nutrient-rich waters of limited extent duckweed can densely cover the entire surface, restricting light penetration to the detriment of submerged aquatic plants; it also limits gas exchange, leading ultimately to anoxic conditions, release of hydrogen sulphide from the lake-bed sediments and death of invertebrate and fish species. Similarly, Canadian pondweed can choke shallow ponds almost to the exclusion of other aquatic plants. Both these species, however, are of value to the ecosystem, duckweed being a direct source of food for many ducks and ducklings and Canadian pondweed supporting a rich fauna of invertebrates which are also valuable waterfowl foods.

In practice, in gravel-pit lakes restored for wildlife, it is unlikely that management of the submerged plant community will be required, though clearance is sometimes required on waters used for fishing or sailing. In ponds, regular intervention may be required to maintain some areas of open water or to prevent the development of complete cover by tall emergent plants such as reeds and great reedmace, which spread rapidly in waters less than 1 m deep, or form floating mats extending over deeper water. There are no circumstances in which extensive cover by these plants would be desirable, since there would be resultant losses of aquatic productivity and habitat diversity. In unmanaged sites where these plants become dominant, the variety of birds declines. However, some emergents are very important for dragonflies or as nesting cover for several kinds of waterfowl, so they should never be cleared entirely even from ponds.

In the very long term, the annual die-back of marginal plants leads to a build-up of vegetable matter which may rise above the watertable to a point where it can be colonised by plants tolerant of drier conditions. The wind-borne seeds of willows will readily germinate on ground which has been exposed to late summer draw-down, but is still damp. Once they begin to grow, they accelerate the process by drying out and the transition into woodland. Though such transitional habitats are themselves of conservation value, management intervention may be necessary by excavating the vegetation litter to restore original soil levels.

Herbicides can offer precise and cost-effective methods of control of marginal plants, though physical control of the latter is also practicable. Grazing and trampling by cattle will break up stands. Cutting is rarely effective unless repeated or followed by flooding to 'drown' the plants. Dredging or scraping the vegetation away is preferable in older sites where many years of plant litter have accumulated, raising the bed level and reducing the extent of shallows. In any event, the need for control should be anticipated,

so that it can be carried out in limited areas of a site on rotation, rather than all at once. Wholesale clearance may lead to algal blooms caused by release of excessive levels of nutrients into the water column, either through the decay of plant matter killed by herbicides or through physical disturbance of organic sediments.

Spoil should be deposited only where organic nutrient-rich materials will be beneficial and should not be placed in low-lying hollows which may be of wildlife value in their own right.

Reedbeds

A number of emergent plants will, if unmanaged, spread to form large single-species stands. This reduces habitat diversity and is generally undesirable but in the case of reed, the deliberate creation of a large reedbed is likely to have conservation benefits.

The main value of reedbeds is for birds. Reed warblers will occur in very small stands or fringes, but the rare bearded tit, bittern and marsh harrier probably require stands larger than 20 ha. There are about 20 reedbeds of this size in Britain and less than 100 larger than 2 ha, with only a handful away from the coast.

Reeds will grow in water down to 1 m deep and the leaf and stem litter produced annually by them builds up on the bottom at a rate of up to 1 m in 20 years. Therefore, to delay the need for management intervention, the proposed site should be 0·75–1 m deep. If designed for bitterns, it must contain areas 1·5–2 m deep, so excluding reeds but encouraging other aquatic plant growth. These areas will be the habitat of fish, especially eels, which are the birds' main food resource. As hunting takes place at the reed/open water interface, the edge-to-area ratio should be as large as practicable. A system of 1·5 m deep, submerged trenches is ideal (see Fig 3.15).

If the introduction of reeds is contemplated in a site where it is desired to retain areas of shallow open water, they should be separated from the proposed reedbed by deeper (minimum 2 m) trenches created prior to flooding.

Reeds cannot be planted into water as this kills them. Therefore a marginal shelf should be created and topsoiled so that the ground is wet but not inundated. Reeds may then be introduced by:
(a) planting rhizome clumps into the moist soil from mid February to early April. They should be firmed in place but not trampled as this breaks off new buds;
(b) cutting new shoots in early summer and

Infrequently managed reeds

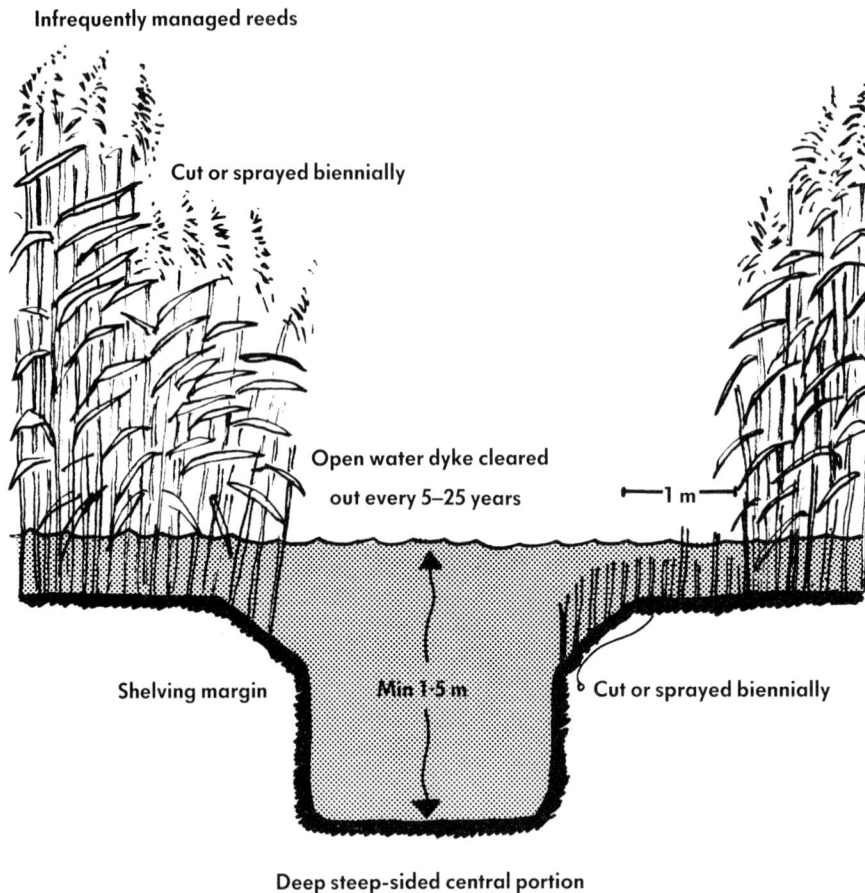

Cut or sprayed biennially

Open water dyke cleared
out every 5–25 years

⊢—1 m—⊣

Shelving margin

Min 1·5 m

Cut or sprayed biennially

Deep steep-sided central portion

Fig 3.15 Generalised management of reedbed dyke (from Burgess et al, 1989).

inserting them in a slot in the soil 10–20 cm deep with nodes buried and the growing tip above the surface;

(c) bending over existing reeds in early summer and pinning them down to root from the nodes, so accelerating their spread.

Once the accumulation of litter raises the bed level above the summer water surface, reed growth is less vigorous and invasion by willow and alders is likely, converting the area into carr woodland. This is a much commoner habitat than reedbed and of less conservation value. It is therefore desirable to prevent the succession by one of the following methods. In no case treat more than 10% of the site in any one year.

(a) Dig out litter by mechanical means.

(b) Cut annually before mid March and remove the material, which may be saleable. Later cutting will damage new buds and kill the reeds.

Burning is a traditional management system but not generally recommended because of the difficulties of control. The herbicide Dalapon is a very satisfactory approved control which kills few other plants but is not at present manufactured for sale in the UK.

Where carr invades reeds, the bushes should be cut down and, unless the stumps can be drowned by raising the water level, they should be treated with the herbicide ammonium sulphamate (Amcide). Alder is easily killed; willow less so: treat any regrowth with a glyphosate weed-wipe. However, a substantial fringe of carr should be retained, ideally with additional, individual bushes within the reedbed which may be coppiced on rotation, as these will increase the ornithological value of the habitat.

Herbicides

Before deciding to use herbicides, consider other options to ensure that the most appropriate method is followed. Depending on the target vegetation and the herbicide formulation used, it may be possible to achieve complete eradication,

126

remove growth for a single season, reduce the total area of vegetation or control a particular plant species. In gravel pits being managed for wildlife, only selective control of a limited area or particular species is likely to be required. Both these aims may also be achieved by physical means. While cutting may be less effective, and dredging more costly, they have the virtue of minimal risk of damage due to inadvertent misuse or secondary effects. By contrast, herbicides have the potential, as a result of their ease of use and efficiency, to destroy aquatic flora and thereby fauna more extensively than is required. Where extensive areas are treated, recolonisation by the original flora may be impossible either because potential source material has been destroyed or because the plants that colonise are species resistant to herbicides. Of particular concern is the potential to turn a balanced plant community into one dominated by algae.

There are two main methods of controlling algae: use of herbicides (which is a palliative) and lowering available nutrient levels. As the herbicide formulations available for use against algae also kill submerged plants, and submerged plants are important in reducing free nutrient levels, the use of herbicides against algae is not advisable, at least where wildlife conservation is an aim. In other words, the use of herbicides against submerged plants in any site where nutrient levels are likely to be high, as is the case with most lowland gravel pits, may lead to dominance by algae which will be extremely difficult to correct. Fortunately, there are few circumstances where control of submerged vegetation will be a desirable aim in a wildlife site.

On the other hand, control of vigorous, invasive marginal vegetation will be necessary in order to keep areas of exposed mud or shallows for use by waders and dabbling wildfowl. Here, the disadvantage of herbicide use is that the litter and sediment trapped by root systems is not removed so that in time bed levels may rise above the normal water level, with a consequent loss of shallows. If this is potentially a problem, mechanical extraction will be necessary.

In all herbicide uses, if large amounts of plant material are killed at one time, the decomposition process will use oxygen from the water. Oxygen depletion is particularly noticeable in slow-flowing and stationary waters and in warm weather. Where significant depletion occurs, it may cause fish deaths. It can be minimised by applying aquatic herbicides when the plant biomass is low, usually in spring and by limiting applications to a small area each year. This timing may conflict

with greatest efficacy, which is at the time of maximum growth in summer.

Herbicides may have effects on non-target vegetation. Thus glyphosate, which is the formulation likely to be used to control emergent vegetation, also kills grass, herbs, shrubs and trees. The possibilities of spray drift onto important adjoining habitats must therefore be taken into account.

Similarly, aquatic herbicides may be translocated through the waterbody, so that the susceptibility and importance of areas adjoining the treatment site must again be considered. The user of herbicides has a responsibility to ensure that other interests including fisheries and water abstraction are not adversely affected. Anyone intending to treat aquatic weeds with herbicides must inform the National Rivers Authority, or the Department of the Environment in Northern Ireland or River Purification Boards in Scotland. If the site is a Site of Special Scientific Interest, the consent of the Nature Conservancy Council will be required.

Despite their limitations and dangers, herbicides when used correctly have considerable advantages – a wide variety of aquatic plants can be spot controlled, no disturbance is caused to bottom sediments, there is little or no disturbance or damage to adjoining terrestrial habitats, they do not cause direct mortality of invertebrates, fish or other animals, they may be used where control by machinery or by hand is impracticable and they are highly cost-effective.

Table 3.8 lists the choice of herbicide formulations currently available and their spectrum of weed control. It will be seen that herbicides may be target-specific or broad spectrum. The latter have more potential for inadvertent damage. Unfortunately, Dalapon is not currently manufactured for UK sale and control of reeds necessitates the use of glyphosate, with attendant hazards to many other plant species.

Intending users are strongly recommended to read *Guidelines for the use of herbicides on weeds in or near watercourses and lakes* (MAFF, 1985) which gives comprehensive information on consultation, choice of formulations, the range of plants which may be controlled, appropriate timing of applications, toxicological data and instructions to operators. Current lists of brand names are best obtained from *Pesticides*, published by HMSO.

If doubt exists over the identity of the vegetation which it is desired to control, and hence the choice of appropriate formulation, specialist advice should be sought. Some aquatic plants are extremely difficult to identify with certainty and

Table 3.8
The choice of herbicide formulations and their spectrum of weed control

Plants	Fosamine Ammonium	Asulam	2,4-D-Amine/Chlorpropham mix	2,4-D-Amine	Maleic Hydrazide with 2,4-D-Amine	Maleic Hydrazide	Glyphosate	Dalapon*	Diquat/Diquat Alginate	Dichlobenil GSR	Dichlobenil	Terbutryne
Algae	K			MR								
Submerged plants	K	K	K	K								
Free-floating plants (small leaf area)	K			K								
Floating-leaved plants (large leaf area)		K	K			K				MR	MR	
Reeds				K	MR							
Sedges				MR	K							
Grasses/Rushes					K		K	K			K	
Broadleaved weeds					K		K	K		K	K	
Docks					K						K	
Trees and Shrubs												K

K=killed.
MR=moderately resistant.
*Dalapon is not currently manufactured for UK sale.

they include a number of rare species whose eradication would be undesirable.

Only products which carry specific recommendations for control of aquatic weeds should be used. Even cleared products can cause pollution if not used in accordance with the manufacturer's recommendations.

References

Anon *Wildfowl Management on Inland Waters.* Game Conservancy, Fordingbridge, 108pp.

Bibby, C J, & Lunn, J, 1982, Conservation of reedbeds and their avifauna in England & Wales. *Biological Conservation 23.*

Burgess, N D, & Evans C E, 1989, *The management of reedbeds for birds.* RSPB.

Cooke, A S, The use of herbicides on nature reserves. *Focus on Nature* **14**. NCC.

Fryer, J D, & Makepeace, R J, 1978, *Weed Control Handbook.* Blackwell.

Le Cren, E D & Lowe-McCornell, R H (Eds.), 1980, *The Functioning of Freshwater Ecosystems* (Int. Biol. Prog. 22) CUP. 588pp.

MAFF, 1985. *Guidelines on the use of herbicides on weeds in or near watercourses and lakes.*

MAFF & Health & Safety Executive, 1989, *Pesticides 1989. Pesticides approved under the Control of Pesticides Regulations 1986.* HMSO.

Moss, B, 1980, *Ecology of Freshwaters.* Blackwell, London. 332pp.

Newbold, C, 1984, Aquatic & bankside herbicides. *Rivers & Wildlife Handbook.* RSPB/NCC.

Scott, A D (Ed.), 1982, *Managing Wetlands and their Birds.* Int. Waterfowl Research Bureau Pubs. 368pp.

Spencer-Jones, D, & Wade, M, 1986, *Aquatic Plants: A Guide to Recognition.* Pubs. ICI Farnham, Surrey. 169pp.

Street, M, 1985, *Ponds & Lakes for Wildfowl.* Game Conservancy, 1989.

Svedarsky, W D, & Crawford, R D, 1982, *Wildlife Values of Gravel Pits.* Misc. Pubs. 17 Agric. Exp. Station, Univ. Minnesota, 249pp.

ROUGH GRASS AND TALL HERBAGE

Summary

1. Areas of rough grassland are very valuable habitat for insects, amphibians, small mammals, birds of prey and nesting waterfowl. They should be retained or created.
2. In most sites they will develop naturally on uncompacted subsoils or topsoil.
3. Ideally, plan for the development of such an area on a south-facing slope down to water and if possible incorporate a pond.
4. Prevent scrub take-over. If mowing or grazing is necessary, manage no more than one-third of the area each year.

(See photographs 8 and 9)

General

Any area of ground with reasonable drainage and uncompacted soil will quickly develop a growth of self-sown herbs and grasses which will form a rank cover of vegetation 0·3–1 m high if it is not mown or grazed. This cover provides good habitat for shrews and short-tailed voles which are an important prey for weasels, barn owls and kestrels. In damp sites, tall grasses, especially the tussock-forming kinds such as bush grass *Calamagrostis epigejos* may develop and be colonised by harvest mice. The caterpillars of several butterflies from the brown and skipper families feed on wild grasses. Damselflies and spiders use the structure of tall stems as hunting habitat. Some kinds of ducks and waders prefer to nest where there is overhead cover provided by grass tussocks and tall plant stems: they have better breeding success when concealed from predators in this way. Amphibians and grass snakes also make much use of the habitat.

Vegetation of this type can also be deliberately created by sparsely sowing a mixture of native grasses, ideally in late summer. The initial aim is for a rather open sward which wild plants can invade naturally.

For butterflies and damselflies, site such areas where they have a sunny aspect and, ideally, are fairly sheltered. For breeding wildfowl avoid creating narrow strips which are easily searched by foraging foxes. Perhaps the ideal is a south-facing slope rising from damp ground at the water's edge, where growth will be vigorous and dense, to well-drained higher land where the cover will be sparser and subject to summer drought. Many insects use patches of bare ground for sunbathing or egg laying. If a pond is to be included in the restoration, it could beneficially be located in the lower part of the area.

Sometimes such grasslands need no management for several years, but often bramble and thorn scrub appear rapidly. Initially, this will enhance cover at ground level but as stands of bramble or scrub grow they shade out the growth beneath them and become 'hollow'. This is not satisfactory cover. Limit the amount of this type of cover to a scatter of small, dense bushes. It may be practicable to hand-pull seedlings as they appear: otherwise occasional cutting or grazing will be necessary. As most shrubs regrow when cut down, spot-treatment with herbicide may be required. Do not treat the whole site with herbicide. If the site is cut or grazed, confine the operation to no more than one third of the area in any one year so that populations of insects, small mammals or nesting birds are not entirely displaced. If the area does include important variation (eg from wet to dry ground), apply the one-third rule to take account of this.

WILDFLOWER GRASSLANDS

Summary

1. Relocation of existing herb-rich grasslands prior to over-burden stripping is practicable and very desirable on conservation grounds. Creation of new wild flower grassland has less conservation value but is much more beneficial for wildlife than the conventional rye-grass sward.
2. Existing grasslands can be relocated by transferring turves together with topsoil in an excavator bucket or on pallets to a receptor site which should be weed-free, uncompacted and provide similar watertable conditions to the donor site. Existing topsoil should be stripped or subsoil restored to provide a low-fertility and weed-free substrate.
3. Creation from seed requires selection of species which are suitable to site conditions, good pollen and nectar sources for insects, not so vigorous as to out-compete other required plants and lacking dormancy mechanisms which will delay germination.
4. Ideally, obtain seed from local sources such as surviving hay meadows. A mix of 85% wild grasses and 15% wildflowers is sown at about 2·5 g/m^2 together with about 3 g/m^2 Westerwolds rye-grass as a nurse crop.
5. A firm seedbed with a good tilth and good drainage is essential. Repeated harrowing and rolling will be required. The bed must be weed-free and of low fertility so freshly-exposed subsoil is ideal.
6. The best sowing time is late August to mid September. In the following year, cut at least three times and remove cut material. Subsequently, cut once or twice annually depending on the conservation aim.
7. On free-draining gravel-pit soils expect an open sward: this is beneficial, permitting other native plants to colonise.
8. Existing swards can be diversified by inserting pot-grown specimens or by slot-seeding in herbicided strips. The latter technique is still experimental.

General

The land in many river valleys was traditionally used for hay production and subsequent grazing by livestock, activities which could be accommodated within and benefit from a high watertable and winter or spring flooding. This led to the development of grasslands rich in wildflowers, especially those which require moist ground. Such grasslands were also important for a wide range of creatures including butterflies, harvest mice and grass snakes. Efficient land drainage and agricultural development has destroyed almost all of these areas. Even where grassland remains, the use of fertilisers and herbicides has largely eradicated the wildflower component.

Where wildflower grasslands do still exist, but retention is not possible due to extraction requirements, relocation of the vegetation to specially-restored sites should be considered.

In all gravel workings the opportunity will also exist to create new grasslands containing a colourful diversity of wildflowers. In strict conservation terms, this is only a cosmetic measure because the newly-created sites will not contain the range of creatures, especially insects such as grasshoppers, which were present in the original. However, some colonisation will occur and it certainly enhances the beauty and amenity value of areas put down to grass. By contrast, rye-grass swards, though capable of withstanding heavy public use, have negligible wildlife value and should not be created in conservation sites.

Considerable experience has been gained in habitat creation since the mid 1970s when grass and herb (wildflower) mixtures were first sown in experimental plots. Since then several techniques have been used for restoring swards after gravel extraction:

(a) the use of turf transplants or turf fragments and the relocation of existing vegetation;
(b) sowing herb-rich mixtures into prepared seedbeds by:
    (i) using suitable mixtures purchased from wildflower seed merchants;
    (ii) using hay seeds obtained from nearby wildflower grasslands;
(c) diversifying existing species-poor grassland by:
    (i) slot-seeding;
    (ii) inserting pot-grown plants.

Relocation of existing vegetation

Where planning permission has been given for extraction beneath surviving botanically-rich grasslands, it may be possible to save them by relocating the sward using heavy earthmoving equipment. To minimise costs, the distance between the donor site and the receptor site should be kept to a minimum but it is essential that the receptor site provides environmental conditions favourable for turf growth; in particular, the watertable must be at the correct level. Measurements must be made at the donor site, at least to establish typical levels in the summer months, and the receptor site profiled to match. Bear in mind that final water levels in a restored site are likely to be somewhat lower than those which existed prior to extraction and it is this final level which will be critical. In profiling the site, allowance must be made for the substantial thickness of the turves themselves (30–50 cm). Typically the summer watertable should be within 70 cm of the final soil surface.

The receptor site should be of subsoil, free of compaction and without weeds. Freshly-exposed subsoil is likely to be weed-free but if weeds have colonised, herbicides should be used prior to the transfer operation.

For best results, the soil profile should be maintained during pickup and setdown operations. Turves 30–50 cm thick should be cut using a bucket with half-arrow cutting edge side plates. The thickness of the turves is necessary to maintain the existing root system as intact as possible and to retain the associated soil fauna. For these reasons, care must be taken not to break them up in handling.

Turves are either transported directly in the bucket, which minimises risk of breakage, or can be laid on pallets and moved on a trailer. Experience so far suggests that in one hour, 20–25 m² can be moved over distances up to 800 m.

To prevent unwanted weeds becoming established in the interstices between the laid turves, subsoil from the donor site should be used for filling the spaces which are then rapidly colonised by the plants in the turves.

A wide variety of plants, including bee, pyramidal and common spotted orchids, has been translocated successfully by this technique. There is also evidence that some invertebrates survive the move.

Where the area of land available for meadow creation exceeds the area from which turves can be removed, it is useful to lay them in chequerboard arrangement, sowing a low-density *Festuca/Agrostis* grass mixture in the intervening areas, which should be levelled up with subsoil from the donor site. The aim is to establish a fairly open turf which will be receptive to seeds shed in future years by plants in the adjoining turves, thereby enabling desirable species to spread.

Establishment from seed

The key to the establishment of wild flower mixtures from seed is attention to four points:
(a) selection of species suitable for site conditions;
(b) a weed-free seedbed;
(c) good seedbed preparation;
(d) careful management of the site, especially in the first year after sowing.

The selection of species for inclusion in the seed mixture will be determined by the aim. If it is to create a replica of a semi-natural grassland, specialist advice should be sought on the choice of species appropriate for the area. However, the cost may prevent the inclusion of a number of species whose seed is expensive and it is perfectly valid to sow simple mixtures of common plants to create colourful communities which may have no counterpart in the 'natural world'. A list of species which have proved successful on clay, alluvial and sandy soils is given in Table 3.9. Provided the right plants are selected, seeding does work on new, free-draining gravel pit soils. In general, plants for inclusion in wildflower mixtures should be:
(a) ecologically suitable for the local soil and water conditions;
(b) common: rare or locally distributed plants are likely to be difficult to establish;
(c) preferably perennial and long-lived;
(d) attractive in flower;
(e) good pollen and nectar sources for insects;
(f) not highly competitive or invasive because they will come to dominate the whole area and suppress other desired plants;
(g) have seed which germinates easily over a range of temperatures. In particular, avoid those with dormancy mechanisms which delay germination over winter or even for a period of some years.

Where meadows containing such wildflowers exist near to the restoration area, attempt to obtain seed from the local source. The species will be best suited to local conditions and are therefore more likely to succeed. A normal-sized (21 kg) hay bale obtained from a species-rich meadow contains on average about 450,000 seeds, of which about 90% are grasses and the remainder herbs

Table 3.9. Species suitable for inclusion in seed mixtures for sowing on clay, alluvial and dry acid soils likely to be encountered in gravel pits

Grasses		Clay	Alluvial	Dry acid
Agrostis capillaris	Common bent	●	●	●
Aira caryophyllea	Silver hair-grass			●
Alopecurus pratensis	Meadow foxtail		●	
Anthoxanthum odoratum	Sweet vernal-grass	●	●	●
Bromis commutatus	Meadow brome	●	●	
Cynosurus cristatus	Crested dog's-tail	●	●	●
Deschampsia flexuosa	Wavy hair-grass			●
Festuca ovina	Sheep's-fescue			●
Festuca rubra	Red fescue	●	●	●
Festuca tenuifolia	Fine-leaved sheep's-fescue			●
Hordeum secalinum	Meadow barley	●	●	
Phleum nodosum	Smaller cat's-tail	●	●	
Poa pratensis	Smooth meadow-grass	●	●	
Poa trivialis	Rough meadow-grass	●	●	
Trisetum flavescans	Yellow oat-grass	●	●	
Herbs				
Achillea millefolium	Yarrow	●	●	●
Centaurea nigra	Common knapweed	●	●	
Conopodium majus	Great pignut		●	
Crepis capillaris	Smooth hawk's-beard			●
Daucus carota	Wild carrot	●	●	
Erodium cicutarium	Common stork's-bill			●
Galium saxatile	Heath bedstraw			●
Galium verum	Lady's bedstraw	●	●	●
Geranium molle	Dove's-foot crane's-bill			●
Geranium pratense	Meadow crane's-bill	●		
Hypochoeris radicata	Cat's-ear	●	●	●
Knautia arvensis	Field scabious	●		
Leontodon hispidus	Rough hawkbit	●		
Leucanthemum vulgare	Oxeye daisy	●	●	
Lotus corniculatus	Common bird's-foot trefoil	●	●	●
Lychnis flos-cuculi	Ragged-robin	●	●	
Malva moschata	Musk mallow	●		
Medicago lupulina	Black medick	●		
Ononis repens	Common restharrow	●		
Plantago lanceolata	Ribwort plantain	●	●	
P. media	Hoary plantain	●		
Potentilla erecta	Tormentil			●
Primula veris	Cowslip	●	●	
Prunella vulgaris	Selfheal	●	●	
Ranunculus acris	Meadow buttercup		●	
R. bulbosus	Bulbous buttercup	●		
Rhinanthus minor	Yellow rattle	●	●	
Rumex acetosa	Common sorrel	●	●	●
Rumex acetosella	Sheep's sorrel			●
Sanguisorba minor	Salad burnet	●		
Sanguisorba officinalis	Great burnet		●	
Saxifraga granulata	Meadow saxifrage	●		
Silaum silaus	Pepper-saxifrage	●	●	
Silene alba	White campion	●	●	
Silene dioica	Red campion	●		
Stachys officinalis	Betony	●		
Stellaria graminea	Lesser stitchwort		●	●
Trifolium arvense	Hare's-foot clover			
T. campestre	Hop trefoil	●		
T. dubium	Lesser trefoil	●		
Vicia cracca	Tufted vetch	●	●	
V. sativa	Common vetch	●	●	
V. tetrasperma	Smooth tare	●	●	

and sedges. The main problem is to separate the seed. For small areas, it can be sieved from bales. For larger sites, it may be necessary to get a specialist seeds firm to harvest the seed. Alternatively, the hay may simply be spread over the ground to be sown and raked up after a month when the seeds have dropped from it. If left on site, it will tend to smother the germinating seedlings. Alternatively, the hay may be chopped or macerated to reduce its smothering effect when spread on the soil. Note that hay for use in this way should have been harvested reasonably rapidly: hay which has lain long after cutting will have shed much of its seed.

Where wildflower seed is to be sown, it should be mixed with grasses in a proportion of about 85% grasses to 15% wildflowers, for sound ecological and economic reasons. Grasses form the matrix in which broad-leaved plants and sedges are distributed in natural grassland. Grasses are able to withstand compaction, mowing and grazing and remain winter-green, whereas many herbs die down in the winter months and leave areas of bare ground. Grass seed is available in large quantities commercially and is relatively cheap. Herbs, on the other hand, are more expensive and it is not economically possible to include large quantities in a mixture.

Experience has shown that wildflower mixtures often do best with a nurse crop. This is usually a quick-growing annual, which grows rapidly to produce a green or colourful vegetation and then dies back, allowing those species which will form the basis of the wildflower meadow to replace it. Westerwolds rye-grass has these characteristics and is most widely used. It should not be used where the soil is exceptionally fertile as it will grow quickly and may swamp other species. In such conditions, possible nurse crops include common oat, black medick or a mixture of poppies, corncockle and cornflower.

The ideal planting site will be of low fertility and free of weed seeds. Thus, subsoil is preferable to topsoil. Where weeds are present, they should be eliminated with a herbicide such as glyphosate. A fine seedbed with a good tilth and good drainage should be prepared, as the seed of many wildflower species is small. It is a fallacy that wildflower mixtures can be sown in rough seedbeds and a common fault with them is that they are too loose and uneven. A firm bed can be achieved by repeated harrowing and rolling, the timing of these operations in respect of the weather being crucial to the result obtained: avoid wet conditions.

On small areas, seed will normally be sown by hand, but it may be applied by tractor-mounted seed or fertiliser broadcasters. The grass and wildflower seed mixture is usually sown at about 2·5 g/m², mixed with about 3 g/m² of a nurse crop such as Westerwolds ryegrass. As the quantities of seed being sown are often small, it may be necessary to mix the seed with small quantities of an inert substance such as sand, sawdust or barley meal to ensure even distribution. After sowing, a light raking or harrowing, followed by a flat roller, will be helpful in ensuring good contact between seed and soil.

The best time for sowing wildflower mixtures is from the end of August to mid September but good results have been obtained at other times in those parts of the country where rain is plentiful throughout the year.

Subsequent management during the first two years is crucial both to the establishment and the final composition of the sward. It is difficult to make hard and fast rules as each site is different, but generally the newly-sown area may require cutting at least three times in the first year after sowing, with the cut material removed each time to prevent smothering and to reduce nutrient levels. Timing of cuts will depend on the stage of growth of the sown vegetation and any weeds. As a rule of thumb, cut when height exceeds about 15 cm.

After the first year, management will depend on the site's fertility, the type of mixture sown and the effect required. On free-draining gravel pit soils the new sward will often be fairly open and this is beneficial as it will permit other native plants from the surrounding area to colonise. In general, the more fertile the site, the greater will be the requirement for management. Where mixtures are composed mostly of tall and medium-tall herbs and grasses, they should be cut in late July or early August, with the cut material removed, and again in late October or early November, with the cut material left. Where mixtures largely comprise short-growing plants, a single late summer cut and removal will suffice. On large areas, some form of rotational management where different parts are cut at different times will provide the greatest range of conditions for both plants and animals, including butterflies, some of which require short vegetation while others favour long growth.

The cost of maintaining low-fertility grasslands will be less than maintaining other types of amenity grass which are often cut 3–10 times a year, as wildflower meadows will require cutting only once or twice. However, the management input in the first two years may be quite high,

Habitat Management and Creation

depending on the site, and must not be neglected at such a critical stage.

It is sensible to cut paths through meadows to encourage people to use them rather than trample over the whole site. Sinuous paths increase the feeling of space and naturalness in a meadow. The blending of the meadow with other landscape features such as native shrubs and water provides the site manager with a range of possibilities for enhancing visitors' enjoyment and pleasure.

Diversifying established swards

Where land around gravel pits has been sown with a simple grass sward, it is now possible to increase the botanical and conservation interest by introducing plants individually or by slot-seeding.

Native plants can be raised from seed in jiffy pots quite easily using conventional horticultural methods and there is now an increasing number of suppliers. Plants with about four true leaves are ideally sized for inserting into grasslands using a bulb-planter. The technique is suitable for specialist planting schemes, where subtle differences of slope, aspect and drainage may be catered for by using a greater variety of species, selected for the particular habitat conditions, than would be possible when using straightforward grass and herb mixtures. It is also more cost-effective to use pot-grown plants:

(a) where seed is scarce or very expensive;
(b) where the species are slow-growing and likely to be swamped at the seedling stage by surrounding vegetation; or
(c) for species with dormancy mechanisms which prevent them germinating simultaneously with other plants sown in the mixture, thereby putting them at competitive disadvantage when they do germinate.

This method is particularly suitable for enhancing existing grassland either on aesthetic grounds or to achieve particular conservation benefits such as supplying the larval food plant of a butterfly.

An alternative technique, still at the experimental stage, is slot-seeding which also provides a means of enriching existing swards. Essentially, the method consists of spraying a band of herbicide, usually paraquat or gramoxone, to kill a band of the existing sward and drilling the desired species or seed mixture into a slit cut in the ground within the sprayed band. The theory is that, in the absence of competition and with mineral soil exposed, the seed will germinate, become established and grow to a competitive

size before the grass sward recovers and invades the sprayed area. Subsequently, the plants will spread throughout the sward.

It is best to cut or to graze the grassland as hard as possible before the slot seeding is done for two reasons; (i) to create the shortest turf possible, so that competition is reduced to a minimum and so that herbicide which is sprayed effectively kills all surrounding vegetation in the spray band; (ii) to minimise and destroy any accumulated litter at the base of the sward, to enable the seed to reach mineral soil, rather than lodging on organic matter.

The lower the nutrient status the better, so avoid fertiliser applications prior to slot-seeding. Nor should fertilisers be used after slot-seeding, as this will encourage the grasses at the expense of the herbs.

While excellent results have been achieved in some instances, at other sites slugs have been a problem or there has been poor germination. These problems may be attributable to inappropriate timing, management or other factors but, for the present, those considering using this technique should seek specialist advice from the author.

References

Biological Habitat Reconstruction, 1989, G P Buckley (Ed.) *Biological*, Belhaven Press, London and New York.

Wells, T C E, Bell, S, & Frost, A, 1981, *Creating attractive grasslands using native plant species.* NCC. Shrewsbury.

Wells, T C E, Frost, A, & Bell, S, 1986, *Wild flower grasslands from crop-grown seed and hay-bales.* NCC Focus on Nature Conservation. No. 15.

Wells, T C E, Cox, R, & Frost, A, 1989, *The establishment and management of wildflower meadows.* NCC Focus on Nature Conservation. No. 21.

T C E Wells

WOODLAND, TREES AND SHRUBS, SHELTERBELTS AND HEDGES

Summary

1. Woodland is of great conservation value, old woods especially so. Much woodland wildlife does not easily colonise new sites, while provision of new woodland and mature timber is a very long-term process. Retain existing woods and trees wherever possible, and start the planting programme as soon as possible.
2. Hedges support some wildlife also found in woodland and may serve as corridors between woodland blocks. Retain older hedges and those linking woodland and scrub, or create new ones as links.
3. Native trees and shrubs support more wildlife than do most introduced species: favour them in planting schemes and encourage their natural regeneration by preparing suitable receptor sites.
4. Evergreens have special value in visual screening and non-native conifers are often the best choice for this purpose.
5. Aim for diversity in tree and shrub species and for a varied woodland structure with a good understorey of shrubs and herbs. Sheltered sunlit glades are very valuable.
6. For rapid growth select species most suitable to site conditions.
7. The main causes of failure in planting schemes are soil compaction and associated waterlogging, allowing the roots of transplants to dry out, and using trees which are too large. Subsidiary causes of failure are inadequate staking, lack of protection from grazing and poor aftercare, especially weeding.
8. Competition by weeds and grass in particular slows early growth. The need to weed can be reduced by using subsoil for all conservation plantings: most trees grow well in it.
9. Select appropriate fast-growing species for screening and shelterbelts. Establish in topsoil with correct spacing and control weeds for three years.
10. Manage hedges to create a dense structure to ground level, as cover and nesting habitat.
11. By cutting hedges in rotation, both flowers and a berry crop can be produced each year on part of the habitat.

(See photographs 16, 17 and 18)

General

A great range of plants and animals depends primarily on trees, and many wetland creatures including dragonflies, amphibians and some wildfowl use woodlands. New planting may be carried out on extraction sites for several purposes and wildlife can also benefit if the right decisions are made on siting, composition and management. In addition, sites may contain existing woodland, trees or hedges which, because of their greater age, will contribute valuably to the wildlife interest of the restored site if they can be retained, at least in part.

Before human clearance, most of the UK was covered by trees and as a result, most kinds of our native wildlife depend on trees or shrubs. Some can live in small, isolated plantings or features such as hedges, but the majority need the special conditions provided by woodland. Depending on soil types, drainage and local climatic conditions, the tree and shrub composition of ancient woodland varied across the country and, in general, the woods which are most valuable for wildlife today are those which reflect that original composition. Ideally, new plantings should attempt to restore the original woodland type, but all plantings can have some value for wildlife.

In the gravel-pit context, it is particularly valuable to create woods which have a working relationship with the waterbodies. Willows, alder, aspen and poplars flourish in damp sites, and in natural wetlands they will form extensive stands, often fronted by reeds and other emergent plants growing in deeper water. They are important as cover, feeding and breeding habitat for many wetland invertebrates, birds and mammals, while the annual production of leaf litter provides an input of nutrients to the aquatic system.

Whatever the primary aim, the following general principles should be followed as far as possible:

1. Retain existing woodland or hedgerows. Unlike much wetland wildlife, many forms of woodland wildlife, especially plants and invertebrates, are not good at colonising new sites. Woods which are over 400 years old are extremely important for nature conservation. Consent is unlikely to be given for felling, but if it is, seek to retain some portion to be linked to new plantings so that the wildlife it contains

135

will have some chance of expanding into the new habitat.

Hedges may serve as corridors by which wildlife can move between woodland blocks and colonise new plantings. Those on farm or parish boundaries are often of considerable age and tend to be the richest, containing more kinds of trees and shrubs than newer plantings; thus they support more wildlife. They are worth retaining especially if they can be used to connect new tree or woodland plantings together.

Even a relatively recent planting may be many decades old and its wildlife value will take as long again to restore if it is destroyed.

2. Keep old trees. Old timber is especially valuable. In the unmanaged, natural wildwood, old trees and dead wood were much more abundant than they are in managed forests. One-third of all woodland birds nest in holes in old trees. One-fifth of woodland invertebrates are associated with dead wood. Taking a century or more to replace, older trees should be kept wherever possible. Do not remove standing dead timber unless there is a safety problem. Leave fallen timber to rot in place. Do not 'tidy up' woodlands.

3. Take advantage of natural regeneration. Willows and alders will readily colonise damp areas, and birch and Scots pine will appear on well-drained ground. Consider how such 'windfalls' can be incorporated into restoration, perhaps being enhanced by some additional planting. Or simply prepare receptor sites and be patient. Natural regeneration often outperforms planted trees.

4. Favour native tree and shrub species in new plantings. For the most part, they support a much wider variety of insects than do recently introduced trees. In turn, the insects provide food for other creatures, especially birds. Native willows, oak and birch are invaluable: in summer, oak in particular supports thousands of leaf-eating caterpillars which are gathered by many birds including tits, warblers and woodpeckers. Note that native trees may have restricted distributions (eg beech is only native in southern Britain). Where the management aim necessitates using some non-native trees, incorporate as many natives as possible.

5. Plant a diversity of tree and shrub species. This will benefit a wider range of creatures and is particularly important for birds which need a range of food resources coming 'on stream' at different seasons, to support them year round.

Particularly in late autumn and winter when insect food is scarce, berries and other tree seeds are essential. At this season, evergreens provide valuable shelter, especially in the form of nocturnal roost sites protected from wind and rain. Holly, Scots pine and ivy are the native options suitable for most gravel workings. Aim for at least 10% of the area planted to be occupied by shrubs and 10% by non-timber trees or, in commercial timber plantings, have at least 5% of each.

6. Aim for a varied woodland structure. The three-dimensional structure of woodlands is extremely important to wildlife. Woods consist of four main layers – the ground layer (low-growing plants), the field layer (tall flowers and grasses, young shrubs and tree saplings), the shrub layer (mature shrubs and young trees) and the canopy (mature trees) (see Fig 3.16). A new planting is nearly without structure, especially if weeding is undertaken. As soon as possible, allow a natural herb layer to develop, benefiting butterflies and nesting wildfowl. As the trees grow, ground, field and shrub layers should come into existence. From now on, to maintain some open ground or shrubby areas may require management: in general, thinning should aim to permit ample light to reach the lower layers, otherwise they will be shaded out and lost. A new wood with all canopy and no understorey supports little wildlife.

7. Create rides and glades. In larger plantings, glades or rides at least 15 m wide can be managed for wildflowers and butterflies. The centre will be of grass, cut regularly each year, and there will be shrubs at the margins, a third of which should be cut down every three years, so ensuring continuity of vigorous regrowth. More complex regimes may be devised in larger sites, to create an intimate mix of shrub and grassland ages plus sheltered bays or scallops in the side margins (see Fig 3.17). In small plantings, a similar shrub and grass margin can be created outside, on the southern edge where it will receive most sunlight.

8. Inter-link woods, shelterbelts and hedges. Where possible, plan new plantings to create corridors to aid colonisation and movement around the site by woodland species. However, do not plant woodland blocks immediately up-wind of water areas because of the wind turbulence problems they create.

9. Plan and plant as soon as possible. Because of the long time-lapse between planting and maturity, tree-planting should not wait until active excavation has ceased. A general guide-

Fig 3.16 'Natural' structure of woodland.

line would be to start planting as soon as any part of the site is available, ideally as soon as planning permission is received.

Prescriptions for new plantings

(a) Visual screening should be planted well before extraction commences, using fast-growing species such as poplars, larch and birch: some evergreens may also be required, especially if the area available is narrow. These should be interspersed with slower species such as ash and oak which will dominate in later years and greatly increase the wildlife value from quite an early stage. In addition, ground level screening and wildlife will benefit from either under-planting with shrubs or a dense mixed-species hedge along the outer margin. If planted on an earth embankment, the screen gains an early height benefit.

Unless very dense, deciduous species are unsuitable as screening for approaches to hides. Here, a thick conifer hedge is essential for winter cover and more effective for noise reduction.

(b) Noise screening plantings need to be close to the source, dense and preferably evergreen. The most effective noise screen comprises an earth embankment with plantings on the top and sides. This will probably necessitate using non-native conifers. Scots pine and Norway spruce are better for wildlife than the North American species such as sitka spruce.

If space permits, inter-plant with small numbers of shade-tolerant hardwoods, such as beech, which can replace the conifers after their functional requirement ceases.

(c) Dust control is largely a summer problem so deciduous species are recommended as the dust-blanketed leaves are shed each year. The mixtures recommended for visual screening will be appropriate.

(d) Boundary establishment. It is important to install and maintain secure site boundaries where wildlife conservation is an aim, and in the longer-term hedges best perform this function, although fencing may need to be erected initially. Hawthorn is the normal species to plant but other shrubs and trees should be incorporated to maximise the considerable wildlife potential of the habitat. The native black poplar (*Populus nigra*), now rare, is a handsome, fast-growing tree appropriate to hedges in river valleys.

(e) Shelterbelts. To protect waterbodies and certain terrestrial habitats, shelterbelts would normally be created close to the site boundary but large sites, especially those which are elongated in the direction of the prevailing wind, may benefit from internal belts. Composition and management are discussed on page 141.

(f) Landscape enhancement or timber production. Plantings for these purposes may take a wide variety of forms. If Forestry Commission grant aid is sought, a proportion of the planting may be non-crop trees and shrubs without loss of payment.

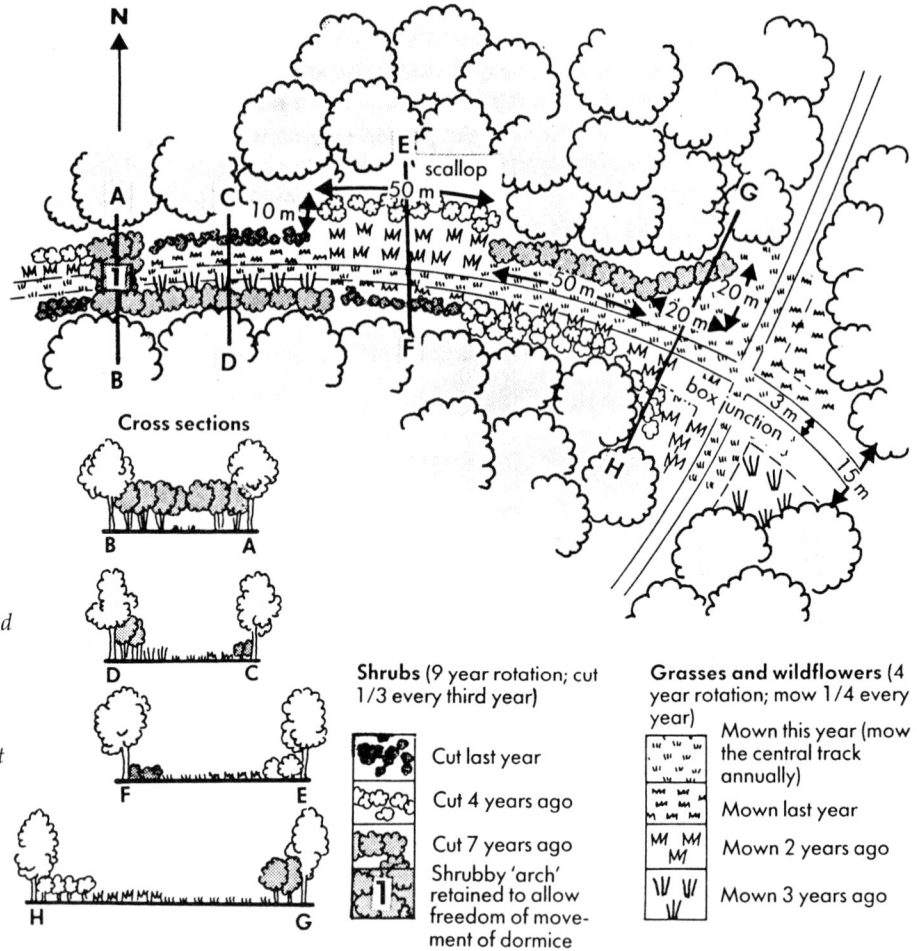

N

scallop

Cross sections

Fig 3.17 Conservation
management of a ride and
ride intersection.
The diagram illustrates an
ideal intimate mix of shrub and
grassland ages. The
management could be
simplified by spreading the
work over a number of rides
and cutting up to half a ride at
at time.

Shrubs (9 year rotation; cut
1/3 every third year)

Cut last year

Cut 4 years ago

Cut 7 years ago

Shrubby 'arch'
retained to allow
freedom of move-
ment of dormice

Grasses and wildflowers (4
year rotation; mow 1/4 every
year)

Mown this year (mow
the central track
annually)

Mown last year

Mown 2 years ago

Mown 3 years ago

Natural regeneration

Most trees have efficient mechanisms for spreading seeds, and natural regeneration is common-
place in gravel workings. To encourage the process, areas of ground may be deliberately cleared
of any existing vegetation to reduce competition
and, if necessary, cultivated to create a suitable
seedbed, though germination often takes place on
any uncompacted ground and through an existing cover of herbage or shrubs (but more rarely
through grass). Several species are adapted to
early colonisation, having windborne seeds
which travel long distances and an ability to grow
in poor soils, so that the provision of top soil is
unnecessary. Birch and, in some areas, Scots pine
will spring up on dry sites while willows and
alder appear on moist areas. The creation of carr –
substantial blocks of willows and alder with
marginal vegetation at the edges of a restored lake
– will be particularly valuable and merely requires
that the ground level is slightly above average

summer water levels so that soil is wet when
seeds arrive. It almost invariably occurs without
any planning on silt lagoons as soon as the silt
level rises above the water.

There are two problems with natural regeneration. It is dependent on the chance combination of
suitable conditions which may not occur every
year. It may be necessary to wait some years for
colonisation of the site (but it often grows much
faster than planted stock). Without fencing, it is
vulnerable to damage from grazing animals but
this is rarely a serious problem on gravel
workings.

In the long term, many native trees and shrubs
may colonise and their presence should be
fostered.

Tree planting and aftercare

Many gravel-pit tree-plantings fail, wasting time
and money. The main reasons for this are:

(a) bad soil conditions, especially compaction below cultivation depth;

(b) allowing roots to dry out during transport or planting;

(c) use of trees which are too large, given the low levels of aftercare which they conventionally receive.

Additional causes of failure include:

(a) selection of inappropriate species for local site conditions;

(b) inadequate staking;

(c) lack of protection from rabbits and hares;

(d) competition by weeds;

(e) planting at the wrong level relative to final watertables.

Choice of tree species

The choice of tree species to be planted must be appropriate to their required function, ie for a hedge, a shelterbelt or for specific wildlife conservation values. The species selected must also be appropriate for the site in question and, for this, information will be required on local meteorology (wind, frost incidence, precipitation), soils (depth, texture, water holding capacity, pH and nutrient status), hydrology (depth and fluctuation of watertable, seasonal water deficit), atmospheric and other pollution. The values, tolerances or requirements of most species likely to be planted are listed in Table 3.10 (page 145).

Ideally, plant mixtures of trees and shrubs as this creates diversity of habitat and food resources. In woodland, use at least four tree and five shrub species. There are wide variations in the composition of old woodlands in different parts of the UK, probably in part reflecting their original, natural character (though oak was very widely planted and lime, for example, is now much rarer than before human intervention). If necessary seek advice from conservation bodies on mixtures suitable to the locality in question.

Stock selection

Younger plants, such as two-year-old forest transplants, are considerably cheaper than older plants and tend to develop a good root system well before the crown of the tree becomes large and affected by wind. Thus, they tend to be much more stable, to require little or no staking and to establish themselves well. In fact, a two year-old tree will often catch up with a tree which was several years older when initially planted. Where an initial visual impact is required, larger standard trees may be planted but they will be much more expensive to buy, plant and maintain, difficult to stake securely and vulnerable to drought in their initial years.

Strong root systems are essential for shelterbelt trees. Open ground, bare-rooted stock normally has good root systems. If containerised trees are used, they must not be pot-bound and roots which are curled around inside the pot must be well teased out before planting. Certain difficult-to-establish species such as oak and beech are commonly available as containerised seedlings, supplied usually in biodegradable pots.

Bare-rooted hedging plants are widely available but sources of native trees are more difficult to find. Advice may be sought from the Forestry Commission, the local authority or the county wildlife trust.

Site preparation

Good 'take' and early growth are much more likely if there is reasonable fertility and a good soil structure, retaining moisture but not waterlogged. Where soils have been compacted they must be deeply ripped, and this should be done beforehand if topsoil is to be spread. Alternatively, individual planting stations must be dug deeply to penetrate any compaction. Compacted or waterlogged soils will inhibit the downward extension of tree roots and the resultant shallow-root development will lead to poor growth or wind blow.

Soil structure and fertility can both be improved through the addition of organic material such as animal manures, mushroom compost or sewage sludge cake, although the nutrient element most likely to be required is phosphorus.

Planting

Broadleaved trees and shrubs are best planted when dormant, in November–March. Evergreens should be planted in October whilst the soil is still warm, or in April when it is warming up. Any planting in March or April may, however, be at risk from drought. Containerised stock may be planted in late spring or summer but will need repeat watering. Planting should not take place when ground is frozen, waterlogged or very dry; at these times plants should be held over and kept moist, if bare-rooted by heeling into a shallow trench out of doors. Plant roots dry out very quickly in cold winter air as well as in sunlight: drying out kills them.

Habitat Management and Creation

The most economical plantings are with bare-rooted transplants (20–40 cm). A notch or slot is made in the soil with a spade and the plant is inserted to the depth at which it had been planted in the nursery. The soil is firmed around the plant with a foot but not trampled hard.

For larger trees such as whips (1 m) and standards (to 3 m) pit-planting is required, the hole being large enough to accommodate all the roots without constriction. If a stake is required, it should be driven in first and the tree placed alongside. The final planted depth must be the same as that at which the tree grew in the nursery. If possible, orientate the tree so that one major root points in the direction of the prevailing wind as this will aid future stability. The pit should be filled with soil mixed with a slow-release general fertiliser. Repeatedly shake the tree up and down to ensure that soil settles around the roots and gently firm each layer. When the infilling is completed, a good final firming should be given. Trees planted in moist positions may benefit from mound planting, which raises them a few centimetres above the local ground level. In contrast, trees planted in dry positions or in late spring may benefit from pit-planting, the shallow saucer around the tree aiding in subsequent watering.

Where aftercare cannot be assured, cut lateral branches back to 3–4 buds each so that early leaf growth will not stress a tree with an unestablished root system.

Willows are generally supplied as cuttings about the size of a pencil, cut square at the bottom and oblique at the top. It helps establishment enormously if they are inserted the right way up. They should be pushed into the soil for half their length and firmed around. Do not make a preliminary hole as the cutting is less likely to root if there is air or water rather than soil around it. Cuttings can be taken in winter from trees on site or from nearby workings. In moist ground a strike rate of 80% should be achieved. If damp, bare ground is available when nearby willows are seeding in summer then the windborne seeds will probably successfully colonise the site.

There are several possible approaches to the spacing of trees and shrubs. If trees are planted at about 4 m centres, interspersed with shrubs at 1–1·5 m, this will encourage the former to develop spreading crowns while permitting light to reach the ground to benefit the shrubs and herbs. It also delays any requirement for thinning. However, on new sites this approach has two drawbacks. Firstly, grass or bramble may come to dominate the ground layer, competing with the planting and locking up nutrients unless managed.

Second, the open structure provides little shelter and leaf litter is blown off site. It may therefore be better to plant at high density (1·5 m for trees and 1 m for shrubs) to shade out grass, create internal shelter and permit natural thinning to take place through competition. A third course is to plant at the wider spacings and at once cut the shrubs right back as this will aid establishment and encourage a bushy form quickly shading the ground. Whichever course is followed, plant in compatible groups of species with similar growth rates. Intimate mixtures of 'fast' and 'slow' species create aftercare problems. In no case is a nurse crop required or desirable.

Staking

Tree-staking is expensive in terms of effort, materials and maintenance. A major benefit of cuttings and transplants is that no staking is required: in addition, stronger root development occurs when a tree is self-supporting from the outset. Normally all standard trees will require staking, as will some of the larger whips. Use short stakes wherever possible, fixing the tie about one third to half way up the trunk; this allows it to flex in the wind, producing a stronger tree. If a standard tree with a well-developed crown is planted, a full-length stake may be essential to prevent the trunk snapping. It is cheaper and better to plant smaller trees sooner.

Stakes will need a life of at least five years and should be of treated timber. Ties should be capable of adjustment as the trunk increases in girth.

Watering and shelter

Do not let roots become dry; keep them bagged or covered by moist sacking until the moment of planting. If the soil is dry, the hole and back-filling soil should be watered before use. Once planting is complete, the site should be well watered.

Subsequent watering will depend largely on weather and time of year. The major danger period is during spring drought following planting. A tree with much leaf will transpire large quantities of water during warm weather and, if root hair development has not proceeded rapidly, this water loss will check growth, cause dieback or even kill the plant. Evergreens planted in the autumn can be damaged or killed in winter during cold, windy weather, losing moisture through their foliage without adequate root growth to replace it, or simply because the soil around their roots is frozen.

At exposed sites it may be beneficial to provide artificial wind shelter for initial tree plantings. A perimeter hedge planting would normally be protected by a stock-proof fence on which can be mounted a 1 m high strip of plastic windbreak netting. This will afford considerable protection to the young plants.

Windbreak plantings themselves may benefit from artificial protection. If they are planted inside the line of a perimeter hedge, the nurse role of the hedge can be extended later when it will infill the lower part of the main wind-break as it becomes thin.

Mulching and weed control

Grass and herbs within 50 cm of any newly-planted shrub or tree compete with it for moisture and nutrients, reducing the growth rate. If allowed to grow unchecked, taller weeds will also compete for light. Healthy, well-planted trees and shrubs will get away in time – it is a state of affairs with which they cope in nature. However, to maximise growth in the year or two after planting, weeds should be controlled by cutting, by hand-weeding or use of an appropriate herbicide. A translocated glyphosate-based herbicide is ideal, but care must be taken not to spray the tree leaves; granular formulations overcome these problems.

Use of a mulch for 50 cm out from any tree will suppress weed growth, reduce moisture loss and protect shallow roots against frosts. Many kinds are available, ranging from synthetic sheet material such as polythene to organic materials such as mushroom compost. Sheet materials may need weighting or pegging; some mulches such as forest bark can be expensive. Ideally, use grass or herbage cut on site; placed around, but not quite touching, the young trees it will fulfil all the benefits expected of any mulch and will also supply a small amount of nutrients as it decomposes. All organic mulches will need topping up each year to remain effective.

Protection against damage by animals

Newly-planted trees may need protection against damage by grazing or browsing animals. If live-stock are present, erect a stock-proof fence 2 m away from the outer rows of planting. Electric fencing must be inspected daily, as failure will quickly result in stock crossing it. Tall (1·8 m) plastic grow-tubes offer protection for hardwood transplants from browsing animals up to roe deer size. They also act as mini greenhouses and may bring about remarkable increases in growth rates. If used, they need strong staking, are visually very intrusive and tend to attract vandalism as well as being rather costly, but they reduce tree losses so that initial planting density may be reduced.

Deer can be extremely destructive, browsing all growth tips and even damaging bark on quite mature trees. They are often very secretive and their presence may not be suspected until damage is done. Advice on risk should therefore be taken before planting. As an alternative to grow-tubes, or where fallow deer are present, a 2 m fence may be required, and this is costly. Where deer numbers are low, a large planting may suffer acceptably small losses, especially if left unweeded so that plants such as bramble protect the young trees and offer alternative foods.

Protection from rabbits and hares can be achieved for whips and standards by using individual tree guards or, for transplants, by using grow-tubes or surrounding the planting with a 25 mm wire mesh fence, 60 cm high, the base being turned outwards so that grass and weeds grow through it and make a reasonably rabbit-proof join.

Aftercare

It should not normally be necessary to water trees and shrubs after their first growing season, but if exceptionally dry weather occurs in their second season then watering may save trees, particularly those planted in free-draining soils. It is usually cheaper to water than to replant.

Trees and shrubs should be kept mulched and weed-free for 2–3 years. Rabbit guards, fences and tree stakes should be regularly checked. Loose stakes should be firmed well in and tree-ties adjusted. Trees which rock in their planting holes often die, yet this can be readily corrected by staking or by firming.

Shelterbelt planting

The composition of a windbreak should reflect its physical state when shelter is most required. For optimum performance against winter winds, an evergreen species is desirable. To achieve equivalent winter shelter from deciduous trees, the screen would need to be so densely planted that it would cause excessive turbulence and down-draughts when the trees were in leaf.

For summer shelter a screen of deciduous trees or a mixed deciduous/evergreen planting is best.

Habitat Management and Creation

In mixed plantings the deciduous species are ideally the lightly-foliaged ones such as ash, aspen, white poplar, birch, hawthorn, willows, *Sorbus* and *Prunus* species. The evergreens are likely to be conifers unless holly, our only native evergreen broadleaf, is chosen. Holly is very hardy, shade tolerant and good for wildlife but it grows slowly compared with many conifers. If shelter is required before the deciduous trees come into leaf, this can be achieved by increasing the proportion of evergreens. Mixed plantings are usually very effective and are visually pleasing, but do not work well as single row screens.

Soil conditions need consideration. For example, in water-logged locations only willows, poplars and alders are likely to succeed. Bear in mind that the native tree cover of most lowland river valleys will have been dominated by these species so there are good wildlife conservation arguments for encouraging them, particularly as suitable conditions can easily be created during land-forming operations, after which establishment and management costs are low and growth rates are likely to be good.

Different tree species put out feeding roots at different depths. Oak, sycamore and silver fir have deep-feeding roots whereas spruce, birch, hornbeam and alder have shallow-feeding roots. Thus the two groups of trees are not significantly in competition and members from each can be planted together.

In a deciduous planting, alternate rows should be of main tree species and of shade-tolerant understorey species, spaced at about 2 m centres in the rows with 3 m between rows. This relatively dense planting will generate early shelter and when the trees are 2–3 m high the planting should form a dense thicket.

Some tree species cast deep shade, suppressing understorey and leading to development of gaps near the ground, where the shelterbelt needs to be at its most dense to be fully effective. In general, species such as beech and hornbeam are best not used as canopy trees, but work well as understorey with, say Scots pine.

Screens of three or more rows of trees present fewer problems than single-row screens; in particular, the failure of the odd tree is not crucial, so less attention is required in the early years. Fast-growing species can be incorporated as nurse trees and later removed, the structure replenishing itself as other species reach maturity.

The outside rows in a multiple screen should comprise fast-growing species which are removed or replaced later – alder, birch, poplars or sitka spruce are ideal. The total planting should consist of a wide mixture of species; the taller and/or faster growing species providing throughout a tall structure with an irregular upper profile. Outside the screen, a hedge should be planted, both to help in the early establishment phase and later to close gaps at the base.

An effective mixed planting would comprise poplars at 3–6 m centres in alternate rows with Lawson's cypress, spruce and silver fir at 1–2 m centres. Other proven mixed plantings would comprise Scots pine with a beech or hornbeam understorey, or larch with oak or sycamore. Note that understorey trees must be reasonably shade-tolerant and that by using species such as beech or hornbeam in the initial understorey, they can take over should the main windbreak trees fail.

Windbreak hedges usually comprise hawthorn or some of the small-to-moderate-size shrub or tree species. An effective structure is achieved by planting transplants at 45 cm centres, usually in a single row or in a double, staggered row, for a low design-height or up to 90 cm apart for a taller hedge. The closeness of the initial planting largely controls the time at which the structure becomes effective.

If space is limited for shelterbelt planting then a single row planting may have to be considered, although for this it is essential that only reliable species are selected. A shrub planting or a hedge at the base may be required and will have wildlife value.

Planting distances for deciduous or deciduous/evergreen shelter belts and for windbreak hedges are shown at Fig 3.18.

Hedges

Hedges are used mainly by wildlife which is adapted to live at the margins of wood or stands of scrub and in glades, where there is a combination of open ground, ample sunshine and thicket cover. They may also be used as corridors by small mammals, invertebrates such as butterflies, and some birds which prefer to remain in cover, enabling them to move between isolated areas of habitat such as woods.

As a general rule, a hedge has greater value for wildlife if it:
(a) contains a wide variety of native shrubs rather than just one or two species;
(b) has a dense bushy structure with foliage virtually down to ground level: this can be created by management;
(c) contains standard trees, the older the better;
(d) has a ditch at its foot. Whether wet or dry, this will extend the area of cover and foraging habitat for wildlife;

(a) Deciduous

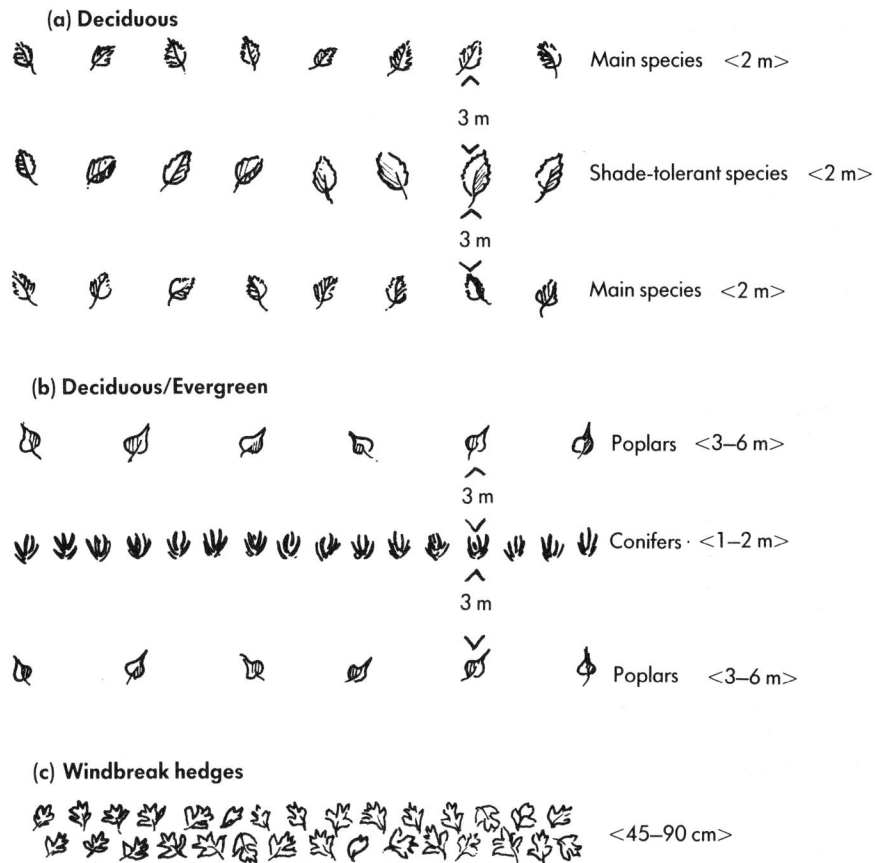

Main species <2 m>

3 m

Shade-tolerant species <2 m>

3 m

Main species <2 m>

(b) Deciduous/Evergreen

Poplars <3–6 m>

3 m

Conifers· <1–2 m>

3 m

Poplars <3–6 m>

(c) Windbreak hedges

Fig 3.18 Shelterbelt planting spacings.

<45–90 cm>

(e) has wide margins with a varied community of herbs.

Features important to birds are shown at Figure 3.19.

Hedges may serve a number of management functions within the site:

(a) to provide a boundary which is stock-proof or discourages trespass;

(b) as a means of channelling public use of a site;

(c) as screening, particularly to prevent disturbance to waterfowl;

(d) to provide shelter from wind.

For wildlife, it is usually better to put resources into the creation of scrub or woodland rather than hedges, the former both being of much greater overall value, but existing hedges should be retained if possible, for several reasons. First, the existing root system and structure is well established so that cover can be provided more rapidly than when planting from scratch. Second, they can be used as part of the structural matrix against which further scrub or woodland can be constructed. Third, they may act as reservoirs for wildlife communities, particularly insects, enabling them to colonise the new site more rapidly.

Managing established hedges

Do not over-manage hedges by cutting more often than is necessary. On sites where shading of agricultural crops is not a problem, hedges can be encouraged to grow tall and bushy. Careful cutting to stimulate growth of side shoots may be desirable from time to time to prevent gaps developing in the lower branches and to maintain a dense covering of foliage.

Avoid cutting hedges during the nesting season (March–July inclusive), or before berries have been eaten by birds. Wherever possible, undertake cutting or trimming in January or February. Do not cut all hedges during a single season. Where possible, manage on a two- or even three-year rotation to ensure that flowers

143

Key
N — nesting
F — feeding
S — songpost

Canopy
S: Yellowhammer, song thrush,
blackbird, robin
S&F: Blue tit, great tit, chaffinch
N: Blue tit, great tit, kestrel, little owl

Hedge
N: Blackbird, song thrush, robin,
greenfinch, linnet, dunnock
N&F: Partridges, yellowhammer,
corn bunting, reed bunting
F: Chaffinch, greenfinch, linnet

Damp ditch
F: Dunnock, song thrush, blackbird

Retain herbage at foot of hedge
Retain/create
wet or dry ditch
Retain/establish standard trees
Create dense structure
without gaps

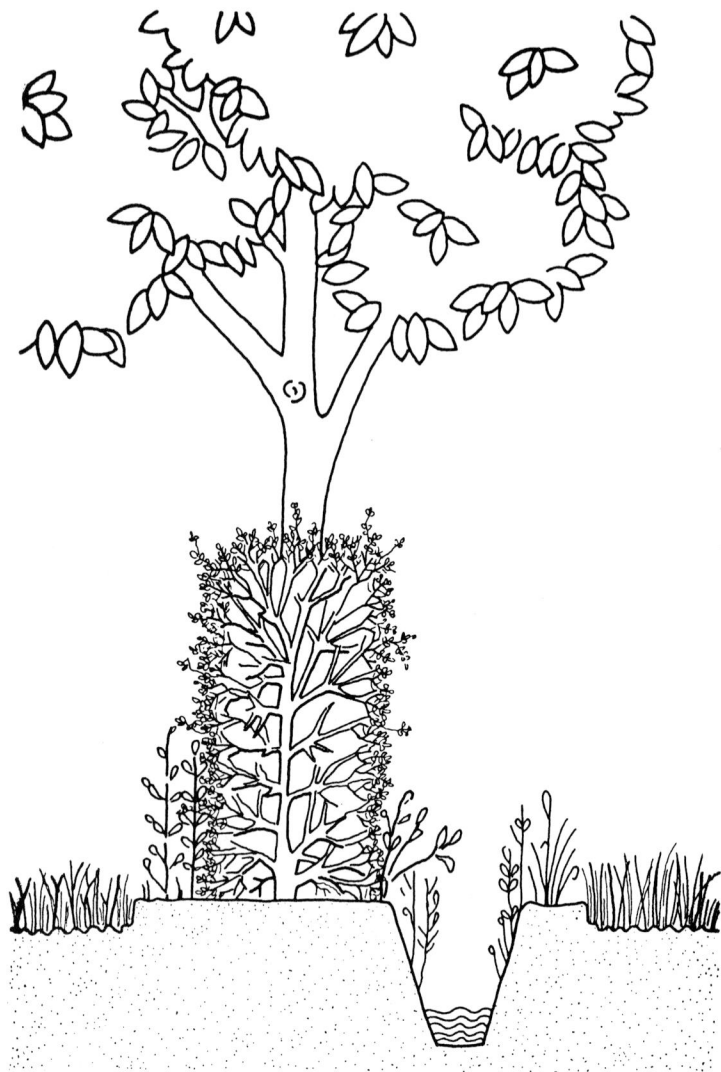

*Fig 3.19 Features of hedge
habitat of importance to
breeding birds.*

and fruit are carried on a proportion of the length each year.

If a hedge has become open at the base or developed gaps, it may be rejuvenated by being laid or coppiced. As coppicing involves cutting the hedge almost down to ground level, it may lead to the extinction of populations of invertebrates, so only do part of the hedge at a time, ideally spreading the whole work over several years.

Leave a margin of perennial herbs and grasses at the base of the hedge at least 1 m wide each side for butterflies and ground-nesting birds, such as partridge and mallard. Cut this on rotation with the hedges, every two or three years only.

Keep existing hedgerow trees. Where few or none exist, identify suitable saplings to be allowed to grow into trees. Ensure that these are rooted directly into the ground and are not simply side shoots. Except for safety reasons, leave dead timber standing.

Planting and gapping-up

When planting a new hedge or gapping-up an old one, choose tree and shrub species appropriate to the locality and to the hedge's function. For example, to deter trespass use thorns: hawthorn and blackthorn are also generally excellent for wildlife. Several trees and shrubs are unsuitable for stock- or human-proof hedges because their growth habit may lead to the creation of gaps, but would be acceptable in a hedge created for wildlife and landscape reasons primarily. These include guelder-rose, elder and privet. Individual hawthorns may be grown on to make good small trees and there are many other suitable species, including crab apple and field maple, as well as traditional farm-timber trees such as oak and ash.

Where screening against disturbance is required, deciduous hedges will be less satisfactory and consideration should be given to the use of evergreens. Holly is excellent but tends to be slow-growing. This is one case where an exception can be made for non-native species but bear in mind that varieties of Lawson and Leyland cypress rapidly become very tall, so that annual cutting may be necessary where height or shading would be a disadvantage.

For most purposes, use 3–4 year-old seedlings up to 60 cm high, ideally from a site with poorer soil than along the proposed hedge line. Seedlings grown on rich nursery soil may not survive on a poor, exposed site.

Plant between October and March, ideally in October or November. Prepare a cultivated tilth 20 cm deep and 30 cm wide for a single-row hedge or 60 cm wide for a double row. The latter is preferred for screening and general wildlife conservation benefits.

Hawthorn and blackthorn benefit from cutting back to within 10 cm of the ground at the end of the first season's growth, so as to bring on vigorous new shoots. Cut other deciduous species back by one-third but only lightly trim holly and other evergreens. Incorporate trees at about 10 m spacing. This allows for some failures and they can be thinned if necessary to reduce shading at a later stage.

Protection from grazing rabbits and hares may be necessary and, if plants are established in good topsoil, competitive weed growth must be expected. Hand weeding or use of herbicides will be necessary if quick hedge growth is desired. Though most young shrubs will get away eventually, if weed growth is not controlled in the early stages, the hedge will develop with a thin base.

The main cause of failure of hedge planting is inadequate care of the seedlings – particularly leaving roots even briefly exposed to drying air and failure to firm them properly into the ground.

References

Bean, WJ, 1970–1980, *Trees and Shrubs Hardy in the British Isles*. 8th edition, 4 vol. 3,410 pp (plus 1988 supplement, Vol A 616 pp) Murray, London.

Backett, K, & Beckett, G, 1979, *Planting Native Trees and Shrubs*. Jarrold, Norwich. 64 pp.

Caborn, JM, 1965, *Shelterbelts and Windbreaks*. Faber & Faber, London. 288 pp.

James, NDG, 1982, *The Forester's Companion*. Blackwell, Oxford.

Pollock, MR, 1984, *Shelter Hedges and Trees*. Leaflet No 2 Rosewarne Experimental Horticultural Station. (MAFF/ADAS) 4th edition, 42 pp.

Rushforth, K, 1987, *The Hillier Book of Tree Planting and Management*. David & Charles, Newton Abbot. 224 pp.

Shepherd, FW, 1979, *Hedges and Screens*. Wisley Handbook 17, Royal Horticultural Society, London. 47 pp.

Smart, N, & Andrews, JH, 1985, *Birds and Broadleaves Handbook*. RSPB, Sandy.

Table 3.10

Tree and shrub species

Note: No list can be exhaustive. The following comprises native trees and shrubs, plus a selection of non-natives which have particular qualities relevant to certain functional uses such as shelterbelts or visual screening. Many species widely used in general landscaping schemes but of no particular wildlife merit have been omitted.

Information on growth rates and final size is not given as both depend on the selected stock and on site conditions. In general, poplars and willows on wet sites grow very rapidly.

A generalised assessment of wildlife value is given for native species only. It is expressed in terms of extensive, moderate and restricted, relating simply to the number of benefits it provides. A species of restricted value may still be highly important for a small number of scarce species or in some special conservation context. No wildlife value assessment is given for non-native trees. This does not mean that they are devoid of value. As with natives, age and form are important considerations. A mature, well-thinned stand of Norway spruce may have more wildlife value than a new planting of oak, for instance.

Name	Wildlife value	Shade tolerant	Soil preference			Comments
			Sands	Clay	Wet	
Alder *Alnus glutinosa*	Moderate	★	★	★	★	Excellent on wet sites. Coppices well.
Alder, grey *A. incana*	–	★	★			Useful for drier sites with low fertility.

Table 3.10 (continued)

Name	Wildlife value	Shade tolerant	Sands	Clay	Wet	Comments
			Soil preference			
Ash *Fraxinus excelsior*	Moderate	★		★		Short season in leaf but light shading. Shade tolerant only at first.
Aspen *Populus tremula*	Moderate		★	★	★	Tolerates exposure.
Beech *Fagus sylvatica*	Restricted	★	★	★		Very subject to squirrel damage. Good for under-planting. Old trees cast very dense shade.
Birch, downy *Betula pubescens*	Extensive		★	★	★	Vigorous colonists of bare ground so not a priority for conservation planting.
Birch, silver *B. pendula*	Extensive		★	★		
Cedar, western red *Thuja plicata*	–	★	★	★		Branched to the ground.
Chestnut, horse *Aesculus hippocastanum*	–			★		Never a woodland tree. Cast dense shade.
Chestnut, sweet *Castanea sativa*	–	★	★	★		Ancient introduction. May have shelterbelt value if coppiced as shoots grow more than 50 cm a year. Shade tolerant only at first.
Cypress, Lawson's *Chamaecyparis lawsoniana*	–	★	★	★		Good for under-planting, clothed to the ground.
Cypress, Leyland *Cupressocyparis x Leylandii*	–	★	★	★		Very quick and excellent screen. Plant small for wind stability. Good for under-planting.
Cherry, bird *Prunus padus*	Moderate			★		Mainly northern distribution.
Cherry, rum *P. serotina*	–		★			Good windbreak species.
Cherry, wild (Gean) *P. avium*	Moderate		★	★		Thrives on most soils.
Fir, Douglas *Pseudotsuga taxifolia*	–	★		★		Dislikes calcareous soils.
Hemlock, western *Tsuga heterophylla*	–	★		★		Dislikes dry, sandy soils.
Holly *Ilex aquifolium*	Moderate		★	★		Good wind break, hedging or woodland undershrub.
Hornbeam *Carpinus betulus*	Restricted	★	★	★	★	Confined mainly to the Southeast and East Anglia. Coppices readily.
Larch, European *Larix decidua*	–		★	★		Greater wildlife value than most conifers because deciduous.
Larch, Japanese *L. kaempferi*	–			★		Less subject to disease than *L. decidua.* Accepts wetter sites. Both species dislike dry sites.
Lime, European *Tilia x europaea*	–	★	★	★		
Lime, small-leaved *T. cordata*	Moderate	★		★		Now rather rare, deserves planting.
Maple, field *Acer campestre*	Moderate	★	★	★		Occurs mostly in hedgerows, where it can be clipped as a shrub, or in mixed oak-ash-maple woods.
Oak, pedunculate *Quercus robur*	Extensive			★		Exceptional value for invertebrates and birds.
Oak, sessile *Q. petraea*	Extensive		★	★		

Table 3.10 (continued)

Name	Wildlife value	Shade tolerant	Soil preference Sands	Clay	Wet	Comments
Pine, Austrian *Pinus nigra austriaca*	–		★			Excellent shelterbelt tree.
Pine, Corsican *P. n. calabrica*	–		★	★		
Pine, lodgepole *P. contorta*	–		★	★	★	Tolerant of wide range of soils.
Pine, Scots *P. sylvestris*	Moderate		★			Dense when young, gappy when older. Only truly native in Scotland.
Poplar, balsam *Populus trichocarpa*	–		★	★		Very quick and widely used in shelterbelts.
Poplar, black *P. nigra*	Moderate		★	★	★	The classic gravel valley tree, now quite rare.
Poplar, downy black *P. n. betulifolia*	–		★	★	★	Quick and widely used for shelterbelts.
Poplar, grey *P. canescens*	Moderate			★	★	
Poplar, Lombardy *P. nigra 'Italica'*	–		★	★		Widely used in shelterbelts. Uniquely ugly.
Poplar, white *P. alba*	Moderate		★	★	★	Quick and good for shelterbelts. Possibly an ancient introduction.
Rowan *Sorbus aucuparia*	Moderate	★	★			Tolerates poor conditions.
Spruce, Norway *Picea abies*	–	★		★	★	Good for under-planting with hard woods. Better wildlife value than most other evergreen conifers.
Spruce, Sitka *P. sitchensis*	–			★	★	Valuable shelterbelt tree but needs high rainfall.
Sycamore *Acer pseudoplatanus*	–	★	★	★		Litter suppresses ground vegetation. Regenerates invasively. Little subject to squirrel damage.
Whitebeam *Sorbus aria*	Moderate		★	★		Good for windbreaks. Favours calcareous soils.
Willow, crack *Salix fragilis*	Extensive		★	★	★	Excellent on wet sites. Initially very quick-growing. Best pollarded.
Willow, white *S. alba*	Extensive		★	★	★	
Yew *Taxus baccata*	Restricted		★	★		Poisonous to livestock. Slow-growing.

Minor trees and shrubs

Name	Wildlife value	Shade tolerant	Soil preference Sand	Clay	Wet	Comments
Crab apple *Malus sylvestris*	Extensive		★	★		Good hedgerow tree.
Blackthorn *Prunus spinosa*	Moderate		★	★		Good for stock-proof hedges.
Broom *Cytisus scoparius*	Moderate		★			Copes with poor acid soils.
Buckthorn *Rhamnus catharticus*	Moderate	★	★	★	★	Calcareous soils only.

Table 3.10 (continued)

| Name | Wildlife value | Shade tolerant | Soil preference | | | Comments |
			Sands	Clay	Wet	
Buckthorn, alder *Frangula alnus*	Moderate		★	★	★	Good for moist sites. Host of a cereal rust.
Dogwood *Cornus sanguinea*	Moderate	★	★	★		Use as woodland under-shrub.
Elder *Sambucus nigra*	Extensive		★	★		Ready colonist of bare ground and new hedges. Hardly justifies planting.
Gorse *Ulex europaeus*	Extensive		★			Useful on poor soils.
Guelder-rose *Viburnum opulus*	Moderate		★	★	★	
Hawthorn *Crataegus monogyna*	Extensive		★	★		Excellent hedging species. Good for windbreaks.
Hawthorn, Midland *C. oxyacanthoides*	Extensive	★		★		A woodland under-tree.
Hazel *Corylus avellana*	Extensive	★	★	★		Coppices. Good woodland understorey.
Osier *Salix viminalis*	Extensive		★	★	★	Valuable in wet sites.
Rose, dog *Rosa canina*	Moderate		★	★		Useful in human-proof screens.
Rose, burnet *R. pimpinellifolia*	Moderate		★			Will grow on very poor soils.
Sallow *Salix cinerea*	Extensive		★	★	★	Valuable in wet sites.
Spindle *Euonymus europaeus*	Restricted	★		★		Woodland undershrub.
Wayfaring-tree *Viburnum lantana*	Moderate			★		Favours calcareous soils.
Willow, goat *Salix caprea*	Extensive		★	★	★	Valuable in wet sites.
Willow, purple *Salix purpurea*	Extensive		★	★	★	Valuable in wet sites.

ISLANDS AND OTHER BIRD NESTING SITES

Summary

1. Predators take a significant toll of nesting birds, their eggs and young. Birds thus seek concealment in cover or holes and, in the case of ground-nesting wildfowl, the relative safety of islands. Provision of good nesting sites greatly increases breeding success.
2. For ducks, herbage cover more than 0·5 m tall must be retained over winter in large, non-linear blocks to conceal nests from avian predators such as crows, as well as from foxes.
3. Islands should be as far offshore as practicable, though even a distance of 3–4 m gives some protection. Several small islands are preferable to one large one.
4. In sheltered locations, shallows all around an island are desirable. In exposed sites, windward shallows will absorb wave effects but the lee of some should fall into deeper water where diving birds may roost in open but sheltered conditions.
5. Erosion protection may be necessary for some island forms or locations.
6. Islands should slope at less than 1:4 for use by nesting wildfowl and be covered by dense herbage. Gulls and some waders require a lower sward, cut in autumn. Islands for terns or ringed plover species should have a very low profile, with a top height of about 50 cm, and be covered by shingle over polythene sheeting which inhibits vegetation establishment.
7. Islands may be created with overburden or inert fill imported onto the site. In existing lakes construct spits by tipping and then cut into sections.
8. Rafts provide good substitutes for islands, and other materials such as straw bales and tree limbs can also be used.
9. Many hole-nesting birds will use correctly designed and placed artificial sites. They include shelduck, sand martins, kestrels, owls, woodpeckers and tits.

(See photographs 19, 20, 21, 22 and 24)

General

Concealment is of great importance to nesting birds. Most ducks nest in deep cover or in tree cavities, the incubating female protected by cryptic plumage. Grebes, coot and moorhen prefer to have their nests surrounded by water – anchored amongst emergent vegetation or on a fallen tree branch. Some waders nest in the open and flee the site at the approach of danger, relying on the camouflage of their eggs to protect them. Many woodland birds nest in holes in trees, gaining both concealment and protection from weather.

Site design and management should take account of these specialised needs if good breeding success is to be achieved.

Vegetation management for nesting wildfowl

Most wildfowl nest close to water. However, mallard will go far to find suitable sites but this increases the risk of duckling loss as they are brought to water after hatching. In order to hatch out ducklings when chironomids in particular are most abundant, some species nest early, before the new season's growth has commenced and when dense cover is in short supply. Nests in vegetation less than 0·5 m tall are much more likely to be found by predators than nests in deeper cover which is most simply created by allowing patches of ground to be colonised by scrub, bramble, dog rose or tall herbs and managing these on a rotation to maintain their density of growth at ground level. In particular, areas of tall growth should not be cut down for tidiness in the autumn or winter as the dead, standing stems provide the necessary early spring concealment. By spreading cut branches, eg from coppicing, a simple physical framework can be created which will help to support grass and herb stems over winter and provide good patches of cover. Cut branches can also be piled in rows or clumps and will provide habitat for invertebrates, small mammals and amphibians as well as foraging and nesting sites for a range of birds.

It is important that areas of cover are large and not linear in nature. The more autumn cutting that is done, the more nests will be concentrated and the smaller the area to be searched by predators. Small patches are easily searched and linear features such as hedge bottoms or a narrow band of vegetation at the water margin are likely to be regularly traversed by foxes, mink and rats, so that the chances of nests surviving are small. Isolated trees close to patches of nesting cover are undesirable as they will be used as lookouts by crows and magpies though where tree cover is generally abundant the problem is less likely to arise.

Wildfowl nestboxes

A number of species naturally nest in cavities in old timber or the tops of the boles of pollard willows. Artificial boxes and baskets are sometimes used by mallard but success is very variable and in general good vegetation management is a more reliable approach. One possible exception to this rule is the shelduck, which usually nests in cavities, including rabbit burrows and gaps in straw ricks. An artificial structure can be built into a low bank or shoreline, with building blocks walling an area about 30×30 cm to a height of 25 cm. The base should be bare ground, scraped into a shallow depression about 5 cm deep. If drainage is poor, the structure may be built on a layer of gravel and in any case the entrance tunnel – a metre length of 20 cm diameter concrete pipe – should slope downwards away from the cavity to provide drainage. The cavity is roofed with a concrete paving slab and buried under a thin layer of gravel, which can be removed in winter to allow access for cleaning.

Islands

Islands are favoured for nesting by waterfowl for two main reasons: compared with sites on land, they are less affected by human disturbance and they are less accessible to mammalian predators such as foxes. For the same reasons, they are attractive to birds which are resting, particularly during the moulting season when wildfowl are flightless and a sense of security is most important. Shelter is also a consideration, and islands always have a lee shore, whilst surrounding shallows offer safe feeding conditions, which may be particularly important for duckling broods.

Several factors influence the type and extent of use which will be made of islands, and the bird species which will benefit from them. These are location, size, shape and surface cover.

Islands should be as far offshore as possible, to minimise the likelihood of access by foxes, which may swim to them, especially where they can see or hear nesting colonies of terns or gulls. The greater the likelihood of predators gaining access, the more important it is to provide dense vegetation cover for wildfowl. Where islands are being created in old gravel workings by cutting through the landward ends of existing spits, the intervening water width may be only 3–4 m but it provides some predator protection and excludes casual human access so it is still worth doing. However, given the choice, birds will nest in larger numbers and have greater breeding success on islands farther offshore.

Cost and material constraints will limit the number of islands which can be constructed. If materials are limited, it is better to use them to create shallows and provide rafts for nesting. Consistent with distance offshore, they should be as widely spaced as possible, bearing in mind that islands in exposed locations will require protection against erosion. Where visitor viewing is a priority, island location and form must not obstruct sight lines: alternatively, they may be deliberately used in order to screen feeding or resting areas from any form of visual disturbance.

Several small islands will hold more nesting birds than a single island of the same total area. A minimum practicable size is probably 100 m² but larger islands, up to 0·1 ha, may be easier to manage.

In sheltered situations, islands may be entirely surrounded by shallows where wildfowl and waders will feed. However, in exposed situations, the island could be profiled to absorb wave effects on the windward side and to provide shelter for wildfowl in the lee. The exposed shore should have a slope of 1:15, with its extent related to wave fetch. Given a fetch of 150 m, waves generated by a 60 kph wind will interact with a bed 1·4 m below the surface. In this case a marginal slope 21 m wide to a depth of 1·4 m may be expected to prevent much erosion. By contrast, the lee shore of some exposed islands may shelve steeply as this will prevent the establishment of emergent vegetation and enable diving ducks to find the sheltered open water they favour for safe roosting. The island profile should rise towards the downwind end to a height of up to 2 m above water level and might ideally be capped by scrub to give the best shelter effect.

In general, the shoreline length should be maximised as the very shallow areas associated with the land/water interface are favoured feeding areas for waders and ducks. Atoll, horseshoe and cruciform shapes are all excellent in this respect (see Fig 3.20). The land beach should be as flat as possible, particularly to allow easy access by ducklings. Overall, slopes should be no greater than 1:4 for use by nesting wildfowl. (However, if

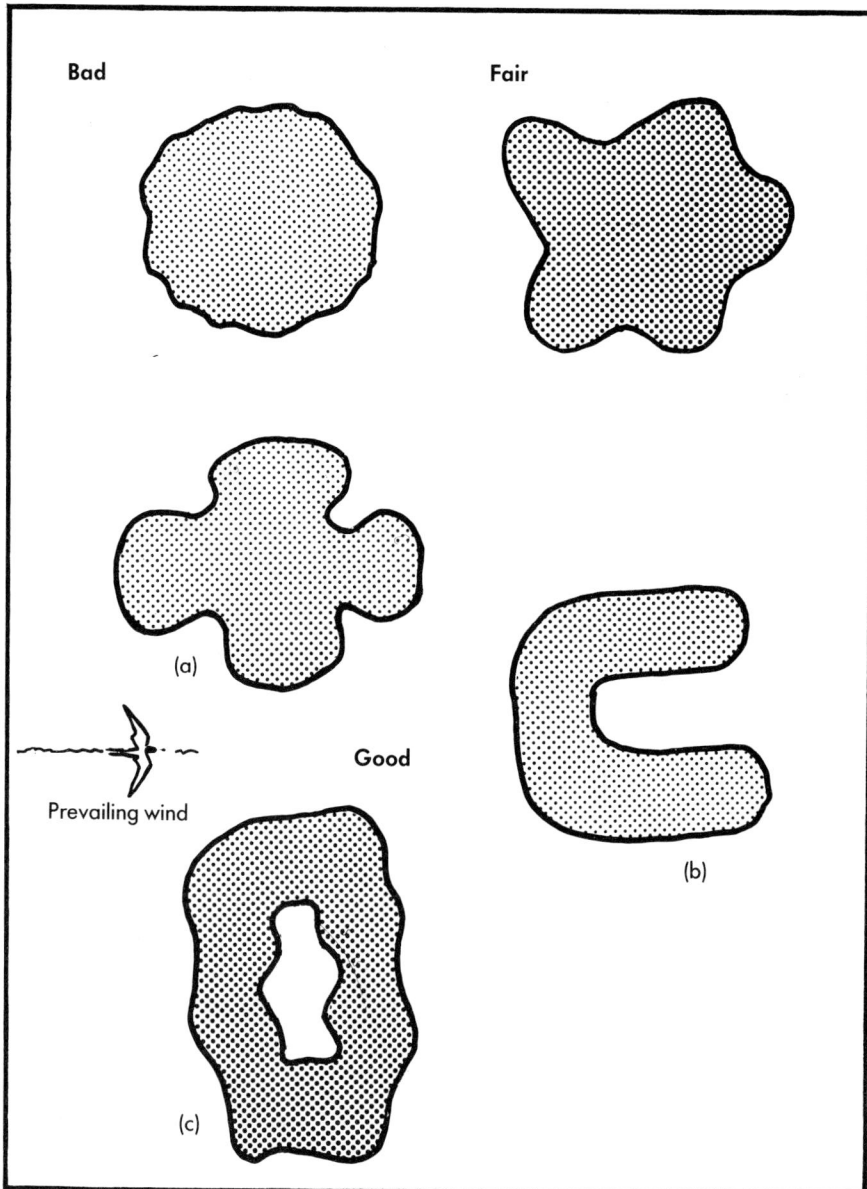

Fig 3.20 Island forms to provide abundant 'edge' for feeding by waders and dabbling ducks.

it is desired to discourage landing by Canada geese on islands prepared for use by common terns, margins should be as steep as practicable provided that the top is relatively level.)

For birdwatchers, islands with shallows towards viewing hides are likely to be ideal. Where different needs potentially conflict, several forms may be provided.

If marginal erosion is a problem or anticipated, physical shore protection may be required. Methods are straightforward and include:

(a) booms such as telegraph poles attached to spaced piles. If attached by chains, they will be free to move up and down with variations

in water level. They also have the advantage that they can be set away from the shore, thus providing some shelter to the inner shallows and plants which may be growing there;

(b) use of large stone material. Infilling tends to wash out, leaving a surface difficult for wild-fowl – ducklings in particular – to cross;

(c) willow staking. This will usually take root and provide quite an effective structure for several years, though it will be necessary to cut the growth regularly;

(d) treated timber or sweet chestnut palings used as piles and backed by brushwood.

Often physical structures are used as a means of

Habitat Management and Creation

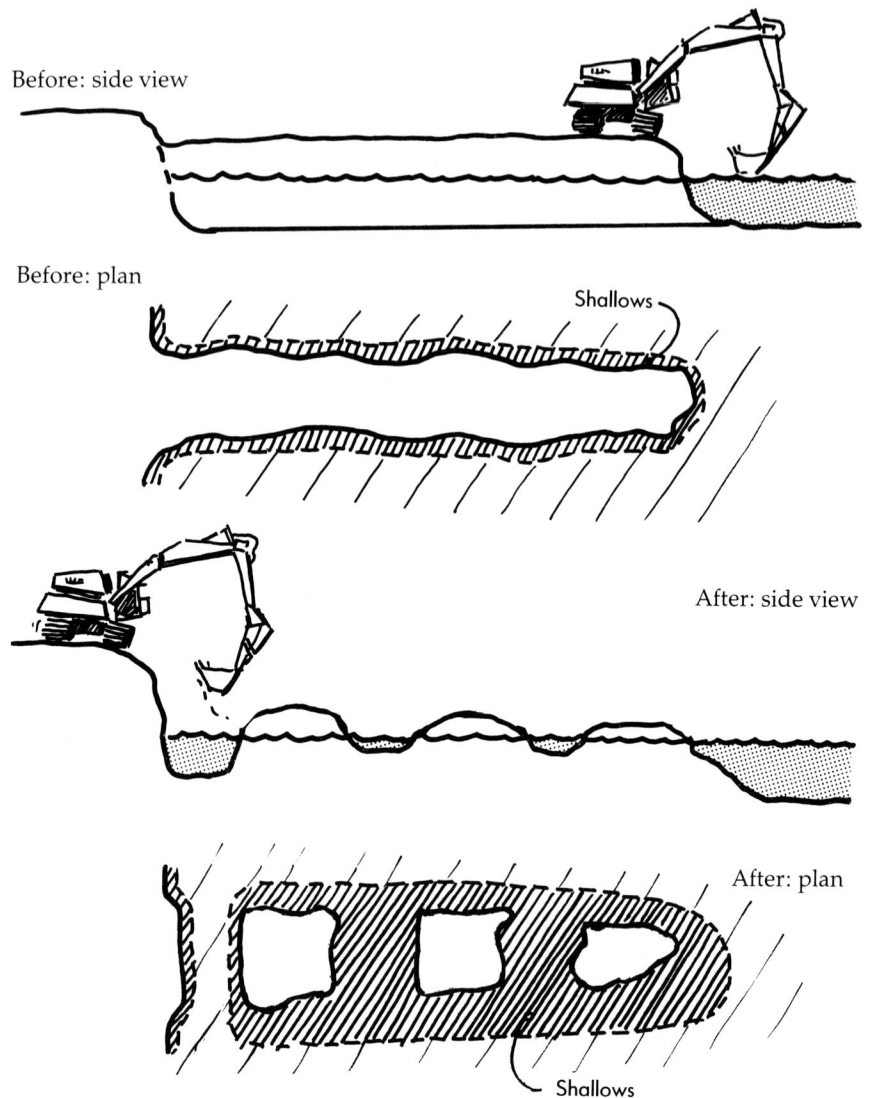

Before: side view

Before: plan

Shallows

After: side view

Fig 3.21 Treatment of spits. In new workings, retention of spits enables access to accurately form islands and shallows after water-level stabilisation. The technique may also be used to improve spits in old workings. Note creation of islands of varying height, surrounding shallows created with material excavated from the spit, and deep water trench to obstruct access from the land.

After: plan

Shallows

temporary protection while marginal vegetation gains a hold. However, as many ducks require direct access to water when breeding, stands of the more vigorous and effective marginal plants, such as reeds, should be allowed to develop only on the windward side.

Trees should not be planted or permitted to grow on islands unless additional wind shelter is required. They will be used as lookout places by predatory birds.

Normally, islands will be profiled before pits are flooded, though fine-scale adjustment may be necessary once final water levels are known.

It is recognised that the volume of material

involved in island construction is considerable. In sheltered locations or where adequate erosion protection can be provided, a steeper underwater profile will greatly reduce costs though with a consequent reduction in the productive feeding shallows. Undisturbed material below the level of wave action can have a steep angle of repose.

Consideration should also be given to constructing islands by the use of inert, clean fill imported onto the site.

On sites which have been worked wet or where it is desired to create islands in workings now flooded, a spit may be constructed by tipping progressively into the lake: this can then be cut into islands by working backwards towards the shore and using the excavated material to increase the area of marginal shallows (see Fig 3.21). Where old workings contain peninsulas, they may be treated similarly.

For nesting wildfowl, a dense vegetation cover is required. Many ducks nest before the new season's growth has begun, so plants which stand over winter and provide good overhead cover in early spring are to be preferred. Dense stands of stems at least 50 cm tall will provide concealment from predatory birds such as crows and magpies. The selected islands should therefore be topsoiled and seeded or allowed to vegetate naturally. Good cover is provided by plants such as willowherb, docks and greater pond sedge.

For nesting by black-headed gull, lapwing and redshank, a lower sward is required and this can be achieved by cutting once or twice in autumn and clearing the litter.

Terns, ringed plover and little ringed plover require islands surfaced by shingle and ideally only a few centimetres above the water. After initial profiling to a low and gently sloping or level form not more than 50 cm above summer water level, the surface should be covered by heavy duty plastic sheeting or old farm fertiliser sacks, ideally to three thicknesses. This is then covered with a depth of at least 10 cm of un-washed aggregate – the natural mix of gravels and sand is usually ideal. The outer edge of the plastic must either end above high water level or be weighted and protected with larger stones or broken concrete.

The purpose of the polythene is to prevent deep-rooting plants becoming established, but periodic autumn weeding or herbicide treatment may also be necessary. Small amounts of annual weed growth are not objectionable as they pro-vide shelter for tern chicks. Where a plastic underlay is not provided, the surface will require annual digging, raking and possibly herbicide treatment. Alternatively, where water levels can be controlled, winter flooding may be effective.

Straw bale islands

In sheltered, shallow areas, groups of straw bales can be anchored by driving in stakes around their perimeter to create small islands. The bales are best soaked in advance until thoroughly water-logged before putting in position. The upper surface of the bales should be roughly level with the water surface. Amongst emergent vegetation or under an overhanging fringe of tree foliage, these will be attractive to grebes, coot and moor-hen as nest sites.

Branch and tree 'islands'

Trees felled into the water, for instance when clearing over-shaded banks, or rough faggots of branches wired together and staked into position, may be used as nest anchorages by grebes and coot, and as roost sites by wildfowl.

Rafts

Where islands cannot be created to the extent desired, for instance due to extreme water depth, cost or lack of overburden, rafts provide an acceptable alternative for breeding and roosting, although they lack the adjoining feeding areas for wildfowl and waders. A compensatory advantage on waters where levels fluctuate widely is that nests on rafts are protected from inundation.

They may be surfaced with vegetation for use by wildfowl, or with shingle for terns. There appears to be no preference for size but larger rafts are more cost-effective and more stable in choppy conditions. In sheltered sites, they may be left out over winter when they will be used by loafing wildfowl but will require a maintenance check in early spring and, on tern islands, the shingle should be cleaned of wildfowl droppings and any vegetation.

Two designs are given, one for terns and one for wildfowl. Many possible variants exist, adapted to material which may be most readily available.

Tern raft design

This raft (Fig 3.22) is a 3 m×3 m platform which will hold up to 10 pairs of common terns. It has raised sides 15 cm high to retain shingle and chicks. A sloping re-entry board is provided so that chicks which do leave the raft can get back again. There are also simple shelters to provide chicks with cover from hot sun. The design has been found satisfactory but variants are possible, depending on available materials for construction and flotation.

General: All timbers tanalised softwood. Assembly time about two man-days.

Main frame: Four 3 m×20 cm×10 cm timbers, bolted together through overlapping corners. One upper timber inset from the ends of the two lower timbers by 15 cm to allow for re-entry ramp.

Deck: Planking 3 m×15 cm×25 mm attached with 75 mm galvanised nails to lower main frame timbers.

(a) Completed raft

Removable protective wire frame bolted at ends to surround all four sides of raft

3·0 m × 230 mm high, externally covered with 25 mm chicken wire

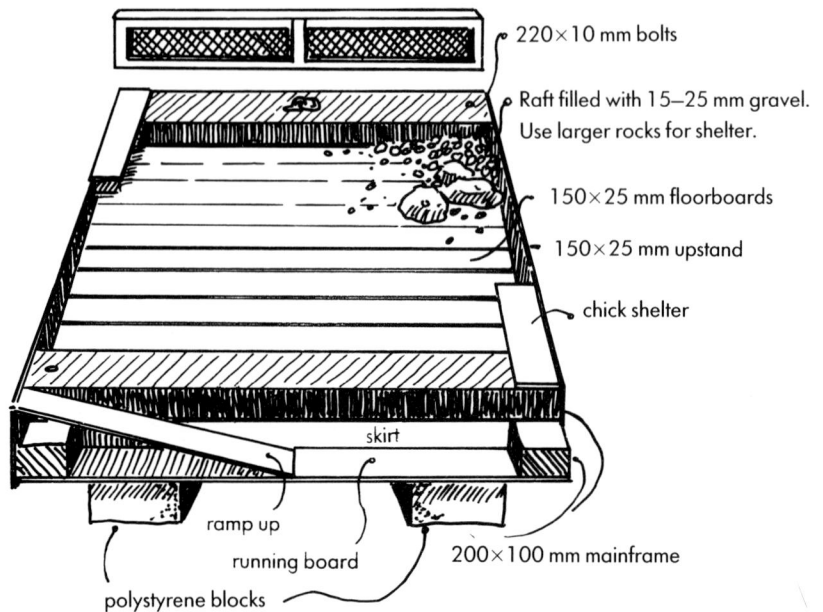

220 × 10 mm bolts

Raft filled with 15–25 mm gravel. Use larger rocks for shelter.

150 × 25 mm floorboards

150 × 25 mm upstand

chick shelter

skirt

200 × 100 mm mainframe

ramp up

running board

polystyrene blocks

(b) Anchorage for raft

760 mm circumference marker buoy

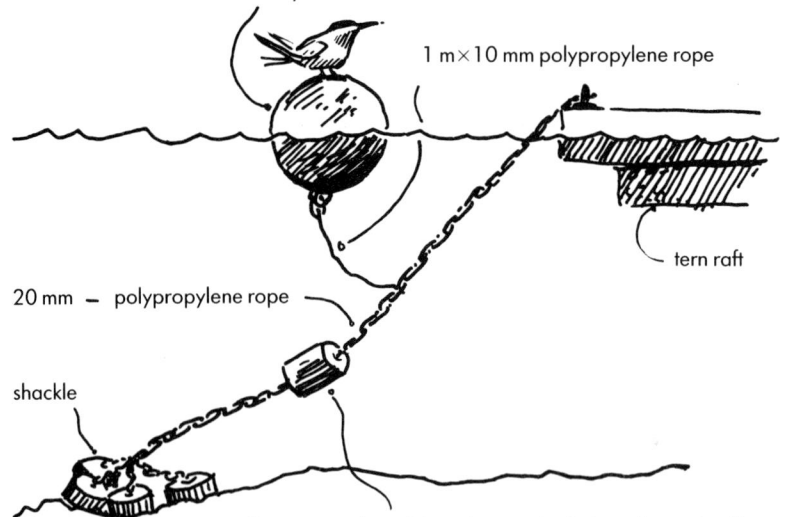

1 m × 10 mm polypropylene rope

tern raft

20 mm — polypropylene rope

shackle

Fig 3.22
Tern nesting raft
(design by K Robert,
RSPB Ryemeads reserve).

If necessary, 'angels' can be attached along the anchor line to damp effects of wave action.

Sub-frame: 3 m × 7·5 cm × 5 cm battens attached flat and parallel to lower main frame members by nailing through planks, the outer two against the inner sides of the main frame members, the inner two each at 45 cm spacing from the outer two.

Main flotation holders: Two 3 m × 10 cm × 5 cm timbers attached on edge against the inner edges of the two inner battens, by nailing through the planking.

Sides: Four 3 m × 15 cm × 25 mm planks; two nailed to the lower main frame timbers with their

154

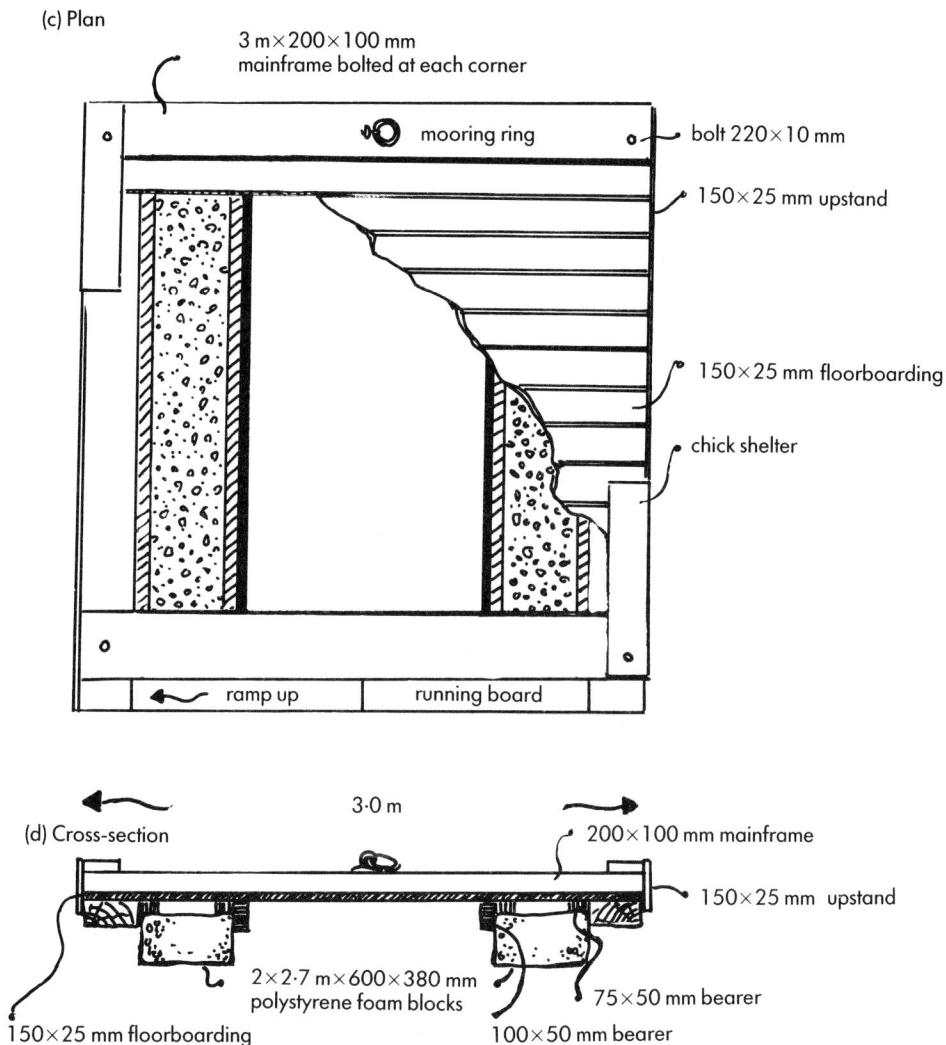

(c) Plan

3 m×200×100 mm
mainframe bolted at each corner

mooring ring

bolt 220×10 mm

150×25 mm upstand

150×25 mm floorboarding

chick shelter

ramp up   running board

(d) Cross-section

3·0 m

200×100 mm mainframe

150×25 mm upstand

2×2·7 m×600×380 mm
polystyrene foam blocks

75×50 mm bearer

150×25 mm floorboarding

100×50 mm bearer

upper edges level with the top of the upper main frame timbers at the corners, thus forming a tray to hold shingle. Two nailed to the ends of the lower main frame timbers and battens with their upper edges level with the deck to hold in the flotation material.

Re-entry system: This enables chicks which fall overboard to regain the raft. It comprises a board 3 m×15 cm×25 mm nailed to the bottom of the two lower main frames at the inset end, with a ramp 1·5 m×15 cm×25 mm sloping up from the middle of this board to the top corner of main frame. The gap behind the ramp should be blocked with planking to prevent chicks getting under the raft.

Security fence: To keep off ducks and geese, four frames 3 m×23 cm of 5×5 cm poles covered with 25 mm chicken wire, bolted around the sides and joined top corners.

Shelters: To protect small chicks from rain, 1 m lengths of plank nailed to the upper edge of the side planks, with one end supported by the main frame timber and the other by a 5×7·5 cm end block. At alternate corners.

Buoyancy: Two blocks of 2·7 m×60 cm×38 cm high density polystyrene foam, optionally painted with Aquaseal 44 bituminous paint to water seal and strengthen them. Located as shown in diagram. For additional security, strips of polypropylene webbing may be passed over the blocks and nailed to the frame but, once in the water, the weight of the raft is sufficient to hold the blocks in place without additional fixings.

Gravel covering: 15–25 mm gravel, plus some rocks, added until the raft floats with the running board at water level.

Mooring: Mooring ring bolted through upper mainframe timber at end opposite to re-entry ramp. Connected to chain or 20 mm polypropylene rope (which will not rot but can chafe or snap) with hard-eyes and shackles each end. A marker buoy should be attached to the raft end of the chain or rope so that the raft can be detached for maintenance.

Anchor: Set four or more buckets, or similar-sized disused drums with concrete, each with an eye bolt set at the centre. These weights will be practicable to transport. They should be connected in pairs by shackles to 30 cm lengths of chain and the chains crossed to provide a single point for shackle connection to the mooring line.

Transport: The raft is a wide load and if transported flat by road the police will require 48 hours' notice.

Waterfowl raft design

The aim here is to create a frame which will hold growing plants with their roots in water. This design (Fig 3.23) is very robust but many alternatives exist.

Main frame: Two telegraph poles held apart by three planks 1·2 m×23 cm×25 mm attached by 75 mm coach screws (two at each plank end), three planks above and three below (see figure).

Flotation: Three polystyrene blocks 75×30× 23 cm, slipped between the pairs of spacing planks and retained by galvanised wire.

Vegetation trays: 1·2 m width of 25 mm chicken wire, stapled to upper surface at sides and ends with sufficient slack to form a shallow tray.

Vegetation: Clumps of vegetation with root systems placed in the galvanised wire tray. Suitable plants include iris, rushes, reedmace, reed sweetgrass and other marginals.

Sand martin banks

Sand martins nest colonially, usually in the sheer faces which develop naturally on river meanders or are created in the course of sand and gravel winning. Sites are abandoned once the face slumps, becomes overgrown with vegetation or accessible to predators such as weasels.

Safe and long-lasting artificial sites can be created by bedding 1 m lengths of 10 cm polythene pipe into a bank constructed from sand and gravel. A sheer front face can be created with a weak or dry mix of concrete built-up against shuttering, which should then be removed. The face should drop into fairly deep water both to prevent colonisation by tall, emergent vegetation which would obstruct the birds' flight paths and also to restrict access by predators and humans. The lowest row of pipes should be 1 m above summer water level, sloping slightly down towards the entrance, with rows 0·3 m apart and pipes at 0·2 m spacings.

Each pipe should be filled with sand and the entrance half-blocked with a cement filler. The birds will then excavate their typical oval tunnel along the top half of each pipe. Ideally, pipes should be scraped out and recharged each winter.

Nestboxes for woodland birds and birds of prey

In most woodlands about a third of the breeding birds nest in holes, gaining both protection from the elements and concealment from most predators. Historically, in the wildwood, such potential nest sites would have been abundant, provided by the large numbers of older trees. In many modern woods, particularly plantations, this element is either missing or considerably depleted. As a consequence, nest holes are often at a premium and the provision of nestboxes is most valuable.

Boxes may be purchased or made. Wood is by far the best material as it is a good insulator against heat and cold, does not produce condensation and can blend with the site. Any type will do; softwood is easier to work but hardwood lasts longer. Solid boards less than 15 mm thick

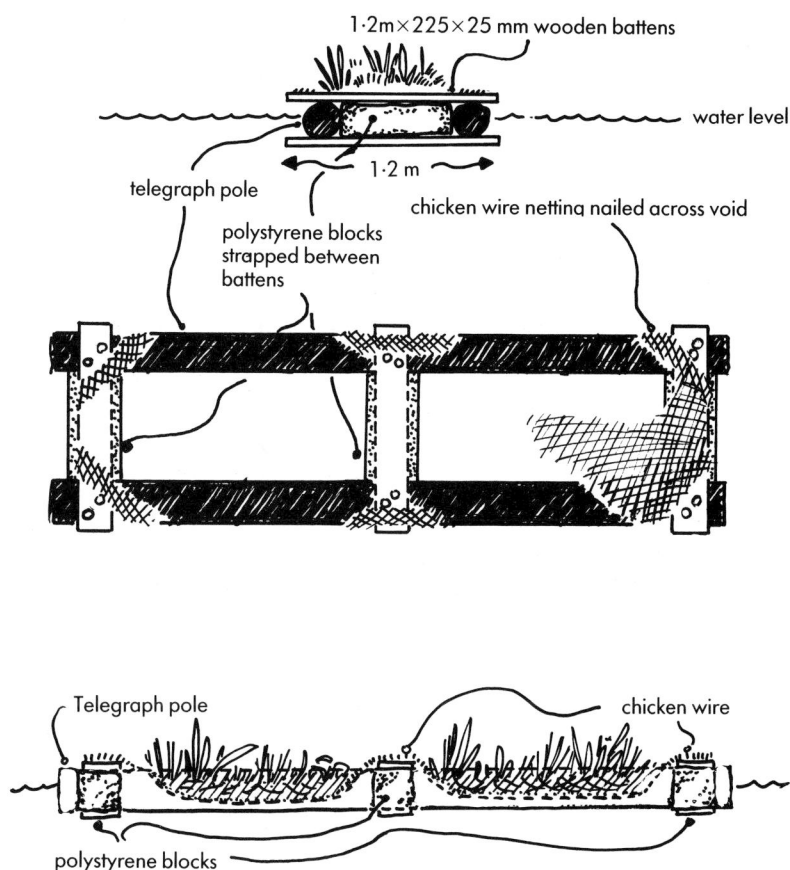

Fig 3.23 Waterfowl nesting raft.

are liable to warp but exterior grade ply of 6 mm or over should last reasonably well without warping. Dimensions are rarely critical (though minimum internal sizes should not be much less than those stated for individual boxes) and it is often easier to make the box fit the wood rather than vice versa. When assembling the box, galvanised nails last longer than wire ones. A good catch to fasten the lid securely is essential. Wood preservatives will help prolong the life of boxes (particularly if built of softwood) but should not be used inside the box because of their toxicity.

Boxes may be attached with a batten on the back of the box and nailed, screwed or tied in place. Nails and screws should not be used if the timber has any commercial value. Nylon, copper, aluminium or hardwood pegs can be obtained and will not damage a saw blade. It is sometimes possible with larger boxes to wedge them in a forked branch.

In sheltered sites, such as within a woodland, the direction a box faces makes little difference; the angle of the trunk, and keeping the box clear of the route water naturally takes down the tree are

more important. In more open sites, the box should face away from the prevailing wind and direct sunlight. A position between north and south-east is usually appropriate. Angle smaller boxes slightly forward to provide additional shelter for the entrance hole. In woods frequented by people the boxes may need to be put out of reach or at least placed where they are not seen from paths. The heights appropriate to different species are given below for the different boxes.

The tree species on which a box is mounted does not appear to affect the chance of its occupation, but good results are often obtained from trees on the edge of woods or along rides, or a single outstanding tree such as an oak in a conifer plantation. For most species, boxes should be located to allow a convenient open flight-line to the entrance. Perches near the box or attached to the box front are undesirable.

The density at which boxes should be erected will vary from habitat to habitat. About 10 assorted small boxes per hectare is a useful starting density. They should be well spaced. Additional boxes can be added at a later stage if

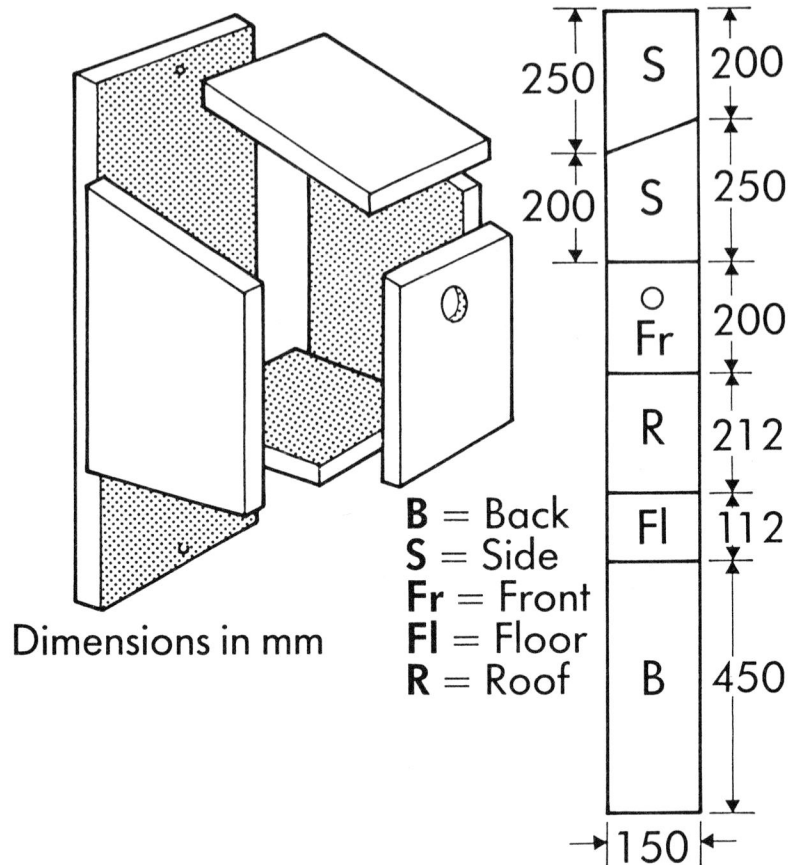

Dimensions in mm

B = Back
S = Side
Fr = Front
Fl = Floor
R = Roof

250	S 200
200	S 250
	Fr (O) 200
	R 212
	Fl 112
	B 450
	150

Fig 3.24a Nestbox designs.
Design 1: Standard tit box.

felt necessary. Larger boxes are obviously required in smaller numbers; there is likely to be only one pair of tawny owls or kestrels in a small wood, but it is worth giving the birds a choice of nest sites to increase the chances of successful uptake of a box. Large boxes can be particularly visible and should be sited with care, so as not to attract the attention of egg thieves.

When setting up a woodland nestbox scheme, the proportion of different boxes should be 50% standard type (Design 1) 25 mm hole, 25% standard type (Design 1) 28 mm hole, 10% standard type (Design 1) 32 mm hole, 10% mix of other box types (Designs 2 and 3) plus a few owl and kestrel boxes.

The following designs (Fig 3.24) are for boxes applicable to a wide range of situations. They are suitable for any woodland and will encourage a number of different species.

Design 1: tits, nuthatch and tree sparrow
This is the archetypal nestbox design with the small, round entrance hole on the front. It is best made from a plank about 150 mm wide and 15 mm thick. The diagram shows the sizes of individual sections of the box and how they fit together. The inside dimensions of the floor of the box should be at least 100 mm square. The bottom of the entrance hole should be at least 125 mm from the floor. The size of the entrance hole will affect the species able to use the box; 25 mm diameter will encourage blue, coal, marsh and willow tits, 28 mm diameter will allow in slightly larger birds such as great tits and 32 mm diameter will allow in nuthatch and tree sparrow. The height at which the box is fixed will also affect the species likely to use it. For blue and great tits, boxes should be placed at 2–5 m. For coal, marsh and willow tits, they should be placed low (1 m) and for nuthatch, rather higher (4–5 m). Willow tits prefer to excavate their own hole so the box needs to be filled with wood shavings. The lid should be hinged with a strip of leather, rubber or plastic and fastened securely.

Dimensions in mm

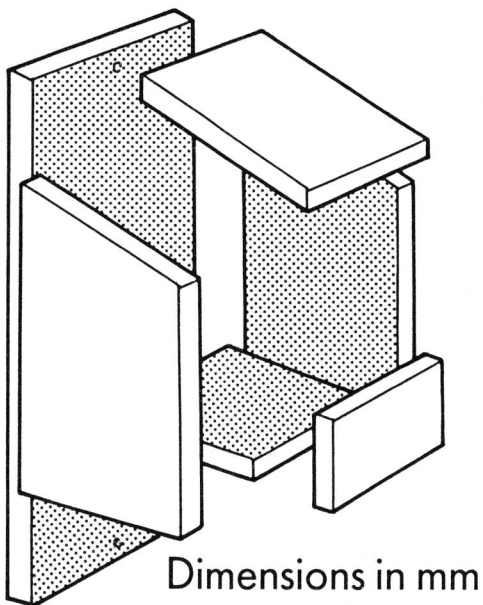

B = Back
S = Side
Fr = Front
Fl = Floor
R = Roof

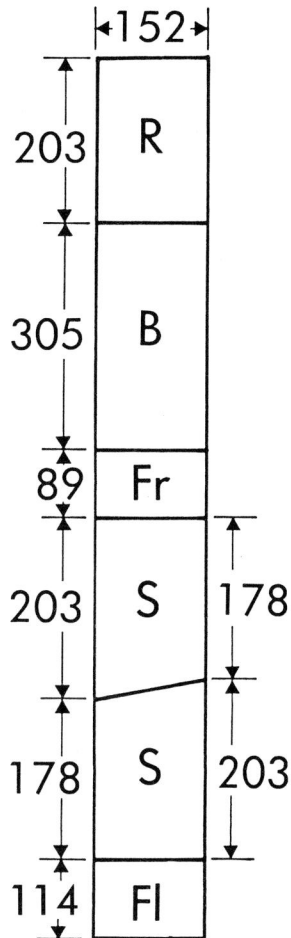

←152→

203 | R
305 | B
89 | Fr
203 | S | 178
178 | S | 203
114 | Fl

Fig 3.24b Design 2: Small open-fronted box.

Design 2: robin, pied wagtail and spotted flycatcher

This box will attract species such as spotted flycatcher, robin and pied wagtail, depending on its location. Robins prefer boxes placed low (1–2 m) in concealed positions amongst vegetation. Spotted flycatchers and pied wagtails will use the box in more open situations at heights of 2–5 m.

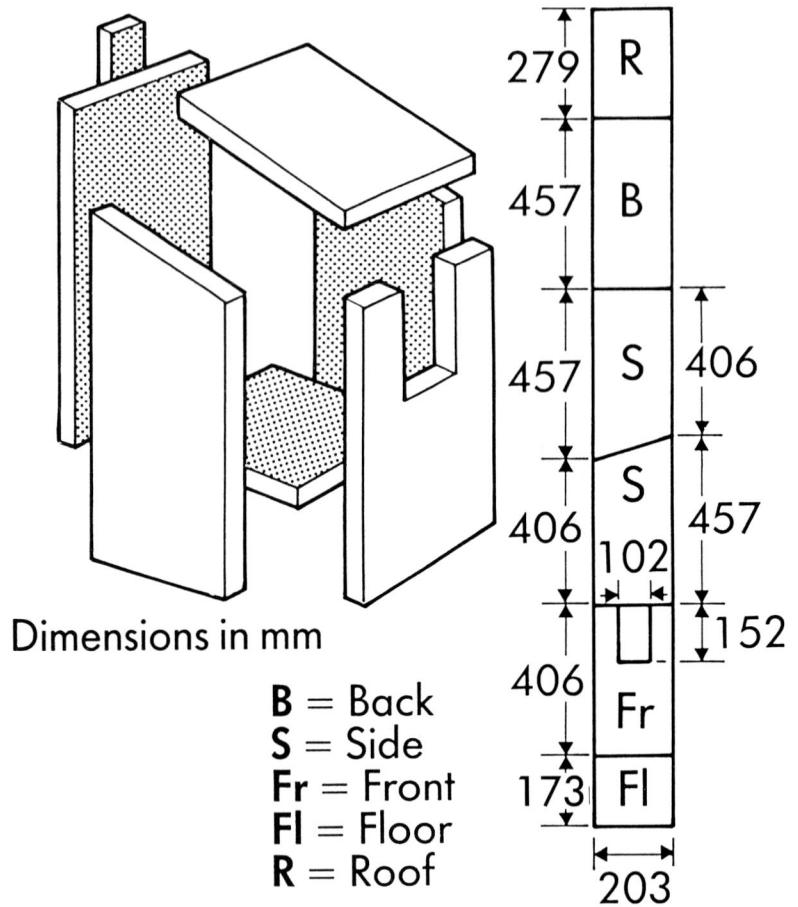

Dimensions in mm

B = Back
S = Side
Fr = Front
Fl = Floor
R = Roof

*Fig 3.24c Design 3: Large
open-fronted box.*

Design 3: jackdaw, stock dove and woodpeckers
An open-fronted box designed for jackdaw and
stock dove. It may also be used by great spotted
woodpeckers, great tits and starlings. The main
material is a plank approximately 2·1 m×20 cm×
19 mm.

An alternative design specifically for great
spotted woodpeckers makes the box rather
deeper, about 400 mm, and replaces the open
front with a hole entrance about 50 mm diameter.
Woodpeckers prefer to excavate their own nest
hole, so the box should be almost filled with a
block of soft inert material (expanded polystyrene
and balsa wood have both been used successfully)
leaving only a small entrance space. The box
should be located high on a tree in an area free
from any disturbance. For the great spotted
woodpecker, the box should be filled and sited
high but on the underside of a branch away from
the main trunk. For lesser spotted woodpeckers,
the box should be approximately the size of that
in Design 2, with an entrance hole of about

32 mm: they will accept wood chips as a box
filling. The box should be at least 2 m from the
ground and may be fixed to a sloping side branch.
Green woodpeckers require a large, filled box,
internal dimensions 450×180×180 mm with a
60 mm diameter entrance hole, sited high on a tree
trunk.

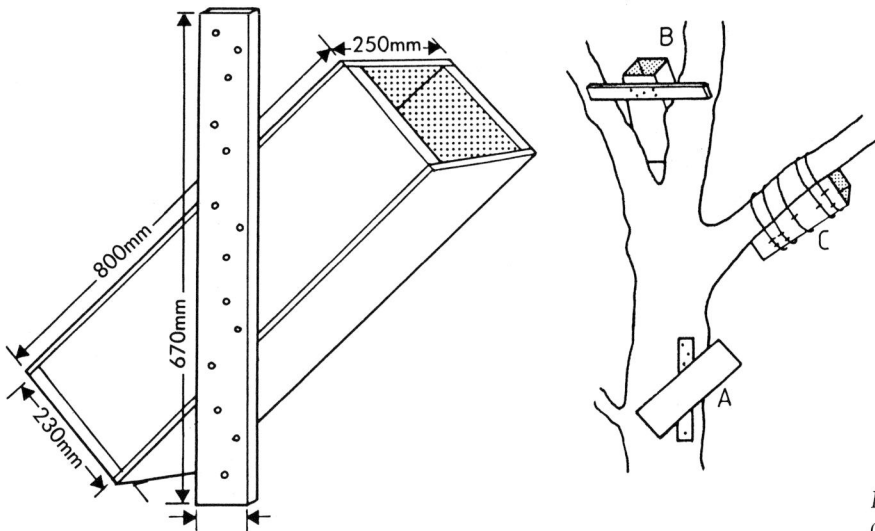

Fig 3.24d Design 4: Tawny owl box.

Design 4: tawny owl

This 'chimney-style' box is designed to mimic the hollow end of a broken branch, a site frequently used by tawny owls. The cavities they choose are usually deep, dark and often surprisingly narrow. Though primarily woodland birds, tawny owls are also found on farmland where nest sites are available. A box placed near the edge of a spinney or covert stands a good chance of being used. Where a known nest site is being felled, a box in its vicinity may help to maintain the owls in an area.

The minimum dimension of the box should be 80×23×23 cm. Using 19 mm timber, the sizes of the individual pieces should be shown in the diagram, though it is possible to use 9 mm exterior ply (WBP) for the larger sides. The batten should be produced from at least 25 mm timber.

About a dozen 5 mm drainage holes should be drilled in the base of the box and a layer of soft material (wood chips, straw, leaf mould etc) spread on the floor. Sawdust is unsuitable as it tends to clog the drainage holes.

The box should be fixed as high on the tree as possible, at an angle of 45°. There are three main methods of attachment. Either (a) wire it to the underside of a branch at the correct angle; (b) fasten it to the trunk via a wooden batten, fixed at 45°; (c) wedge the box into a forked branch using a horizontal batten. It may be possible to manage the last method without nails, but if the box has a tendency to slip, nail one end of the batten only in case of uneven growth of the fork. Where the site is exposed, the entrance should face roughly east. Within a wood, the direction is not critical.

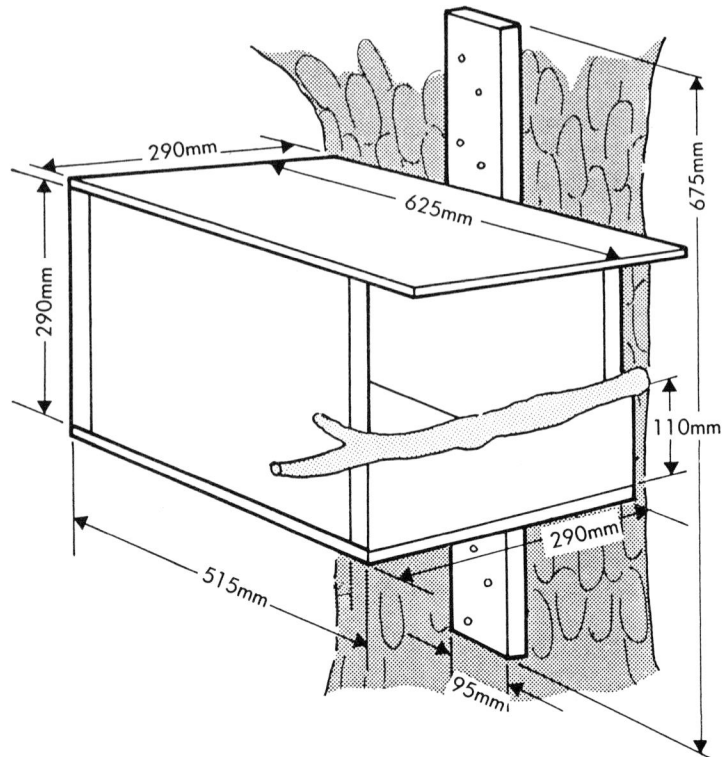

Fig 3.24e Design 5: Kestrel box.

Design 5: kestrel

Kestrels are remarkably catholic in their choice of nest sites, which range from ledges on cliffs or buildings to cavities in trees or the old nests of crows and magpies. This particular design of box reflects the type of cavity they choose; usually large and open with a side entrance. A feature of the design is the perch positioned across the front of the box which allows both adults and young to sit alongside the nest. Kestrels have traditional nest sites, so it may be some time before a box is used. However, other species may make use of this design, for instance tawny owls and stock doves.

The box can be put high on a tree (at least 6 m), nailed (via a batten), wired on or jammed into a fork. It should face away from the prevailing winds and should be sufficiently open to allow free flight to the box and good all-round visibility from the entrance. It may be necessary to prune some branches to allow this. Prominent or isolated trees in undisturbed areas are a good choice.

About a dozen 5 mm drainage holes should be drilled in the floor and a layer of wood chips or straw spread over it. The perch should be a branch about 25 mm diameter nailed across the front.

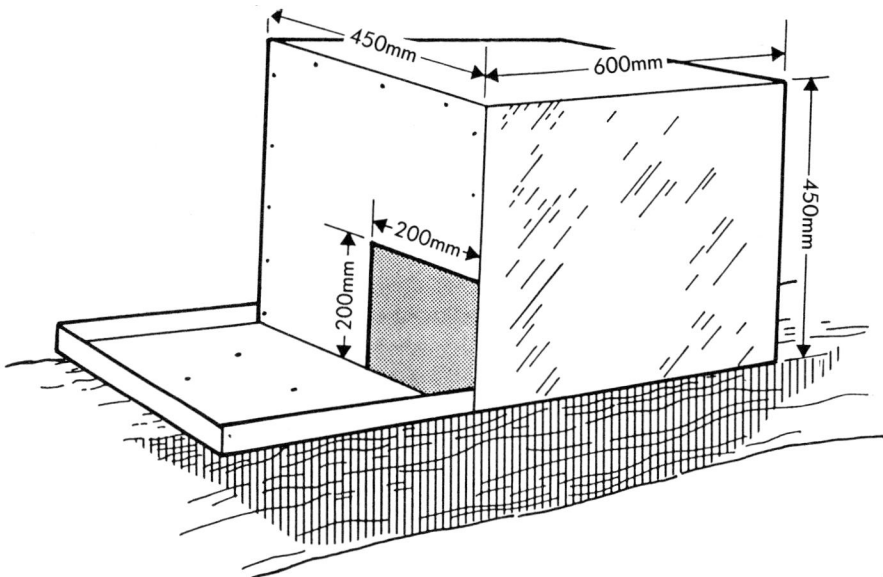

Fig 3.24f Design 6: Barn owl.

Design 6: barn owl

Barn owls readily take to boxes, though they may be used only for roosting for the first year or two. Obviously barns where the owls or their pellets have been seen are good potential sites for box installation. The building should be quiet and undisturbed with permanent access (a hole in the wall or roof is better than an open window or door). Buildings too close to roads are unsuitable as the owls' hunting behaviour makes them susceptible to collisions with vehicles.

Cavities in large oak and elm trees also provide alternative nest sites for barn owls, though Dutch elm disease has depleted potential sites severely. It is possible to site boxes in trees, or erect them on stout poles.

For external use they should be built of similar material to that recommended for kestrel boxes, but under cover an old tea chest or packing case makes an ideal box.

The minimum size should be 45×45×60 cm long, but the bigger the better. The hole entrance (at least 23 cm square) can be at the bottom or half way up one end. A lipped tray about 45×30 cm should be added to the entrance end to provide a safe exercise area for the young owls. The box should be attached by battens or wire in a suitable tree crotch or nailed firmly to a beam or bracketed to a wall, preferably in a dark corner away from the main entrance. No lining material is needed in the box as a thick layer of pellets will accumulate before the eggs are laid. Barn owls have a long breeding cycle, up to 12 weeks, starting at any time between March and September. They are shy birds and should not be disturbed. As they are protected under Schedule 1 of the Wildlife and Countryside Act, it is an offence intentionally to disturb these birds at the nest.

References

Burgess, ND, and Becker, D, 1983, *The Creation and Management of Islands and Rafts on RSPB Reserves.* RSPB, Sandy.
Street, M, 1984, *The Restoration of Gravel Pits for Wildfowl.* Game Conservancy, Fordingbridge.

IMPROVEMENT OF OLD GRAVEL PIT LAKES

There are many older, wet sites from which sand and gravel have been extracted which were either just abandoned or simply left 'neat and tidy'. There was little or no restoration or planting. However, over time, natural colonisation by a variety of trees, shrubs and herbaceous plants has taken place, the aquatic community has developed and some such sites are now of high conservation value. Others would benefit from management to develop their potential or to restore value lost as a result of plant succession.

These older pits were generally either:
(a) rectangular or of simple outline, bounded by straight or gently curving margins; extraction commonly proceeded close against the site boundary and marginal land areas are consequently narrow (10 m or so would be typical);

Banks and lake margins fall away steeply to fairly deep water (3–6 m or more water depth is normal), the lake floor is fairly level and there are few or no islands or peninsulas. Marginal areas support taller trees which may heavily shake lake margins so that growth of aquatic plants is prevented;
(b) the result of 'over the shoulder' working, having highly indentate margins when considered at the coarser (100 m) scale but rather linear margins when considered at the scale of a few metres or so, site margins often narrow, and lake margins steep, preventing development of emergent vegetation; many peninsulas, all accessible to human disturbance and ground predators; tree growth can be densely developed, shading out shrubs, herbaceous plants and aquatic plants.

Both types can be improved in broadly similar ways:

Problem	Solution
1. Steep margins; abrupt land-water interface.	Import clean fill to create shallows. Regrade margins by cutting back where land area permits, dumping spoil into lake.
2. Linear margins; minimum shoreline length.	Make indentations especially along sheltered shorelines, using spoil to make promontories or shallows.
3. Lack of shallow water areas.	Regrade margins. Where spits exist, regrade most to slope from 30 cm below average water level all round, to a top height of 20 cm above it; cut landward trench so that spit is protected from access.
4. No islands.	Where spits exist, cut off at landward end (trench >5 m wide and 1 m deep). Install nesting rafts.
5. Lack of aquatic plants due to shading by trees.	Selectively fell especially on south and east sides but maintain those providing shelter from prevailing winds.
6. Minimal waterfowl nesting habitat; lack of breeding success.	Create islands or rafts. Coppice trees and shrubs: stack cut material in rows to provide cover. Fell trees into water and leave. Clear shading trees to aid marginal plant growth: introduce marginal vegetation. Do not cut tall herbage, brambles, etc. Create sunlit shallows and shoals to aid plant growth and boost chironomid numbers.
7. Lack of marsh, pond or terrestrial habitats.	Clear and reprofile silt lagoon or other areas within site.

(See photograph 23)

ACCESS AND VISITOR MANAGEMENT

Summary

1. Different human activities disturb wildlife to different degrees. Some species are more susceptible than others. The impact of the disturbance can be significant, notably by causing breeding failure or preventing use by moulting, migrant and wintering waterfowl.

2. Disturbance is most severe on small sites with little vegetation cover and all-round access. A single visitor on the banks can cause waterfowl to leave such sites.

3. From the outset of restoration planning, the aims of conservation and visitor use should be integrated and modified if necessary. Where active recreational use is planned, restoration for wildlife should not be a primary aim except on lakes larger than 10 ha which may be capable of accommodating both objectives.

4. Sites to be developed for wildlife should be free of external causes of disturbance, capable of isolation from uncontrolled access (eg public footpaths) and suitable for use by birdwatchers and other naturalists.

5. Boundaries should be proof against livestock and casual trespass: well-maintained thorn hedges are good but a 3 m wide ditch may be necessary in some situations.

6. Successful visitor control is achieved by meeting the need to see all habitat types and all major waterfowl concentrations through correct siting and screening of the path network and viewing facilities.

7. The path network should provide extensive, attractive and varied walks with disturbance minimised by location and screening. Discreet fencing, boardwalks and the siting of ditches and marshes may be used to channel visitors unobtrusively.

8. Hides should have different orientation to cope with varied light conditions. Tower hides are valuable as they can be set well back from sensitive areas and provide excellent views into a site. Cars make good mobile hides where there is a suitable road network.

9. Income from conservation sites, including visitor permit charges, does not meet the full costs of acquisition and management. Sites must be restored to high standards if conservation bodies are to be attracted to accept long-term responsibility for them.

General

Where nature conservation is the main goal of restoration, visitor-use will need to be constrained, but with good planning a substantial level of access and enjoyment of the wildlife will be possible. Where public use is the main objective, it will limit the range of species which will co-exist with it but even where, for example, active water-based recreation is the goal, there will be some conservation potential. Thus, grasslands can contain wildflowers and tree or shrub planting can be of native species. In larger sites, it should be possible to cater for both the leisure and amenity needs of people and the seclusion and low-disturbance needs of wildlife. However, significant extra resources should not be used to tinker with areas which, through disturbance, will have limited potential. It is better to concentrate money and materials such as over-burden in the priority wildlife areas.

Visitor-use should be considered from the outset. Unless the site is very remote or in the rare event of a full-time warden being appointed, there will be unmanaged visiting. It is necessary to anticipate this and design for it, particularly by creating plantings and structures which will channel visitors away from vulnerable areas. Factors to be assessed are:

(a) the species for which management is a priority, and their susceptibility to disturbance;

(b) the required habitats and their appropriate location;

(c) the relative disturbance or damaging effects of different human activities;

(d) methods of channelling visitor access;

(e) provision of wildlife viewing facilities;

(f) operational safety considerations in sites where extraction is still in progress and subsequent visitor safety.

Disturbance

In general, different kinds of birds and mammals are variously susceptible to disturbance and different human activities disturb them to varying degrees.

Most woodland birds are little affected by human activity confined to paths as the wood itself provides very efficient visual and noise

165

Habitat Management and Creation

screening. However, some birds of prey in particular are easily disturbed and unlikely to breed in woodland with regular public access. As with waterbodies, small sites such as stands of scrub or hedges are more vulnerable than larger ones. Open-ground birds such as partridge, lapwing and other waders are very vulnerable to disturbance. Adapted to use habitats which provide little cover, their reaction is to move off the site entirely.

A few species of waterfowl accept high levels of disturbance. Under some circumstances, mallard, mute swan, Canada and greylag geese in particular will habituate to humans and become quite tame. This is particularly true of local resident populations. However, mallard arriving as winter migrants from continental Europe, for instance, may be very wary and simply not settle at a site where there is any disturbance.

Most waterfowl species tolerate little disturbance, being most at ease where they can neither see nor hear human activity. Distant noise or visible activity makes them more alert and accordingly reduces their time spent resting or feeding. As the source of disturbance becomes closer or louder, birds will cease all activity to concentrate their attention on it. They will next move to what they regard as a safe distance. Depending on the perceived threat, the wariness of the species concerned, and the nature and size of the site, this may simply mean swimming round the back of a promontory or island or hiding in the cover of marginal vegetation. On larger waterbodies, birds may swim or fly to the undisturbed side; where there is a complex of waterbodies, they may fly from one to another; where no nearby refuge area exists, birds may be forced to move long distances. Once displaced from a pit, bird numbers may not build up again for several days. Where disturbance is repeated, bird numbers may be permanently depressed as a consequence.

Disturbance is therefore at its most severe on small sites with little or no cover, all-round access and no alternative safe areas close by. It has least effect on larger sites, those with substantial cover, and those where birds can withdraw to other nearby waterbodies, returning when conditions are suitable.

Different human activities disturb birds to different degrees. Their reactions are not far different from ours. Low levels of noise are less worrying than loud, and especially sudden, noises. People they can see and hear are more worrying than people they can hear but not see. Small numbers of boats on a water are less

disturbing than a large number. Slow-moving boats are less disturbing than fast ones, so motor-boats cause more disturbance than sailing dinghies. Dogs are less disturbing than people. People in vehicles are less disturbing than people on foot. Thus birdwatchers in cars cause less disturbance than birdwatchers on foot. Nearby vehicle traffic is ignored. A stationary fisherman is probably less disturbing than a moving bird-watcher.

On small, open sites occasional but repeated disturbance, for instance by dog-walkers, may prevent all but the most tolerant species from using the water. On large waterbodies, notably reservoirs, it may be possible to zone activities so that a sufficient area remains undisturbed for birds simply to withdraw into it, spreading out again once disturbance ceases. Most gravel-pit lakes are too small to permit such zoning and retain good bird numbers. Therefore, if the aim is to attract large numbers of waterfowl, particularly the scarcer species, a pit should be set aside for this purpose.

There is ample evidence that disturbance in the breeding season either prevents birds from settling to nest, causes them to desert eggs or increases the risk of predation, for instance, when a duckling brood is disturbed and scattered. Dogs as well as humans can be a source of disturbance and will readily eat eggs and young birds.

Outside the breeding season and in reasonable weather conditions, disturbance at one particular site may have no effect on overall bird numbers in a county or nationally. However, it is obviously the case that if all sites were heavily disturbed there would be an effect on bird numbers both locally and nationally. In fact, a large number of waterbodies in lowland Britain are disturbed, many of them to an extent that they are virtually uninhabitable by birds. Thus the creation of new sanctuary sites does have real conservation value.

In conclusion, disturbance is an under-rated problem. Birds have remarkably keen senses of hearing and sight and many, particularly waterfowl, waders and birds of grassland, may leave a small site or one lacking cover in response to a single human visit, possibly not returning for hours or even days. A regular low level of human use may therefore sterilise a site. Birdwatchers themselves are a significant cause of disturbance, even where hides are provided, unless approaches are adequately screened.

Physical damage to habitats

Uncontrolled access causes major modification to wildlife habitats through the trampling and destruction of vegetation. Thus a heavily trampled wildflower sward is likely to lose most of its interesting plants and revert to those grasses and common lawn weeds which are resistant to trampling: where bank fishing is permitted, tree branches, marginal vegetation and beds of aquatic weeds will be intentionally cleared.

These and other effects should be minimised by site design, management and other measures. For instance, good path siting can virtually eliminate undesired habitat damage. Even in grassland, people will tend to keep to short mown tracks. On any site where formal leisure activity takes place, including sailing, fishing and birdwatching, lease provisions can include habitat safeguards and matters such as litter control.

Site selection

In addition to the appropriate physical habitat creation and management, sites in which conservation management will be the priority aim should be:
(a) remote from obvious significant causes of disturbance, notably visible pedestrian movement especially on sky lines, and intermittent high levels of noise such as clay pigeon ranges;
(b) capable of isolation from most uncontrolled access, although the ideal is unattainable!
(c) capable of providing controlled and adequate access for birdwatchers and others without causing disturbance.
Note that planning authorities normally expect existing public footpaths and bridleways to be reinstated in or close to their original locations. Significant relocation will need serious justification. As one has little control over use and abuse of public rights of access, their presence may be very influential in determining the goals and form of restoration.

Boundary management and entry points

Boundaries of sites restored for wildlife conservation should be made secure against uncontrolled access or misuse. Those shared with farmland used by livestock must be stockproof as cattle, sheep and horses can be very destructive of young trees, scrub and marginal vegetation. Initially, post and wire fences may be necessary but a well-managed hedge, primarily of hawthorn or black-

thorn, is much more resistant to human access than any fence. It will also visually screen the site, offer some degree of wind protection and be of positive wildlife value. Where a large amount of uncontrolled access is anticipated, a water-filled ditch at least 3 m wide may be constructed and the spoil used to create a screening bank on the inner side. Suitably planted, both ditch and bank will have wildlife value and be visually attractive.

Ideally, the entry point to a wildlife area should be as close as possible to viewing facilities so as to minimise intrusion and disturbance. In order to give good views over water, hides should be placed with the light behind them – ie on the southern rather than the northern perimeter. If access from the highway will be remote from the main viewing area, it may be better to bring people through the site in vehicles rather than on foot. In general, cars are a much less significant cause of disturbance than pedestrians and, indeed, make quite satisfactory viewing hides. If such an access road passes areas where people will wish to look at birds, then provide suitable laybys and signs – 'This layby is for birdwatching only. Please stay in the car to avoid disturbance to waterfowl'. Tree planting and subsequent vegetation management would need to take account of sight lines for viewing. Wildlife viewing from vehicles has been successfully developed in the USA and is informally practised on many UK gravel pits. It certainly has potential for development, given the good road networks which often exist on sites: disabled and elderly people, particularly, will benefit.

Site facilities – car parking, toilets, picnic areas and interpretative material – should ideally be located together and screened for noise and visual disturbance. At the facility point provide a map showing clearly the location of hides and the distances involved, and indicate conditions of use. These cover what constitutes sensible behaviour in a reserve. Some visitors may not realise that loud music, fires and free-running dogs are inappropriate but 'sign psychology' suggests that it is better to list what people should do rather than what they shouldn't; for example 'This is a nature reserve. Much of the wildlife is wary. Please leave your dog in the car, keep to the paths and talk quietly'. Conditions are more likely to be accepted if they seem reasonable. Thus, 'Please keep out of this area to avoid disturbing nesting birds' is quite convincing in spring but implausible in mid winter.

Overall, a site should contain as few signs as possible. A surfeit of admonitory material is a sure way of getting it ignored!

Habitat Management and Creation

Paths

The management of visitors within the site is accomplished by the routing of paths, by screening and by viewing facilities. A good path network will provide access to points from which the major concentrations of birds can be seen, enable visitors to sample all the wildlife habitats, cause minimal disturbance to shy species and be intrinsically pleasing to walk. Thus the location of paths, viewing facilities and the whole experience must be considered together.

The siting of paths will depend greatly on how much dry land exists between the boundary and the water's edge. Paths around a narrow site periphery, although well screened from the wildlife areas on one side, can have open views out to the adjacent countryside beyond a low boundary hedge or fence. If the excavation extends close to the boundary, then in the worst case no access may be possible. If a reasonably wide area of marginal land is available, a meandering path may be installed which at some places approaches the shore and provides a good viewpoint but at others is more distant, leaving a stretch of undisturbed shoreline and associated terrestrial habitat.

On larger sites, alternative footpath routes should be constructed, some shorter, some longer and more demanding. Where possible, circular routes should be developed but avoid creating paths all round a lake margin and thus potentially causing all-round disturbance. With ingenious planting and variations in level, a long and enjoyable walk can be accommodated in a small area. The path and its immediate surround should be as varied as possible and should make the site seem bigger than it really is, the overall aim being to provide interesting access for visitors with good viewing of as much of the site as is consistent with the wildlife objectives.

Paths should be reasonably level, wide and well drained. Even in late summer, when vegetation is at its most luxuriant, one should still have easy access. Bear in mind the need for access also by management machinery. Some paths may need to accommodate tractors, trailers or mowing machinery. If paths are fenced, the fences should lie back and be hidden by herbage or shrubs. The aim is to avoid people realising that they are being excluded from places, as they may then deliberately trespass or at least feel shut in and lose the pleasurable illusion of being in a wild and natural place.

In certain areas, wooden boardwalks may be considered. Although these are relatively expensive to install and maintain they are much more fun than paths, providing visitors with a very enjoyable experience in crossing, for example, flooded marsh, reedbed or other shallow-water areas, and permitting a closer contact than is normally available with these interesting habitats.

There are several techniques for keeping people on paths in sensitive areas. First and foremost is the provision of adequate viewing facilities, so that there is no need to trespass. Where necessary, water-filled ditches or strips of marsh no more than 1 m wide will keep most people on a path without them realising they are being deliberately constrained. Thickets or hedges of thorny shrubs – hawthorn, blackthorn, bramble, dog rose or gorse – are excellent wildlife habitat, delightful when in flower and virtually impenetrable.

It may be necessary to restrict access in certain seasons in order to prevent disturbance to areas important for nesting birds, duckling broods, passage waders or winter wildfowl, for instance. Practical management aspects of the site must be capable of responding to these changing priorities, with paths and hides located to provide adequate alternative facilities when particular areas are zoned off.

As an invariable rule, the very shallow water areas used intensively by ducklings, waders and other waterbirds should be effectively inaccessible to the general public, though always capable of being viewed from hides.

Screens

For visual screening, broad bands of shrubs or trees will be effective, bearing in mind that an evergreen component or fringe may be necessary to give adequate winter cover. In addition, even the densest scrub eventually grows up and becomes open towards the base so that periodic cutting back is necessary; a wide planting can be cut on rotation in strips parallel to the path so that some cover is always present.

Earth embankments are excellent both for noise and visual screening provided that people cannot obtain access to them. They are tempting viewing points which maximise disturbance by putting the viewer on the skyline. They should therefore be sited behind broad ditches or covered by thorn scrub.

Depending on their distance from areas likely to be used by waterfowl, open viewpoints may need a measure of screening. Simple screens can be created with wattle hurdles, fence panels, straw bales or reed sandwiched between wire-netting and held in a wooden frame. A more pleasing, natural screen is provided by chest-high shrubs, bearing in mind that the main waterbird interest may be during the winter months when much vegetation will have died down. Use of evergreens such as holly or gorse is therefore advisable. Conifers such as Leyland Cypress will give quick results but require frequent trimming. Viewpoints should never place people against a skyline from the birds' point of view. It is important therefore that they are also screened at the back by vegetation at least 2 m high.

Hides

Hides should be sited to provide good viewing conditions of all the main areas likely to be used by waterfowl. As looking into the sun across water is particularly difficult, especially when the sun is low in the morning, evening or during winter, ideally there should be several hides with different orientations. A small promontory is an ideal site, potentially offering a 180° arc of viewing. However, hides should not be sited where visitor access would cause unacceptable levels of disturbance, nor where inadequate views encourage trespass. Hides themselves are potentially a main source of disturbance: they are a focal point of visitor access and approaches must be screened. Screening must be 2 m high; earth banks, formal solid fencing or evergreen planting reinforced by a wire fence. As most visitors have binoculars, hides need not be right at the water's edge but can be set well back if necessary. Height is valuable, however, as even low vegetation or ground features can conceal birds when viewing from ground level. Tower hides, built on stilts, afford excellent views into a site and may be necessary where extensive winter flooding is a possible cause of damage to the structure.

A standard hide design is given in Fig 3.25. If the hide is to be intensively used by school parties, installation of sound-absorbing materials may be considered.

At any site, efforts should be made to provide a rewarding hide for use by disabled visitors. For wheel-chair access, paths must be hard-surfaced and the hide entrance level, or approached by a gentle ramp. Viewing slits must be positioned for easy approach and use from a chair.

Where site restoration has visitor enjoyment as a primary aim, a diversity of good quality bird habitats will be visible from each hide. These might include open water, shallows, islands, a reedbed and marsh.

Income

All experience in the UK is that levels of income from visitor-use of wildlife sites do not meet the costs of the provision of facilities and the management of habitats. Those which come closest to it have the following characteristics:
(a) a varied and abundant bird community including scarce species;
(b) good viewing facilities;
(c) part of a larger site or complex offering either all-day birdwatching for the enthusiast or a range of facilities for the general visitor;
(d) full-time wardening to collect payment, advise or guide visitors and undertake management.

Proximity to major urban centres is not a necessity. People will travel long distances to good sites.

Minor amounts of income can be obtained from the management of conservation sites – for instance from grazing licences, sale of timber or removal of coarse fish but these are never adequate to offset overall management costs.

Conservation bodies are most likely to be prepared to take on a management, and thus a financial, commitment or to provide volunteer labour where the conservation potential of the site justifies the costs to them of its purchase or rental and management.

Reference

Ward, D, 1990, Recreation on inland lowland waterbodies: does it affect birds? *RSPB Cons. Rev.*

FRONT ELEVATION – Standard **12' 3600** Section
showing nailing frame   *measurements in inches and millimetres*

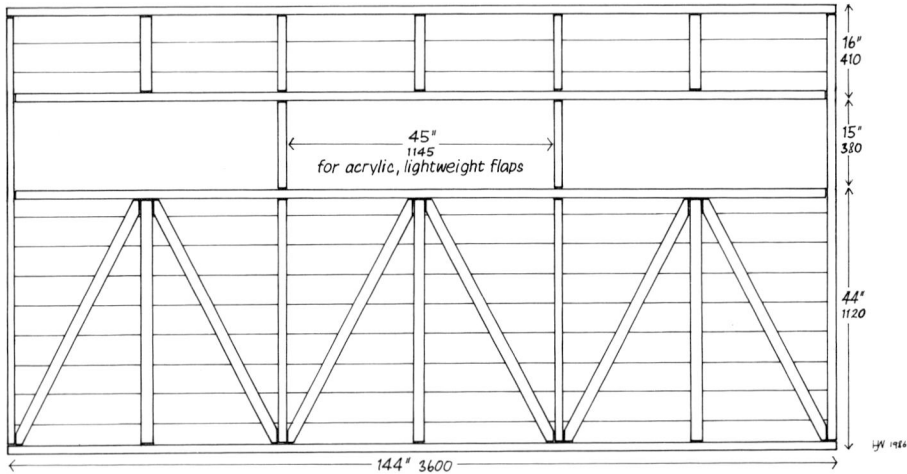

16"
410

15"
380

45"
1145
for acrylic, lightweight flaps

44"
1120

144" 3600

24' HIDE
with one section adapted for wheelchair users

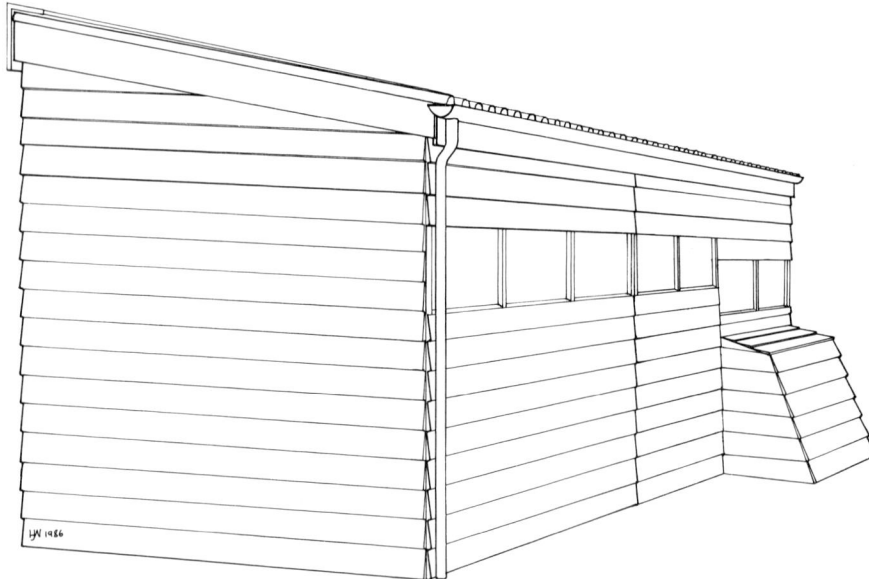

12' 3600 Section   with 34" 865 viewing slots to take heavier glazed or wooden flaps & two flaps
adapted for wheelchair users

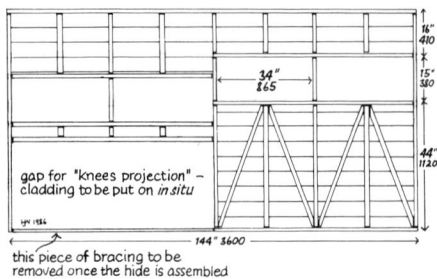

16"
410

15"
380

34"
865

44"
1120

gap for "knees projection" –
cladding to be put on *in situ*

144" 3600

this piece of bracing to be
removed once the hide is assembled

*Fig 3.25 A standard
birdwatching hide.*

SECTION – Standard Hide
measurements in inches and millimetres
(measurements not interchangeable)

Onduline sheeting

17¾"
450

2"× 2" purlins
50×50

4"× 2" rafter
100×50

16"
410

15"
380

87"
2200
inside back wall

75"
1910
inside front wall

8"
200

6"
150

"Sleeping Warden"

44"
1120

10"
250

12"
300

6"
150

9"
230

16"
400

23"
585

67"
1700

BASE SUPPORT FRONT ELEVATION

3"×2"/75×50 floor joists at 16"/400 centre spacing

4"×3"/100×75 "sleeper-beam

4"×4"/100×100 stanchions
at max. 72"/1830 centre spacing

30"
760

3"×2"/75×50 foot-plate if required or –

diagonal cross-struts as necessary

171

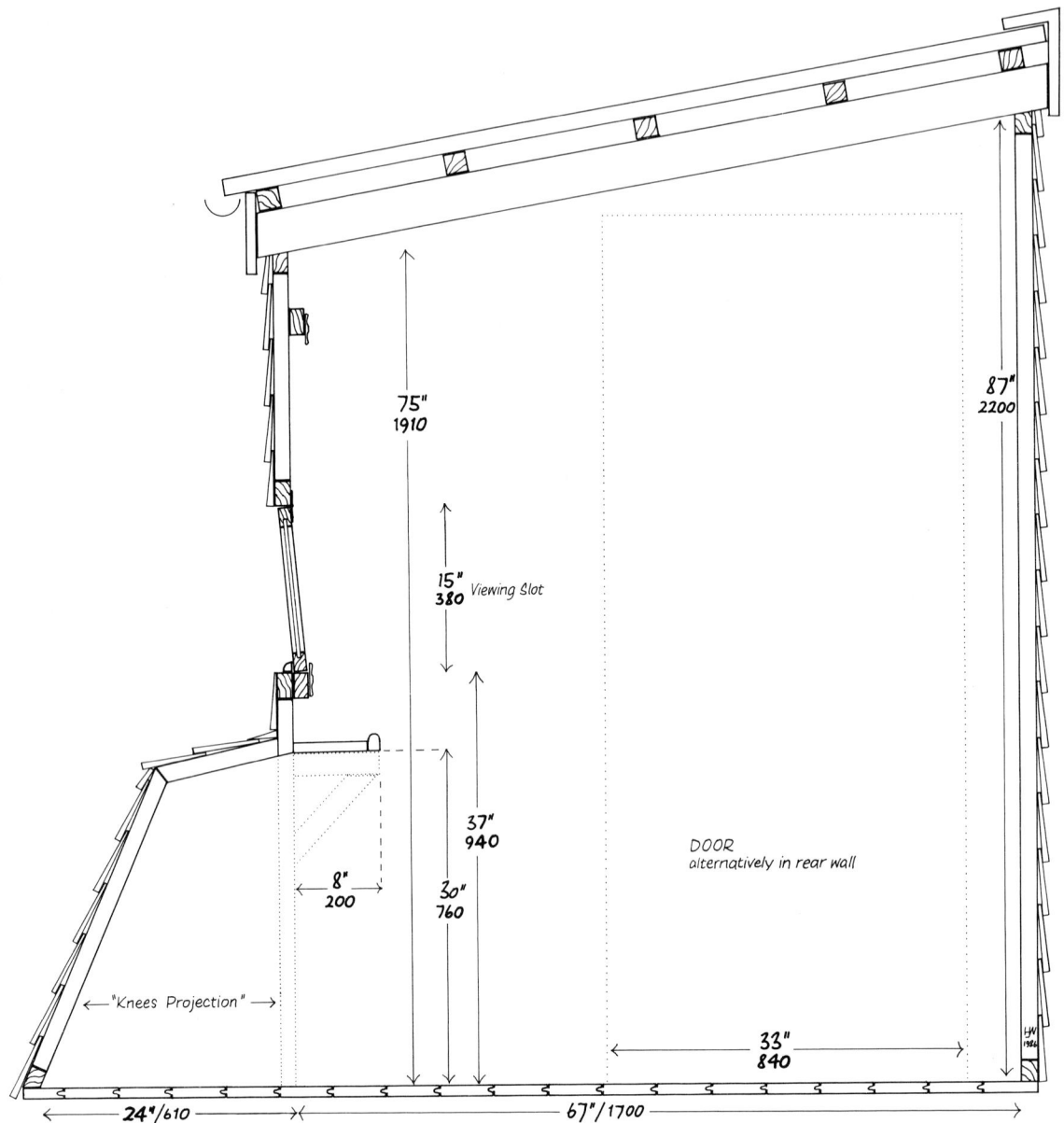

Dimensions shown on the diagram:
75" / 1910
87" / 2200
15" / 380 — Viewing Slot
37" / 940
8" / 200
30" / 760
"Knees Projection"
DOOR — alternatively in rear wall
33" / 840
24" / 610
67" / 1700

Capacity

A standard 3·6 m section will accommodate six birdwatchers comfortably. The hide length can be any multiple of this standard 'module'. It is advantageous to fix a narrow bench (660 mm height) to the rear wall in a busy hide which will permit waiting birdwatchers to sit and partially view over shoulders.

Elevation above ground level

Depends on the location but should be the minimum 760 mm shown, with steps or ramp to the door(s).

Entrance

Normally one door 760–840 mm wide is sufficient, positioned in the rear or one side; but two are recommended for a hide over 12 m long. A side door or one which is 'cloaked' (ie baffle inside door of correspondingly deeper hide) prevents silhouetting to birds.

Materials

Use 'sawn timber' except for handrails, seats and elbow-rests, which should be 'planed all round'.

Walls: Nailing frame 38×50 mm in tanalised timber at 600 mm centres.

Cladding: 19×150 mm horizontal tanalised feather-edging boarding with Cuprinol finish.

Roof: Brown corrugated 'Onduline' sheets on 38×50 mm rafters at 600 mm centres. Alternatively, mineralised roof-felt on boarding which may be thatched overall with bundles of reed. Brown plastic guttering and downpipes as shown.

Floor: 18 mm chipboard or 19 mm tongued-and-grooved floorboards. Ex-conveyer belt or sisal matting can be laid to deaden feet noise.

Bench: Should be hinged at one or both ends to permit those who wish to take their seat without having to swing their legs over the bench.

Viewing slot

A slot 380 mm deep is generally acceptable but this can be reduced to, say, 250 mm where birds are more vulnerable to disturbance. In that case the mid-point of the slot should still be 1300 mm above the floor.

The width of the slot depends on the weight of the materials used: safely, 1145 mm for acrylic sheeting in a lightweight frame (or hinged direct to the wall); or 865 mm for wooden or glass-filled flaps. The glass should be inclined vertically

to avoid rainwater drip. Condensation can be avoided by drilling holes to outside above frame at 150 mm intervals.

'Sleeping wardens' are angled plywood boards running the length of the hide on which are mounted pictures of birds to be seen and other information – repeated for each viewing flap.

Base platform

100×100 mm tanalised corner and intermediate posts with 100×75 mm bearers to support floor-joists. In soft ground a 50 gallon oil drum may be sunk beneath each post and filled with concrete to 225 mm in depth. Once the post is positioned, fill the drum to ground level with concrete.

Wheelchair access

If the hide can be made accessible to wheelchairs (ie level access or ramp to door maximum 1:12 in firm material, omitting door threshold if possible), it is usually sufficient to adapt one 1800 mm section, as shown on the drawings. This will accommodate two adult wheelchairs side-by-side. Two 865 mm flaps should be installed at the lower position (shown). The bench will be either removable or absent.

PREDATOR AND PEST MANAGEMENT

The activities of a small number of mammals and birds may appear to conflict directly with conservation aims, for instance because they kill desired species, take eggs or displace other species through aggression. Always attempt preventative measures before embarking on any form of predator or pest control. Consider the following:

(a) can predator or pest damage be minimised? Before considering control, improve habitat design and management, for instance to create cover to benefit desired species;

(b) can predator or pest damage be off-set? Before considering control, provide better feeding habitat for desired species, so improving their breeding performance or winter survival;

(c) is human disturbance a factor aiding predators? If birds are put off nests or broods are scattered it is easier for crows, magpies and foxes to find and take eggs or chicks;

(d) can predator or pest habitat be removed? For instance crows may use an isolated tree as a look-out post. Will removing it make life harder for them?

(e) can pest species be deterred by scaring? Bear in mind that scaring programmes may be labour-intensive and affect other species too;

(f) moderate losses to predators are normal. Many creatures produce large numbers of young in order to offset losses from this and other causes. If predation ceases, other forms of mortality may take its place. In other words, if large numbers of ducklings survive, more of them are likely to starve in the following winter;

(g) heavy losses of some species are normal occasionally. For instance, the entire egg or chick production of a tern or gull colony may be destroyed in one night by a single fox, but the adults are long-lived birds and will have the opportunity to breed again. Only if heavy losses occur in successive years should you consider action;

(h) killing predators or pests in a limited area usually creates a vacuum into which others move, so that a control programme is likely to be a continuous commitment;

(i) killing one species of predator or pest may simply improve feeding opportunities for another, which may be more damaging or harder to control;

(j) if predator or pest activity is considered to be a problem, is it only significant for a brief period annually eg for about eight weeks when waders are nesting or when ducks are looking for nest sites? If so, control should be concentrated immediately before that period starts so as to achieve maximum effect and minimise the likelihood of other predators or pests moving in before the danger season is over;

(k) have you identified the culprit? In some instances only one individual may be the cause of loss eg a gourmet fox which is prepared to swim to off-shore islands.

APPENDIX I

EXTRACTS FROM GUIDELINES FOR AGGREGATES PROVISION IN ENGLAND AND WALES (MPG 6) AND THE RECLAMATION OF MINERAL WORKINGS (MPG 7)

'There is always a presumption in favour of allowing applications for development, having regard to all material considerations, unless that development would cause demonstrable harm to interests of acknowledged importance. However, minerals can only be worked where they occur and mineral extraction often has, by reason of its scale, duration and location, more impact on the environment than other forms of development. In some cases, these effects may be only temporary but in others they are irreversible although adequate restoration and aftercare conditions can reduce the impact and secure a beneficial after use. In all areas therefore, policies for mineral extraction including the release of land must balance the need for the development against environmental, social, agricultural and other relevant considerations.' (MPG 6 para 12.)

In general, applications for aggregate extraction in National Parks, National Nature Reserves, Sites of Special Scientific Interest, Areas of Outstanding Natural Beauty and other environmentally important areas 'must be subject to the most rigorous examination', and extraction must be demonstrated to be in the public interest. Mineral working in Green Belt areas requires 'that high environmental standards are maintained and that the site is well restored'. (DOE Circular 27/87, Welsh Office Circular 52/87 on Nature Conservation Para 35 says 'Where consent is given careful consideration should be given to the need to impose conditions relating to the process of extraction and the restoration and aftercare of the site.') (MPG 6 paras 19–23.)

'When proposals for development are likely to have significant effects on the environment they will need to be subject to an assessment of those effects under the Town and Country Planning (Assessment of Environmental Effects) Regulations 1988. Whether or not aggregate mineral

workings would have sufficient significant environmental effects to warrant an EA will depend upon such factors as the sensitivity of the location, size, working methods, the proposals for disposing of waste, the nature and extent of processing and ancillary operations, arrangements for transporting products away from the site and proposals for restoration and aftercare of the site. The duration of the proposed workings is also a factor to be taken into account. . . .' (MPG 6 para 26.)

'Some form of restoration and aftercare will be required to make mineral workings fit for beneficial after-use and environmentally acceptable. This may include restoration to agriculture, forestry, management for nature conservation, provision of public open space, recreation or other development. Standards of restoration have generally improved over recent years. Continuation of this trend will enable a wider range of sites to be restored to appropriate standards leading to the release of land which has not so far been made available for mineral working. Wherever practicable, the mineral planning authority and the mineral operators should agree a scheme for the progressive restoration of mineral workings unless to do so would be likely to affect adversely the standard of restoration achieved. . . .' (MPG 6 para 32.)

'Where minerals are worked below the watertable and it is not desirable or practicable to fill the void or to consider "low level restoration", permissions will normally include conditions which will enable one or more appropriate water-based after-uses to be established. The conditions will need to be based on information obtained from pre-application site investigations and working and landscaping plans, which may be subject to more detailed schemes submitted and agreed from time to time during the life of the mineral operations. The information may need to include

Appendix I

depths and areas of water to be created, hydrology, water quality, bank profiles into the water, creation of islands, prevailing wind direction, preservation and use of soils, the treatment and planting of water and land margins, and subsequent management of the area.' (MPG 7 para 87.)

'Different water recreational uses have different requirements, whilst water areas for wildfowl and nature conservation again need specific consideration. It will therefore not be satisfactory to propose a scheme which only anticipates in general the creation of a lake which might be suitable for a water recreation after-use or for nature conservation. The dual use of water areas for some form of recreation and nature conservation may often be attractive, but such mixing of uses is in practice rarely compatible unless they can be physically separated within the configuration and area of water concerned.' (MPG 7 para 88.)

'Advice on lagoon areas intended for wildfowl breeding and feeding may be obtained from the British Association for Shooting and Conservation, the Game Conservancy, and the Royal Society for the Protection of Birds; and for nature conservation from the Nature Conservancy Council and the Royal Society for Nature Conservation (RSNC).' (MPG 7 para 89.)

'When imposing planning conditions for water areas, surrounding banks and islands to be formed as a result of mineral working, it will be important to take account of the available powers under the 1971 Act. Formation of a lake to a specified configuration and depth may be properly required under Section 29. However given the definition of a restoration condition under S.30A(2), a requirement to allow an excavation to fill with water would not come within this and provide the basis for an aftercare condition (or scheme) for the water areas. Whilst, therefore, use of soil materials on banks and islands would provide the basis for requiring aftercare for these areas for amenity use, it may be more appropriate to use voluntary agreements, (eg under Section 52 of the 1971 Act) to achieve reclamation and initial management of water areas – particularly for wildlife and nature conservation.' (MPG 7 para 90.)

'Amenity use includes the conservation or promotion of landscape and wildlife. In this context the NCC may have an interest in many of the possible after-uses of reclaimed mineral working. DOE Circular 27/28 (WO 52/87) (Nature Conservation) sets out policies for the protection of flora, fauna and their habitats, outlines the role of the Council, and draws attention to the need for local authorities to have regard to considerations of nature conservation in drawing up planning policies and in determining individual planning applications. Extraction of minerals can create new types of habitat where they were formerly absent or rare, while quarry faces may provide a valuable supplement to natural rock outcrops. Many of the existing important biological nature conservation sites in mineral workings have regenerated naturally, a process which takes many years. It may be possible for this process to be speeded up using some more recently developed ecological techniques, which might be included in the preparation of schemes for working and reclamation.' (MPG 7 para 91.)

APPENDIX II

WILDLIFE PROTECTION LEGISLATION

In Great Britain, wildlife protection legislation is contained in Part I of the Wildlife and Countryside Act 1981: similar legislation applies in Northern Ireland. The following summarises the main provisions but is not exhaustive. Gamebirds, ground game (hares and rabbits), deer and badgers are the subjects of separate legislation.

Birds

Most birds occurring in gravel pits are fully protected at all seasons. It is an offence to kill, injure or take them, or to take or destroy eggs or occupied nests. Problems sometimes arise with birds nesting in the way of extraction operations (for instance, sand martins may have colonised an exposed quarry face) and damage to, or destruction of their nests is unlawful unless it can be shown that the act was an incidental result of a lawful operation and could not reasonably have been avoided, or unless a licence has been obtained (see below). The definition of 'reasonably' depends on circumstances.

A number of rare breeding species are protected by higher penalties and it is also an offence intentionally to disturb them while nest building, at or near an occupied nest or with dependent young. The little ringed plover and kingfisher are regular breeders at gravel pits which enjoy this level of protection. Licences cannot be issued to permit the destruction of the nest of any of these rare species for commercial operational reasons which should therefore be timed to avoid the risk of their destruction.

Some of the commoner wildfowl, such as mallard and Canada goose, may be hunted during an open season which extends from 1 September–31 January inland.

It is also legal to kill or destroy the nests or eggs of listed pest species which include carrion crow and magpie at any time of year provided that the consent of the owner or occupier of the land has been obtained.

No bird may be killed by unlawful means which are defined in the Act.

Mammals

A small number of mammals, including the otter and all bats, are fully protected. It is an offence to destroy 'any structure or place' used by them for shelter or protection, or to disturb any protected animal while it is in such a resting place. Thus it may be an offence to destroy cover known to contain an otter holt or a hollow tree containing bats, or to block off bats' access to the roof of a building. Again, licences may be sought to give exemption if required.

Plants
It is an offence intentionally to uproot any wild plant without the consent of the owner or occupier. A very small number of the rarest plants are fully protected and may not be picked or uprooted. None is likely to be encountered in normal gravel operations.

Licences

A number of authorities are involved in the provision of licences. Advice should be sought from the Nature Conservancy Council, Northminster House, Peterborough.

Offences

Offences should be reported to the police and, in the case of offences against birds, to the RSPB which also provides advice on the legislation as it affects birds.

APPENDIX III
ADDRESSES OF RSPB, NCC AND NATURE CONSERVATION TRUST OFFICES

RSPB

RSPB Headquarters
The Lodge,
Sandy,
Beds, SG19 2DL.
Tel: 0767 680551.

Scottish Headquarters
17 Regent Terrace,
Edinburgh,
EH7 5BN.
Tel: 031–557 3136.

Highland Office
Munlochy,
Ross and Cromarty,
IV8 8ND.
Tel: 046–381 496.

Northern Ireland Office
Belvoir Park Forest,
Belfast,
BT8 4QT.
Tel: 0232 491547.

Wales Office
Bryn Aderyn,
The Bank,
Newtown,
Powys,
SY16 2AB.
Tel: 0686 626678.

East Anglia Office
97 Yarmouth Road,
Thorpe St Andrew,
Norwich,
NR7 0HF.
Tel: 0603 700880.

East Midlands Office
The Lawn,
Union Road,
Lincoln,
LN1 3BU.
Tel: 0522 535596.

Midlands Office
44 Friar Street,
Droitwich Spa,
Worcs.,
WR9 8ED.
Tel: 0905 770581.

North of England Office
'E' Floor,
Milburn House,
Dean Street,
Newcastle upon Tyne,
NE1 1LE.
Tel: 091–232 4148.

North-West England Office
Imperial House,
Imperial Arcade,
Huddersfield,
West Yorkshire,
HD1 2BR.
Tel: 0484 536331.

South-East England Office
8 Church Street,
Shoreham-by-Sea,
West Sussex,
BN4 5DQ.
Tel: 0273 463642.

South-West England Office
10 Richmond Road,
Exeter,
Devon,
EX4 4JA.
Tel: 0392 432691.

Thames and Chiltern Office
The Lodge,
Sandy,
Beds,
SG19 2DL.
Tel: 0767 680551.

Nature Conservancy Council

ENGLAND
NCC Headquarters
Northminster House,
Peterborough,
PE1 1UA.
Tel: 0733 40345.

South-East Region
Zealds,
Church Street,
Wye,
Ashford,
Kent,
TN25 5BW.
Tel: 0233 812525.

South Region
Foxhold House,
Thornford Road,
Crookham Common,
Newbury,
Berkshire,
RG15 8EL.
Tel: 063–523 8881.

South-West Region
Roughmoor,
Bishop's Hull,
Taunton,
Somerset,
TA1 5AA.
Tel: 0823 283211.

West Midlands Region
Attingham Park,
Shrewsbury,
Shropshire,
SY4 4TW.
Tel: 074–377 611.

East Anglia Region
60 Bracondale,
Norwich,
Norfolk,
NR1 2BE.
Tel: 0603 620558.

East Midlands Region
Northminster House,
Peterborough,
PE1 1UA.
Tel: 0733 40345.

North-East Region
Archbold House,
Archbold Terrace,
Newcastle-upon-Tyne,
NE2 1EG.
Tel: 091–281 6316/7.

Appendix III

North-West Region
Blackwell,
Bowness-on-Windermere,
Windermere,
Cumbria, LA23 3JR.
Tel: 096–62 5286.

SCOTLAND
NCC Scotland Headquarters
12 Hope Terrace,
Edinburgh,
EH9 2AS.
Tel: 031–447 4784.

North-East Region
Wynne-Edwards House,
17 Rubislaw Terrace,
Aberdeen,
AB1 1XE.
Tel: 0224 642863.

North-West Region
Fraser Darling House,
9 Culduthel Road,
Inverness,
IV2 4AG.
Tel: 0463 239 431.

South-East Region
Research Park (Avenue 1),
Riccarton,
Edinburgh,
EH14 4AP.
Tel: 031–449 4933.

South-West Region
The Castle,
Loch Lomond Park,
Balloch,
Dunbartonshire,
G83 8LX.
Tel: 0389 58511.

WALES
NCC Wales Headquarters
Plas Penrhos,
Ffordd Penrhos,
Bangor,
Gwynedd,
LL57 2LQ.
Tel: 0248 370444.

Dyfed-Powys Region
Plas Gogerddan,
Aberystwyth,
Dyfed,
SY23 3EE.
Tel: 0970 828551.

North Region
Plas Penrhos,
Ffordd Penrhos,
Bangor,
Gwynedd,
LL57 2LQ.
Tel: 0248 370444.

South Region
43 The Parade,
Roath,
Cardiff,
CF2 3UH.
Tel: 0222 485111.

Nature Conservation Trusts

Avon
Avon Wildlife Trust
The Old Police Station,
32 Jacob's Wells Road,
Bristol,
BS8 1DR.
Tel: 0272 268018/265490.

Beds & Cambs
The Wildlife Trust,
Fulbourn Manor,
Fulbourn,
Cambridge,
CB1 5BN.
Tel: 0223 880788.

Berks, Bucks & Oxon
Berkshire, Buckinghamshire & Oxon
Naturalists' Trust
(BBONT), 3 Church Cowley Road,
Rose Hill,
Oxford,
OX4 3JR.
Tel: 0865 775476.

Birmingham
Urban Wildlife Group (Birmingham)
(UWG), Unit 213,
Jubilee Trade Centre,
130 Pershore Street,
Birmingham,
B5 6ND.
Tel: 021–666 7474.

Brecknock (Brecon)
Brecknock Wildlife Trust
Lion House,
7 Lion Street,
Brecon,
Powys,
LD3 7AY.
Tel: 0874 5708.

Cambridgeshire
See Beds & Cambs.

Cheshire
Cheshire Conservation Trust
c/o Marbury Country Park,
Northwich,
Cheshire,
CW9 6AT.
Tel: 0606 781868.

Cleveland
Cleveland Wildlife Trust
The Old Town Hall,
Mandale Road,
Thornaby,
Cleveland,
TS17 6AW.
Tel: 0642 608405.

Cornwall
Cornwall Trust for Nature
Conservation
Five Acres,
Allet,
Truro,
Cornwall,
TR4 9DJ.
Tel: 0872 73939.

Cumbria
Cumbria Wildlife Trust
Church Street,
Ambleside,
Cumbria,
LA22 0BU.
Tel: 0966 32476.

Derbyshire
Derbyshire Wildlife Trust
Elvaston Castle Country Park,
Derby,
DE7 3EP.
Tel: 0332 756610.

Devon
Devon Wildlife Trust
35 New Bridge Street,
Exeter,
Devon,
EX3 4AH.
Tel: 0392 79244.

Dorset
Dorset Trust for Nature Conservation
39 Christchurch Road,
Bournemouth,
Dorset,
BH1 3NS.
Tel: 0202 24241.

Durham
Durham Wildlife Trust
52 Old Elvet,
Durham,
DH1 3HN.
Tel: 091–386 9797.

Dyfed
Dyfed Wildlife Trust
7 Market Street,
Haverfordwest,
Dyfed,
SA61 1NF.
Tel: 0437 5462.

Essex
Essex Naturalists' Trust
Fingringhoe Wick Nature Reserve,
Fingringhoe,
Colchester,
Essex,
CO5 7DN.
Tel: 020628 678.

Glamorgan
Glamorgan Wildlife Trust
Nature Centre,
Fountain Road,
Tondu,
Mid Glamorgan,
CF32 0EH.
Tel: 0656 724100.

Gloucestershire
Gloucestershire Trust for Nature
Conservation
Church House,
Standish,
Stonehouse,
Glos GL10 3EU.
Tel: 045–382 2761.

Guernsey
La Societe Guernesiaise (LSG)
c/o F G Caldwell,
Candie Gardens,
St Peter Port,
Guernsey,
C.I.
Tel: 0481 25093.

Gwent
Gwent Wildlife Trust
16 White Swan Court,
Church Street,
Monmouth,
Gwent,
NP5 3BR.
Tel: 0600 5501 (9 am–1 pm).

Hants & Isle of Wight
Hampshire & Isle of Wight Naturalists'
Trust
71 The Hundred,
Romsey,
Hants,
SO5 8BZ.
Tel: 0794 513786.

Hereford
Herefordshire Nature Trust
Community House,
25 Castle Street,
Hereford,
HR1 2NW.
Tel: 0432 356872.

Herts & Middx
Hertfordshire & Middlesex Wildlife
Trust
Grebe House,
St Michael's Street,
St Albans,
Herts,
AL3 4SN.
Tel: 0727 58901.

Isle of Man
Manx Nature Conservation Trust
Ballamoar House, Ballaugh,
Isle of Man.
Tel: 062489 7611.

Kent
Kent Trust for Nature Conservation
The Annexe,
1a Bower Mount Road,
Maidstone,
Kent,
ME16 8AX.
Tel: 0622 53017/59017.

Lancashire
Lancashire Trust for Nature
Conservation
The Pavilion,
Cuerden Park Wildlife Centre,
Shady Lane,
Bamber Bridge,
Preston,
Lancs,
PR5 6AU.
Tel: 0772 324129.

Leicester & Rutland
Leicestershire & Rutland Trust for
Nature Conservation
1 West Street,
Leicester,
LE1 6UU.
Tel: 0533 553904.

Lincs & Sth Humberside
Lincolnshire & Sth Humberside Trust
for Nature Conservation
The Manor House,
Alford,
Lincs,
LN13 9DL.
Tel: 05212 3468.

London
London Wildlife Trust
80 York Way,
London,
N1 9AG.
Tel: 01–278 6612/3.

Montgomery
Montgomeryshire Wildlife Trust
8 Severn Square,
Newtown,
Powys,
SY16 3AG.
Tel: 0686 624751.

Norfolk
Norfolk Naturalists' Trust
72 Cathedral Close,
Norwich,
Norfolk,
NR1 4DF.
Tel: 0603 625540.

Northamptonshire
Northants Wildlife Trust
Lings House,
Billing Lings,
Northampton,
NN3 4BE.
Tel: 0604 405285.

Northumberland
Northumberland Wildlife Trust
Hancock Museum,
Barras Bridge,
Newcastle-upon-Tyne,
NE2 4PT.
Tel: 091–232 0038.

North Wales
North Wales Wildlife Trust
376 High Street,
Bangor,
Gwynedd,
LL57 1YE.
Tel: 0248 351541.

Nottinghamshire
Nottinghamshire Wildlife Trust
310 Sneinton Dale,
Nottingham,
NG3 7DN.
Tel: 0602 588242.

Appendix III

Oxfordshire
See Berks, Bucks & Oxon

Radnorshire
Radnorshire Wildlife Trust
1 Gwalia Annexe,
Ithon Road,
Llandrindod Wells,
Powys,
LD1 6AS.
Tel: 0597 3298.

Scotland
Scottish Wildlife Trust (SWT)
25 Johnston Terrace,
Edinburgh,
EH1 2NH.
Tel: 031–226 4602.

Shropshire
Shropshire Wildlife Trust
St George's Primary School,
Frankwell,
Shrewsbury,
Shropshire,
SY3 8JP.
Tel: 0743 241691.

Somerset
Somerset Trust for Nature Conservation
Fyne Court,
Broomfield,
Bridgwater,
Somerset,
TA5 2EQ.
Tel: 0823 451587/8.

Staffordshire
Staffordshire Nature Conservation
Trust
Coutts House,
Sandon,
Staffordshire,
ST18 0DN.
Tel: 088–97 534.

Suffolk
Suffolk Wildlife Trust
Park Cottage,
Saxmundham,
Suffolk,
IP17 1DQ.
Tel: 0728 603765.

Surrey
Surrey Wildlife Trust
The Old School,
School Lane,
Pirbright,
Woking,
Surrey,
GU24 0JN.
Tel: 0483 797575.

Sussex
Sussex Wildlife Trust
Woods Mill,
Shoreham Road,
Henfield,
West Sussex,
BN5 9SD.
Tel: 0273 492630.

Ulster
Ulster Wildlife Trust
Barnett's Cottage,
Barnett Demesne,
Malone Road,
Belfast,
BT9 5PB.
Tel: 0232 612235.

Warwickshire
Warwickshire Nature Conservation
Trust (WARNACT)
Montague Road,
Warwick,
CV34 5 LW.
Tel: 0926 496848.

Wiltshire
Wiltshire Trust for Nature
Conservation
19 High Street,
Devizes,
Wiltshire,
SN10 1AT.
Tel: 0380 5670.

Worcestershire
Worcestershire Nature Conservation
Trust
Hanbury Road,
Droitwich,
Worcestershire,
WR9 7DU.
Tel: 0905 773031.

Yorkshire
Yorkshire Wildlife Trust
10 Toft Green,
York,
YO1 1JT.
Tel: 0904 659570.

APPENDIX IV

SCIENTIFIC NAMES OF SPECIES MENTIONED IN TEXT

Plants
Waterplants
See Table 3.7 page 121

Grasses and herbs
See Table 3.9, page 131
Bramble — *Rubus sp*
Common nettle — *Urtica dioica*

Trees and shrubs
See Table 3.10, page 145

Dragonflies and damselflies
Emerald damselfly	*Lestes sponsa*
Red-eyed damselfly	*Erythromma najas*
Azure damselfly	*Coenagrion puella*
Variable damselfly	*Coenagrion pulchellum*
Common blue damselfly	*Enallagma cyathigerum*
Scarce blue-tailed damselfly	*Ischnura pumilio*
Southern hawker	*Aeshna cyanea*
Emperor dragonfly	*Anax imperator*
Four-spotted chaser	*Libellula quadrimaculata*
Black-tailed skimmer	*Orthetrum cancellatum*
Keeled skimmer	*Orthetrum coerulescens*
Common darter	*Sympetrum striolatum*

Butterflies
Small skipper	*Thymelicus sylvestris*
Essex skipper	*Thymelicus lineola*
Large skipper	*Ochlodes venata*
Dingy skipper	*Erynnis tages*
Grizzled skipper	*Pyrgus malvae*
Brimstone	*Gonepteryx rhamni*
Green-veined white	*Pieris napi*
Orange tip	*Anthocharis cardamines*
Small copper	*Lycaena phlaeas*
Common blue	*Polyommatus icarus*
Holly blue	*Celastrina argiolus*
Red admiral	*Vanessa atalanta*
Painted lady	*Cynthia cardui*
Small tortoiseshell	*Aglais urticae*
Peacock	*Inachis io*
Comma	*Polygonia c-album*
Speckled wood	*Pararge aegeria*
Wall	*Lasiommata megera*
Marbled white	*Melanargia galathea*
Grayling	*Hipparchia semele*
Hedge brown	*Pyronia tithonus*
Meadow brown	*Maniola jurtina*
Ringlet	*Aphantopus hyperantus*

Molluscs
Zebra mussel	*Dreissena polymorpha*

Fish
Salmon	*Salmo salar*
Brown trout	*Salmo trutta fario*
Rainbow trout	*Salmo gairdnere*
Pike	*Esox lucius*
Carp	*Cyprinus carpio*
Crucian carp	*Carassius carassius*

Tench	*Tinca tinca*
Silver bream	*Blicca bjorkna*
Bream	*Abramis brama*
Bleak	*Alburnus alburnus*
Minnow	*Phoxinus phoxinus*
Rudd	*Scardinius erythrophthalmus*
Roach	*Rutilus rutilus*
Chub	*Leuciscus cephalus*
Dace	*Leuciscus leuciscus*
European catfish (wels)	*Silurus glanis*
Eel	*Anguilla anguilla*
Stickleback – three-spined	*Gasterosteus aculeatus*
Ten-spined	*Pungitius pungitius*
Perch	*Perca fluviatilus*
Ruffe	*Gymnocephalus cernua*
Bullhead	*Cottus gobio*

Amphibians
Great crested newt	*Triturus cristatus*
Palmate newt	*Triturus helveticus*
Smooth newt	*Triturus vulgaris*
Common toad	*Bufo bufo*
Natterjack toad	*Bufo calamita*
Common frog	*Rana temporaria*

Snakes and lizards
Slow-worm	*Anguis fragilis*
Sand lizard	*Lacerta agilis*
Common lizard	*Lacerta vivipara*
Grass snake	*Natrix natrix*
Smooth snake	*Coronella austriaca*
Adder	*Vipera berus*

Birds
Little grebe	*Tachybaptus ruficollis*
Great crested grebe	*Podiceps cristatus*
Grey heron	*Ardea cinerea*
Mute swan	*Cygnus olor*
Greylag goose	*Anser anser*
Canada goose	*Branta canadensis*
Shelduck	*Tadorna tadorna*
Wigeon	*Anas penelope*
Gadwall	*Anas strepera*
Teal	*Anas crecca*
Mallard	*Anas platyrhynchos*
Shoveler	*Anas clypeata*
Pochard	*Aythya ferina*
Tufted duck	*Aythya fuligula*
Kestrel	*Falco tinnunculus*
Moorhen	*Gallinula chloropus*
Little ringed plover	*Charadrius dubius*
Ringed plover	*Charadrius hiaticula*
Lapwing	*Vanellus vanellus*
Dunlin	*Calidris alpina*
Snipe	*Gallinago gallinago*
Woodcock	*Scolopax rusticola*
Whimbrel	*Numenius phaeopus*
Curlew	*Numenius arquata*
Redshank	*Tringa totanus*

Appendix IV

Greenshank — *Tringa nebularia*
Green sandpiper — *Tringa ochropus*
Common sandpiper — *Actitis hypoleucos*
Black-headed gull — *Larus ridibundus*
Common tern — *Sterna hirundo*
Stock dove — *Columba oenas*
Barn owl — *Tyto alba*
Tawny owl — *Strix aluco*
Kingfisher — *Alcedo atthis*
Sand martin — *Riparia riparia*
Robin — *Erithacus rubecula*
Sedge warbler — *Acrocephalus schoenobaenus*
Reed warbler — *Acrocephalus scirpaceus*
Pied flycatcher — *Ficedula hypoleuca*
Nuthatch — *Sitta europaea*
Magpie — *Pica pica*
Jackdaw — *Corvus monedula*
Carion crow — *Corvus corone*
Tree sparrow — *Passer montanus*

Mammals
Shrew sp — *Sorex/Neomys sp*
Bats
  Greater horseshoe bat — *Rhinolophus ferrumequinum*
  Daubenton's bat — *Myotis daubentoni*
  Pipistrelle — *Pipistrellus pipistrellus*
  Barbastelle — *Barbastella barbastellus*
Rabbit — *Oryctolagus cuniculus*
Water vole — *Arvicola terrestris*
Harvest mouse — *Micromys minutus*
Brown rat — *Rattus norvegicus*
Fox — *Vulpes vulpes*
Stoat — *Mustela erminae*
Weasel — *Mustela nivalis*
Mink — *Mustela vison*
Otter — *Lutra lutra*